WAFFEN-SS KNIGHTS AND THEIR BATTLES

Also by the Author

Dietrich's Warriors: The History of the 3. Kompanie 1st Panzergrenadier Regiment 1st SS Panzer Division Leibstandarte Adolf Hitler in World War II

WAFFEN-SS KNIGHTS AND THEIR BATTLES

The Waffen-SS Knight's Cross Holders Volume 2: January-July 1943

Peter Mooney

Schiffer Military History
Atglen, PA

Book design by Robert Biondi.

Library of Congress Catalog Number: 2008928022.

Printed in China.
ISBN: 978-0-7643-3527-3

Published by Schiffer Publishing Ltd.
4880 Lower Valley Road
Atglen, PA 19310
Phone: (610) 593-1777
FAX: (610) 593-2002
E-mail: Info@schifferbooks.com.
Visit our web site at: www.schifferbooks.com
Please write for a free catalog.
This book may be purchased from the publisher.
Please include $5.00 postage.
Try your bookstore first.

In Europe, Schiffer books are distributed by:
Bushwood Books
6 Marksbury Ave.
Kew Gardens, Surrey TW9 4JF
England
Phone: 44 (0)20 8392-8585
FAX: 44 (0)20 8392-9876
E-mail: info@bushwoodbooks.co.uk
www.bushwoodbooks.co.uk
Free postage in the UK. Europe: air mail at cost.
Try your bookstore first.

CONTENTS

	Foreword	7
	Introduction	9
Chapter 1	Accomplishments to Date and the Next Steps	12
Chapter 2	Stopping the Tidal Wave	38
Chapter 3	Retaking the Prize	86
Chapter 4	Build up Strength – March to June 1943	139
Chapter 5	The Kursk Offensive	197
Appendices		
Appendix 1	List of *Waffen-SS* units raised in 1943 (to end of July)	262
Appendix 2	Overview of awards of the *Waffen-SS* Knight's Crosses, Oakleaves, Oakleaves and Swords during 1943 (to end of July) & 1940-1943 (to end of July)	263
Appendix 3	Ranks of *Waffen-SS* Knight's Cross Holders (plus Oakleaves, Oakleaves and Swords) 1943 (to end of July) & 1940-1943 (to end of July)	264
Appendix 4	Skills of *Waffen-SS* Knight's Cross Holders (plus Oakleaves, Oakleaves and Swords) 1943 (to end of July) & 1940-1943 (to end of July)	266
Appendix 5	List of deceased *Waffen-SS* Knight's Cross holders in 1943 (to end of July) and 1941-1943 (to end of July)	267
	Bibliography	268

Map List

Map 1	Places of Origin, January-July 1943	13
Map 2	*Waffen-SS* Positions, January 1943	16
Map 3	Army Group North, January-March 1943	19
Map 4	Kharkov Phase 1, January to mid-February 1943	25
Map 5	Army Group South, January-February 1943	27
Map 6	German Front Line, mid-February 1943	40
Map 7	Kharkov Phase 2, mid-February to 9th March 1943	43
Map 8	Army Group Centre, November-December 1942	83
Map 9	Kharkov Phase 3, 10th to 18th March 1943	93
Map 10	Yugoslavia, January-July 1943	147
Map 11	Army Group North, January-December 1942	186
Map 12	German Front Line, June 1943	196
Map 13	Kursk Offensive, July 1943	205
Map 14	Isjum Area, late July 1943	207
Map 15	Central Russia, July 1943	209

SS-Hauptsturmführer Eberhard Heder photographed after the award of his Knight's Cross in 1944. His award will be detailed in later volumes of this project.

FOREWORD

During the Second World War the *Waffen-SS* was part of the German armed forces. Its' *Divisions* and units stood shoulder to shoulder with and fought under the command of the *German Army* at nearly all focal points of the European front lines, where often amazing achievements were reached. This becomes apparent in the many-recorded hymns of praise by *Army Commanders*, has been pointed out in a glorifying way by some authors and mirrors a generally existing conception.

Due to the media and common historiography the public hardly ever hears about all this. The *Waffen-SS*, a phenomenon in the history of the armed forces, is being abandoned from the recognition of military achievements and is condemned as an "army of the outlaws". Its' undeniable courage and steadfastness during the battle is being stereotyped and devaluated as a sign of lack of consideration and a raw attitude of mind.

The *Waffen-SS* together with the *General SS (Allgemeine-SS)*, the *Security Service (Sicherheitsdienst)* and the police was part of the entire *SS (Gesamt-SS)*. It's also known under the name of "the *SS*", which became a synonym for force and suppression. However, depending on its' structure and characteristics it has been different to the part of Himmler's area of command where horrible and disgraceful deeds have been done. As a military unit, being trained in times of peace under the control and principles of the armed forces and during the war being used on the battlefield, it was totally independent.

The soldiers of the *Waffen-SS* found themselves confronted with a war they haven't wanted and for which they weren't responsible. With trust in the political leadership and being convinced that they had to work for the good of their fatherland, they fought and fulfilled their military duties. It should be possible to get to a non-prejudiced and objective acknowledgement of the achievements of this unit that does justice to the sacrificing commitment, attitude and convictions of its' soldiers.

To this, Mr. Mooney has made an important contribution with his book *Waffen-SS Knights and their battles,* which is of even higher significance as it is written from the distanced position of a Non-German, an Englishman (*Irishman*) without the bias of a German author. For this the former soldiers of the *Waffen-SS* give him recognition and gratitude.

Eberhard Heder

INTRODUCTION

In Volume 1 of this project, we gave the definitions for the words, Bravery, Courage, Valour, Hero, Honour and Loyalty. We highlighted how these words and their meanings are not the sole possession of any one nation or any one period in history. We then went onto state that the words above are usually found associated with successful battles. We covered the actions of the *Waffen-SS* in their formative, per-war years and then carried on with their actions during the initial years of victory of the Second World War from 1939 through to the end of 1942. In this volume, we will cover the critical year of 1943, up to the end of July, when the soldiers of the *Waffen-SS* fought in some of their most reputation-defining battles. These particular battles will demonstrate the qualities that these words define, so the use of them is as important, if not more so, in this volume.

This second volume will continue the focus on a select group of individuals who number less than 500 people, but who, without any doubt, have left their mark upon the military history of our human race, that is, the Knight's Cross holders of the *Waffen-SS*. The purpose of this work is not just to list each person and their deeds, but to give an overall view of the situation from the start of the Second World War in September 1939 until its' end in May 1945 (viewed from the German perspective). Then within this overall global conflict, focus on the battles that they took part in. The main final focus will be upon the actions that resulted in the award of their country's highest award for bravery.

The award in question is that of the Knight's Cross to the Iron Cross and also the higher grades of this award including the Knight's Cross with Oakleaves, the

Knight's Cross with Oakleaves and Swords and finally, the Knight's Cross with Oakleaves, Swords and Diamonds.

This second volume will cover from January until the end of July 1943 and detail the continued awards of the Knight's Cross, Knight's Cross with Oakleaves and the first award of the Knight's Cross with Oakleaves and Swords to soldiers of the *Waffen-SS.*

This work has been compiled over a period of more than 10 years, with the help of surviving holders of the awards listed above that include, Heinrich Springer, Johannes Goehler, Hans Siegel, Otto Kumm, Albert Frey, Remy Schrijnen, Ernst Barkmann, Karl-Heinz Boska, Karl Brommann, Karl Nicolussi-Leck, Paul Egger, Friederich Blond, Eberhard Heder, Karl-Heinz Euling, Siegfried Brosow, Heinrich Sonne, Harald Nugiseiks, Rudolf von Ribbentrop, Walter Girg, Karl-Heinz Lichte, Alois Schnaubelt, Heinz Jurgens, Oskar Schafer, Josef Rolleke and Kurt Sametreiter. Unfortunately, since starting this project, the majority of these men have died. I am indebted to all of them, alive or dead and count myself as a lucky person to have met each of them or had correspondence with them.

In addition, the following *Waffen-SS* soldiers, who served alongside the holders of the Knight's Cross, also helped to compile this record, Erwin Bartmann, Robert Soulat, Jan Munk, Werner Volkner, Max Schmidt, Hans Maguscher, Adolf Schaafs, Helmut Hinze, Sepp Bischoff, Paul Rosch, Gerhard Dilling and Manfred Thorn.

The photographs you will see in this volume have come from a variety of sources that include the Knight's Cross holders themselves and the *Kameraden* who served alongside them. Some of these are listed above, but equally, some of them have been handed to me at re-unions by *Kameraden* who did not provide their names, a few of these photographs were even posted to me by a *Kameraden* who did not provide any contact details at all! One of the key sources was the extensive and impressive collection held by my long-time friend, Justin Horgan. Justin is a fellow enthusiast of the history of the *Waffen-SS* and someone who introduced me to my first *Waffen-SS* Knight's Cross holder. He has had the good fortune to have met, or had correspondence with, many of men that this project will focus on and I am indebted to him for his continued help and support. I have made every effort to obtain original photographic sources for this work.

Further help has directly come from Eberhard Heder, the former *SS-Sturmbannführer* and holder of the Knight's Cross, who very kindly agreed to write the foreword for this second volume. Also, Richard H who, once again, took my map sketches and turned them into the maps you will see within these pages.

A special mention must go to John P. Moore who gave me his permission to use information contained within his *Führerliste Der Waffen-SS, Parts 1-4.* This excellent publication contains information on around 26,000 *Waffen-SS* officers and also the personal files of the Knight's Cross (and other high award) holders of the *Waffen-SS.* Without his permission, this work would not have been completed. I will take this opportunity to thank Mr. Moore and would advise anyone to invest in his publication as it provides a superb insight into the lives of the men who served in, and shaped, the reputation of the *Waffen-SS.*

I will finish this introduction by giving special mention to the most important people of all, that is my son Karl, daughter Alanna and of course, my wife Sandra. They provide continued and unyielding support to my hobby. They have joined me on some of my trips to the homes of the *Waffen-SS* Knight's Cross holders, have remained patient and understanding as I have slaved over notes for hours – after coming home from long days at work, thereby leaving little time to spend quality time with them. This work is dedicated to my children and my wife, without whose support this project would not have been completed.

The work on this project began ten years ago and the intervening years have seen the completion of my first book, *Dietrich's Warriors,* and the first volume of this project. The work on this project continues and I am pleased to see the second volume of this work now complete. I hope you, the reader, will find this book interesting, informative and a worthy continuation of what you read in the first volume.

Peter Mooney
Folkestone, Kent, April 2009.

CHAPTER ONE

ACCOMPLISHMENTS TO DATE AND THE NEXT STEPS

Draw Breath and Expand

In *Volume 1* of this series, we detailed the birth of the *Waffen-SS* and followed this by covering their pre-war political based activities. The advent of war changed all of that and thrust, what became the *Waffen-SS,* into a combat role. The success of the initial *Regiments* was good enough to warrant the raising of further units and the advent of the first *Waffen-SS Divisions*.

We followed these *Regiments* and *Divisions* as they conquered Poland in 1939, then crossed westwards in 1940 as they also conquered Holland, Belgium and France, where the first *Waffen-SS* Knight's Crosses were awarded. A short detour south-east into Yugoslavia and Greece came in early 1941, where additional Knight's Crosses were earned, before they engaged in their biggest struggle to date – the invasion of the Soviet Union – in mid-1941.

Volume 1 covered their many battles in the western territories of the Soviet Union through 1941 and into 1942. These battles swallowed thousands of soldiers from the *Waffen-SS* and almost finished some of the units off as effective fighting machines! The vast majority of the Knight's Crosses (and all of the Oakleaves) awarded to soldiers of the *Waffen-SS* up to the end of 1942 were given for actions conducted in the depths of Russia. Countless acts of bravery were witnessed and some of these were recognized with the award of the Knight's Cross to the Iron Cross.

The men of the *Waffen-SS* had pushed themselves to the extreme and their efforts had paid off. They had been at the vanguard of the *German Army's* advances

Map I **Places of Origin: January - July 1943**

No.	Unit	Place	Date
17	SS-Panzer Korps	France	June 1942
18	SS-Karstwehr Kompanie/Battalion	Dachau	August 1942
19	Estonian SS-Legion	Debica	August 1942
20	Hohenstaufen	Reims	December 1942
21	Frundsberg	Alsace	January 1943
22	Latvian SS-Freiwilligen Legion	Latvia	February 1943
23	Sturmbrigade Reichsfuhrer-SS	Rennes	February 1943
24	Croat SS-Freiwilligen Division	Yugoslavia	March 1943
25	Sonderkommando z.b.v. Oranienburg	Berlin	April 1943
26	II SS-Panzer Korps	Kharkov	April 1943
27	III SS-Panzer Korps	Grafenwohr	April 1943
28	Nordland Division	Grafenwohr	May 1943
29	Latvian SS-Freiwilligen Brigade	Leningrad	May 1943
30	SS-Sturmbrigade Langemarck	Debica	May 1943
31	SS-Sturmbrigade Wallonie	Wildflecken	June1943
32	Hitler Youth Division	Beverloo	June 1943
33	IV SS-Panzer Korps	Potiers	June 1943
34	SS-Freiwilligen Division Galizien	Debica	July 1943
35	I SS-Panzer Korps	Beverloo	July 1943
36	V SS-Gebirgs Korps	Yugoslavia	July 1943

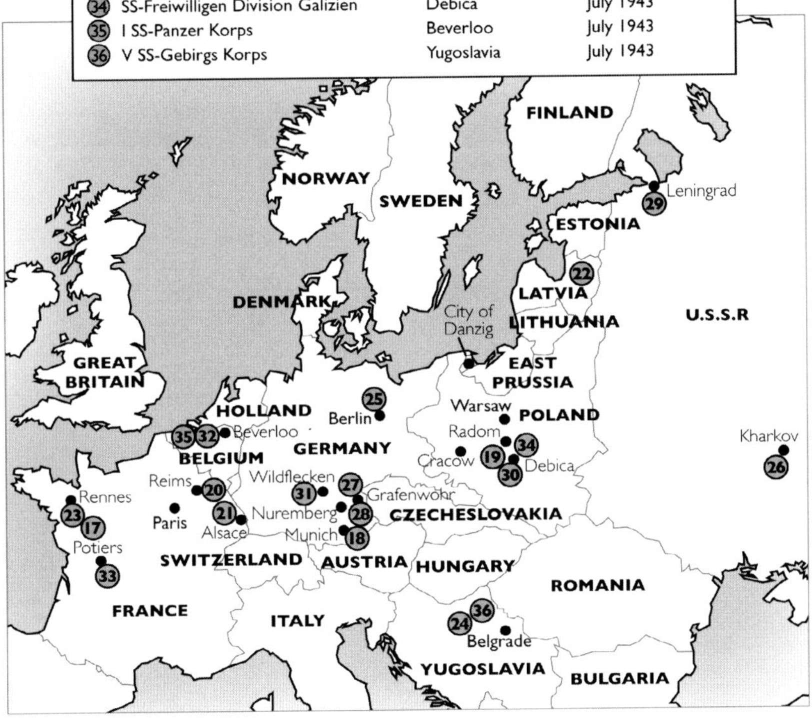

northwards to Leningrad, eastwards to Moscow and southwards across the Don at Rostov and on into the Caucausus. However, this had not been enough to claim victory over the Soviets. If this were to be achieved, more would be needed.

These additional efforts took various forms. The three principle *Waffen-SS* units, *Leibstandarte Adolf Hitler, Das Reich* and *Totenkopf* were extracted from the U.S.S.R., sent to France for a refit and given their own integral *Panzer Regiments.* New *Waffen-SS* units were raised, although their training period would mean they would see little action in Russia in 1942, if at all!

Volume 1 covered the formation and expansion of sixteen separate *Waffen-SS* fighting units. Volume 2 will cover their continued expansion, but also the formation of an additional twenty *Waffen-SS* units. These additional units were as follows:

SS-Hohenstaufen-Division
SS-Frundsberg-Division
Sturmbrigade Reichsführer-SS
Lettisches-SS-Freiwilligen-Brigade
SS-Lettisches-Division
Croat SS-Freiwilligen Division
SS-Sturmbrigade Langemarck
SS-Sturmbrigade Wallonie
SS-Nordland Division
SS-Hitler Youth Division
SS-Freiwilligen-Division Galizien
Estonian Brigade
SS-Karstwehr Kompanie/Battalion
SS-Freiwilligen-Brigade Nederland
SS-Sonderkommando z.b.v. Friedenthal
SS-Panzer-Korps/II. SS-Panzer Korps
I. SS-Panzer Korps
III. (Germanisches) SS-Panzer Korps
IV. SS-Panzer Korps
V. SS-Freiwilligen Gebirgs Korps

Before we go into detail covering the actions in the first half of 1943, we need to start with the situation at the start of that year and the locations of the units in existence at that time:

Leibstandarte SS Adolf Hitler – France
Das Reich – France
Totenkopf – France
Polizei – Leningrad area (northern Russia) and Boguchar Valley (southern Russia)
Wiking – Simowniki (southern Russia)
Nord – Finland
Prinz Eugen – Serbia (former Yugoslavia)
SS-Kavallerie Division – Belij (central Russia)
Kampfgruppe Schuldt – Skassykaja (southern Russia)
Kampfgruppe Fegelein – Boguchar Valley (southern Russia)
2. SS-Infantry-Brigade (mot.) – Leningrad area (northern Russia)
SS-Legion-Norwegian – Leningrad area (northern Russia)
SS-Freikorps-Denmark – Leningrad area (northern Russia)
SS-Legion-Niederlande – Leningrad area (northern Russia)
SS-Legion-Flanderen – Leningrad area (northern Russia)
1. SS-Infantry-Brigade (mot.) – Velikiye Luki (central Russia)

Head First into a Tidal Wave

The above list details where each unit was, but not what situation they were facing at the start of 1943. The focal point of the German war as 1943 opened was situated in the extreme southern part of Russia, namely around Stalingrad. This city had taken on an importance that was in excess of its' probable strategic significance, but assumed more of a political significance for both Hitler and Stalin. It seemed as though the whole outcome of the war pivoted on this one city.

The situation for the Germans worsened rapidly during January 1943 as the Russians completed their deep encirclement of the *German 6th Army*. As dozens of Russian Divisions tasked themselves with completing the destruction of the Germans at Stalingrad, other strong Russian units focused on rolling up the southern front heading west towards Kharkov and southwards into the Caucausus. With the encirclement and imminent destruction of the *6th Army*, a huge gap was left in the German southern frontline. It was into this gap that the Russians poured, what can only be described as, a human tidal wave that was set to engulf all before it. Some of the *Waffen-SS* units were in the direct path of this tidal wave and others would also soon find themselves positioned in it's way. *Field Marshall* Erich von Manstein was placed in command of this southern region at that time.

The forces within the Caucausus were in immediate danger, so those units made a hasty move northwest towards Rostov; one of these units was *SS-Division Wiking*. North east of there, *SS-Kampfgruppe Schuldt* was fighting against the

Map 2 **Waffen-SS Positions: January 1943**

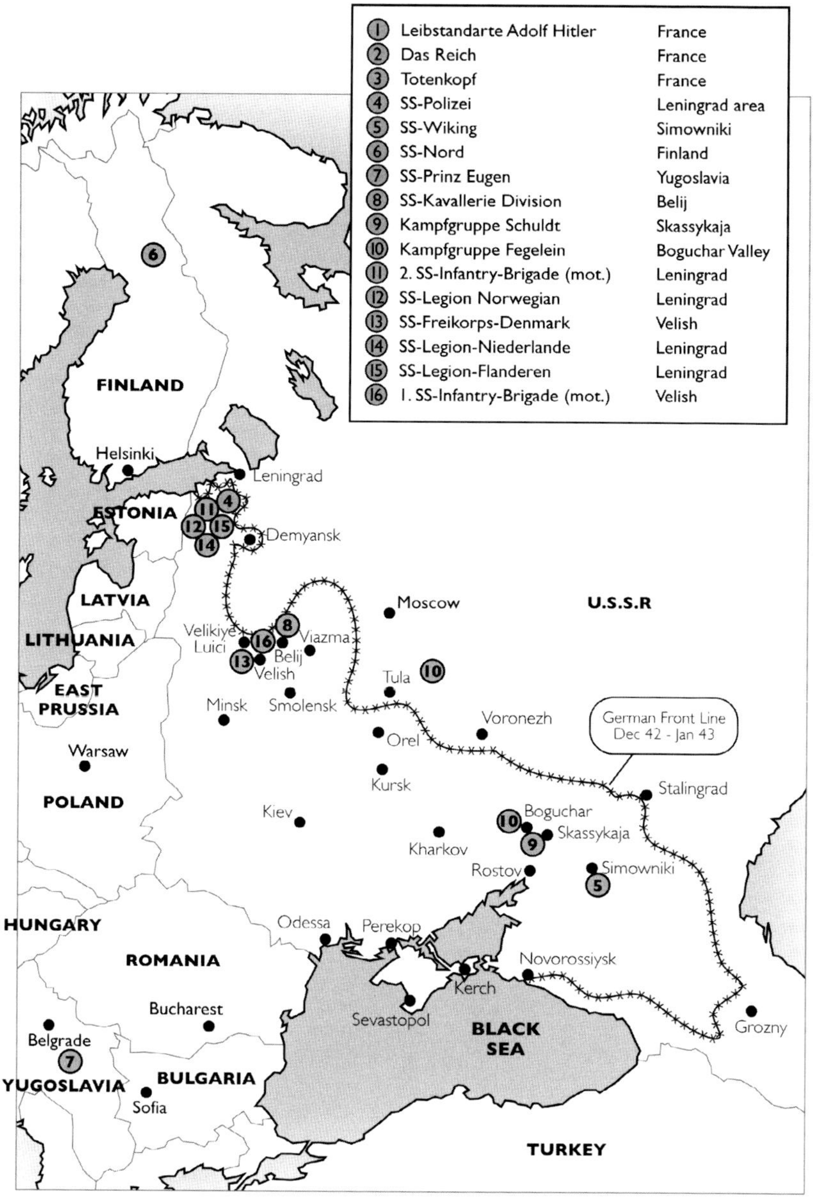

above mentioned Russian tidal wave. The Germans searched for a suitable solution to try to stem the flow of enemy troops and machinery. The potential solution was soon identified as the *SS-Panzer Korps* containing the *LAH, Das Reich* and *Totenkopf Divisions*. They were rushed to this area during late January and early February 1943 and were given the objective of holding Kharkov. *LAH* and *Das Reich* arrived first, but instead of being used in a coordinated combined assault, they were placed under almost immediate pressure by the Soviet forces and forced into a piecemeal defense. The Russians attacked in the north and south of this city during February and it appeared as though these freshly equipped *SS-Panzergrenadier Divisions* would be swallowed up and annihilated before being able to make a difference.

Now let us detail each of these units in the opening months of 1943. As the first Knight's Crosses for the *Waffen-SS* in 1943 came from *Wiking,* we will highlight their actions first before briefly covering their northern *Kameraden*.

SS-Division Wiking

In the final chapter of Volume 1 we highlighted the fact that *Wiking* were moved from the Caucausus, north to the Simowniki area in the closing days of 1942. This was due to the general worsening situation in the east at that time.

SS-Regiment Nordland was the first to arrive, followed by elements of *SS-Regiment Westland.* They had to prepare for defense immediately and as 1942 closed and 1943 opened, *Wiking* became engaged in a bitter struggle in this area. Fighting raged around the town of Orlowskaja from the 5th to the 8th of January and one *SS-Officer,* Hugo Eichhorn, conducted actions that would result in him being awarded the Knight's Cross (details to follow). The *Division* suffered casualties during this fighting and its' aftermath, one notable loss was Harry Polewacz, who had been awarded the Knight's Cross just over two weeks earlier. He was killed at the head of *Nordland* on the 12th of January in Orlowskaja, Wolfgang Joerchel (future Knight's Cross holder) took over command of *Nordland.* Two future Knight's Cross holders also fought in this intense battle, they were Eberhard Heder and Gunther Wannhofer. They were then ordered to give up this area and conduct a fighting retreat, initially southwest towards Ssalsk.

During this fighting retreat towards Ssalsk, further bitter fighting took place around a bridgehead at Prolekarskaja and Manytsch. The *Wiking Pioneer Battalion Commander, SS-Sturmbannführer* Max Schafer led actions that resulted in his award of the Knight's Cross (details to follow). After reaching Ssalsk, they then proceeded northwest towards Rostov, this city itself was reached in the first few days of February 1943.

Wiking did not get to stay in Rostov long and were sent further westwards to Stalino at the end of week one. Instead of having some respite, they were thrown into another struggle, this time further northwest towards Krasno Armaiskoje (*Krasnoarmijs'k*). Positions were taken up south of this objective as the second week of February drew to a close. *SS-Obersturmbannführer* August Dieckmann conducted actions around this objective on the 12th of February that formed part of this Knights's Cross recommendation. They initially held the Soviet advance then pushed it back, taking Krasno Armaiskoje by the 19th of February 1943. (By this stage the *SS-Panzer Korps* had evacuated Kharkov). During the fighting they inflicted significant destruction upon the Russian tank forces in this area. *Wiking* did not get through unscathed during this fighting and one significant casualty, in relation to this project, was *SS-Sturmbannführer* Erwin Reichell. He was wounded and would loose his fight for life on the 28th of February, the same day that he was awarded the Knight's Cross (more detail to follow).

We will leave *Wiking* at this stage and briefly cover the *SS* units fighting in northern Russia, as the next Knight's Cross award came from that region, before returning south to cover the intensive fighting in and around Kharkov.

SS-Polizei

We last covered *Polizei* at the end of 1942 in the area between Kolpino and Mga on the Leningrad front. They enjoyed a relatively quiet time as 1943 dawned. The Soviets launched a fresh offensive on the 12th of January 1943 and this fighting raged for a month. The enemy freed the banks of Lake Ladoga, but they failed to take Mga. Combat died down in mid-February as the Germans held their lines against further enemy aggression and as the Russians counted the cost to them.

Back on the 10th, *SS-Obersturmbannführer* Friedrich-Wilhelm Bock conducted actions around Feklistovo – close to Kolpino – that resulted in his later award of the Knight's Cross. This will be detailed in the next volume of this project and was the only such award for *Polizei* for the whole of 1943!

2. SS-Infantry-Brigade (mot.) & SS-Legion-Niederlande

Both of these units were also positioned in the Leningrad area, west of the positions held by *Polizei* around Krasnoje-Selo and Mga. There was no major occurrences for the *2. Brigade* other than contending with the same Russian offensive as *Polizei*.

For *Niederlande* one of their soldiers, Gerardus Mooyman, conducted actions with his Pak gun on the 13th of February that resulted in his award of the Knight's Cross – the first to a foreign volunteer – detailed shortly.

Map 3 Army Group North: January - March 1943

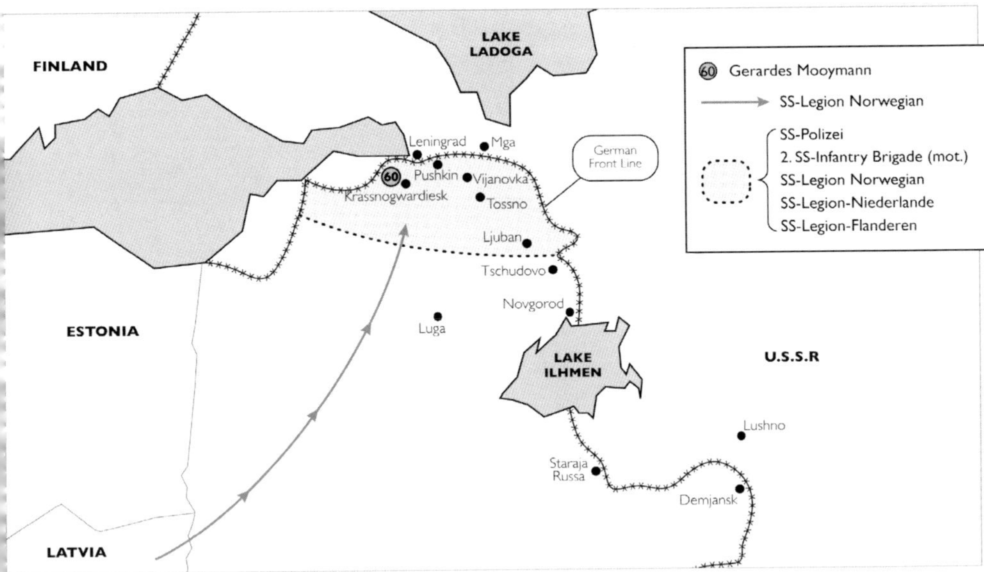

SS-Legion Norwegian

They were initially positioned in Latvia in the early part of 1943, but by February they had moved to Jelgava. They were low in number at this stage and no major occurrences took place for them.

SS-Legion-Flanderen

This unit was in reserve on the Leningrad front in the opening months of 1943.

Now a return south to the Kharkov area and the arrival of the *SS-Panzer Korps*.

SS-Panzer Korps

Leibstandarte SS Adolf Hitler

The worsening situation in the east and the speed of the decline required strong, experienced units to turn the tide. The *LAH* fitted the bill after their refit in France during the second half of 1942. Their new integral *Panzer Regiment* would also be a welcome addition and provide much needed extra strength.

The *LAH* were ordered east and lead elements arrived in the last week of January into the area south east of Kharkov. They detrained at Tschugujew and took over control of Malinowka, as well as Chotomlja to the north and Andrejewka to the south. At this stage the *LAH* were part of the *SS-Panzer Korps,* which was formed in France in mid-1942 under Knight's Cross holder *SS-Obergruppenführer* Paul Hausser.

The *LAH* positions were along the west bank of the Donez and behind the positions of *Das Reich,* who were further east of Kharkov. The lead elements arrived not a moment too soon as the Russian steamroller smashed into these positions in the first few days of February 1943. The initial weight of this enemy attack was focused on the *1. Regiment* in the northern part of the defensive line. The enemy goal was Kharkov and they applied pressure wherever they thought the line was weak. Losses to the *LAH* began to mount in the first week of February, Petschenegi in the north and Andrejewka in the south were particular focal points.

The pressure increased considerably in the second week of February, forcing a retreat to a defensive line closer to Kharkov. Fritz Witt's *1. Panzer Grenadier Regiment* were moved back to Merefa, south west of Kharkov. The *2. Panzer Grenadier Regiment* were positioned from Woljanoje to Ternowo, an area to the south-east of the city.

SS-Regiment Deutschland were positioned to the immediate east of the city. There were deep Russian thrusts to the south of the *LAH* positions. On the 8th of February Hugo Kraas conducted actions in Glinizia that formed part of his Knight's Cross recommendation.

This worsening situation forced an amalgamation of the forces in this area. The *LAH's, 2. Panzer Grenadier Regiment* and other elements were placed under the control of *Das Reich*, holding the northern sector of their overall positions. A second group was under the control of the *LAH* and contained the *1. Panzer Grenadier Regiment,* the *Panzer Regiment,* the *Pioneer, Flak* and *Artillery,* as well as *SS-Regiment Der Führer.* Enemy attacks continued in the days after these moves. *Peiper's* men helped to rescue the *Heer's, 320. Infantry Division.* As the middle of February beckoned, the positions held were as follows; *Das Reich* in the immediate north-east of Kharkov, Wisch's *2. Regiment* in the area between Merefa and Kharkov, with the *1. Regiment* around Merefa.

Orders were issued for an attack to the south by the group positioned around Merefa; this group split into three sub-groups. One group was under the command of Kurt Meyer and included elements of the *Panzer Regiment* under Max Wunsche, they had the objective of taking Alexejewka. The central group consisted of *Der Führer,* under Otto Kumm and they were ordered to take Borki. As they moved towards this objective, Kumm conducted actions on the 11th of February around Jefremowka that resulted in his award of the Knight's Cross to the Iron Cross with Oakleaves (details to follow). The third group under Fritz Witt had to hold the flank to the east and had the objective of Bereka.

By the 12th of February Kumm's group had reached Borki, Witt's group had reached Bereka and Meyer had reached Jefremowka. The day before Hans Reimling, from the *LAH's, Panzer Regiment,* began actions that would result in his award of the Knight's Cross. Meyer reached Alexejewka by the middle of the month, but became cut-off. Otto Kumm reached as far south as Ochotschaje and Witt's group were engaged in fighting around Bereka. This fighting was costly and bravery was the order of the day. This was around the same time as Gerardus Mooyman's Knight's Cross actions further north around Leningrad. On the 14th, Hermann Dahlke conducted actions that resulted in his award of the Knight's Cross. Albert Frey would also receive the Knight's Cross for the actions of his *I Battalion* in their fight around this area at that time. Wunsche led a push from Jefremowka and linked up with Meyer, bringing much needed fuel and ammunition with him.

Exactly sixty years after this action, February 2003, one soldier who was present during this fighing in Bereka wrote a letter to his former *Commander,* Albert Frey. This person was the then *SS-Mann* Gerhard Dilling who was a radio operator and his recollections went as follows:

"On the 14th of February 1943 we became aware of the fact that radio contact with the *3. Kompanie* and *1. Kompanie* had been lost. After repeating this situation to you (Frey) twice, you gave me the order to establish radio contact once again. The *9. Kompanie* of *Der Führer* were moving up on the right hand side, so they were ordered to assist in the attack and the time of the attack was set for 11:00am.

You gave me an accurate description of the way to Bereka. Move along the track towards the small forest, then turn 90 degrees to the left of this forest and continue for 2-3km, where I would find Bereka. As I advanced along this route, there was one Stug from Wiesemann's unit. I advanced through very deep snow and the temperature was freezing. I did take two photos of this area at that time and carried on. Despite the cold, I was sweating and had to use some snow to help cool me down.

After I passed the forest, there was the sound of gunfire and on the right, I seen the village of Bereka. I had to cross two Balkas to reach the village and after crossing the first I noticed a small group of enemy soldiers moving towards my position. They were initially 100 metres away, so I ensured my rifle was fully

The photograph of the LAH Sturmgeschutze described above by Gerhard Dilling

This is another of Gerhard Dilling's photographs and shows the view towards Bereka.

loaded. When they came to within 30 metres I shouted to them to put up their hands. They did not do what I asked and as they came closer, I could see that the wind and snow was forcing them to keep their eyes closed. Thankfully, *SS-Rottenfiuhrer* Fuhring was moving behind them with his machine-pistol, so the situation came out well for us.

I then moved into the village and came across *SS-Oberscharführer* Dahlke. My arrival had come too late, as they had already attacked in the early morning. This attack had produced enormous loss for the *3. Kompanie*, with *SS-Obersturmführer* Gessner, *SS-Untersturmführer* Flocke and many of the *NCOs* being killed. I was very shocked by this news and Dahlke told me to go to a nearby house. In this house were around 10 wounded *Kameraden*. The room was filled with a very bad smell and almost every soldier in there had been shot in the stomach. There was no doctor or first-aiders there, so the situation was very difficult. I used the plentiful snow to cool their heads and wet their lips.

In the darkness a hand took my arm and a voice asked me to shoot them. This request was repeated again and again and I will never forget the sound of this voice. I can only assume that this soldier died shortly afterwards as he stopped asking me whilst I held his hand.

I took part in the continuing attack of the *3. Kompanie* the following morning. I took control of the re-connected telephone contact to you in the evening. The fighting continued over the following day and the battle was hard and heavy, but we succeeded in securing the whole of Bereka by then.

This is how I recall the time of your 30th birthday (16th February 1943). Sixty years have passed, but the memories of those days are like yesterday!"

I have included this letter in full as I feel it provides a good first hand account of one person's perspective of a battle that contributed to two soldiers receiving the Knight's Cross. I hope you the reader agree?

By the 15th the fighting had reached a high point. Kumm and his group could go no further from Ochotschaje, Witt and his men were bogged down in and around Bereka with Meyer and Wunsche coming under increasing pressure in Alexejewka – the extreme point of the overall push southwards. This fighting had been costly, but had delivered the destruction of the fighting capability of the Russian VI Cavalry Corps. This was the start of the reversing of the situation around Kharkov.

I feel it is worth including excerpts from an order issued by Paul Hausser on the 17th of February 1943:

"Since 30.1.1943, the *SS-Panzerkorps* has been engaged in alternating offensive and defensive fighting in an attempt to stop the advance of three Russian

Armies. The enemy's losses have been heavy. One Cavalry Corps was shattered to pieces.

For the first time, *Panzergrenadier Division LSSAH* and *Das Reich,* to which *Panzergrenadier Division Totenkopf* now belongs, were able to fight side by side. Every unit gave its' all during those weeks and, despite the complications in the command process, caused by mixing of the units, decisive defensive successes were achieved.

I offer my deepest respect to the officers and men of all the subordinated units for their performance and conduct in these difficult weeks."

Due to the worsening situation and unrelenting pressure exerted by the Russians, requests were made to withdraw to the southwest of Kharkov. These requests were turned down and the order to hold Kharkov was reiterated. Paul Hausser took the decision to order the evacuation of the city in the early hours of the 16th of February 1943, thereby saving the *SS-Panzer Korps*. The order was given after consultation with *General* Lanz. This order was in direct contravention to an order from Adolf Hitler. By this stage the Russians had already broken into the northwest part of Kharkov. The order from Hausser placed his men behind the Udy River.

Das Reich

Das Reich was one of the units sent into the worsening situation in the east, within the southern sector. They began moving from France on the 9th of January 1943 and traveled through Germany, southern Poland, Tarnapol and onto Kiev. From Kiev they moved onto Kharkov, with their final positions northeast of Kharkov being reached at the end of January.

Although this was the situation for the main bulk of the *Division,* this was not the case for the *I Battalion, SS-Regiment Der Führer.* They were the first unit to arrive in Russia from this *SS-Panzer Korps,* arriving in the third week of January. They were employed immediately into the fight. They were sent to Woronesh and earmarked for a push towards Alexandrowka. They became part of a *Kampfgruppe* under Knight's Cross holder *SS-Standartenführer* Hinrich Schuldt and fought the Russians around Woroschilow at the end of January. The fighting of this *Kampfgruppe* will be covered shortly, but *Der Führer* stayed with them until the end of the first week of March, when they returned to their parent *Division.*

The main part of the *Division* focused on trying to familiarize themselves with the area they were positioned in. They also focused on assessing the situation they were being placed into. As *Das Reich* had been part of *Army Group Centre* during their last trip to Russia, they were not familiar with this area. Their

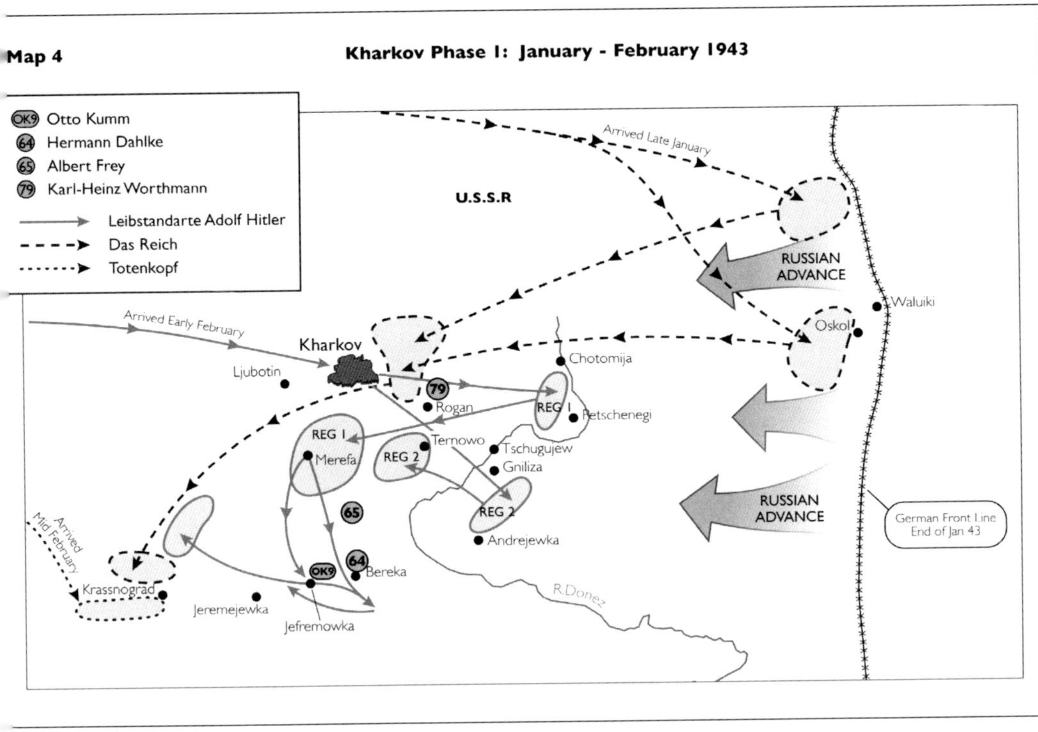

positions placed them around Kosnika, Kamenka, Alexandrowka and Oskol. The first enemy engagements came on the last day of January 1943. At the same time the *6. Armee,* further east, were preparing to surrender.

Heavy defensive fighting raged as February 1943 began. *Das Reich's Panzer Regiment* was committed to battle for its baptism of fire, under *SS-Oberführer* Vahl. At the end of the first week of February the enemy advances in the southern area of Kharkov were presenting a worrying development for the Germans. Riding on a victorious wave in the aftermath of Stalingrad was providing the Russians with a seemingly unstoppable rate of advance. The northern area of Kharkov was also under threat. If this rate of advance continued the Germans would lose an entire *Army Group,* not just an *Armee!*

As the situation worsened, *Das Reich* was withdrawn behind the River Donez and Kharkov itself on the 9th of February 1943. Elements of *Das Reich – Der Führer* – were sent southwards to Merefa and joined the *LAH* there. This was the first attempt by the *SS-Panzer Korps* units to stem and halt the Soviet tidal wave in this region. On the 11th of February Karl-Heinz Worthmann conducted actions around Hill .209 near Kharkov that would result in his award of the Knight's

Cross (details to follow). Christian Tychsen also conducted actions on the 11th at Priwolje that formed part of his Knight's Cross recommendation (details to follow). On the 13th of February Hitler ordered that Kharkov was to be held at all costs.

The attempts to stem the Russian advances at this time were insufficient, so on the afternoon of the 14th of February, *SS-Obergruppenführer* Paul Hausser ordered Kharkov to be evacuated. This was in direct disobedience to a Hitler Order or *Führerbefehl.*

Elements of *Der Führer* were involved in a bitter fight around Ochatschaje. The 15th and 16th of February seen the remaining elements of the *SS-Panzer Korps,* along with other units, being withdrawn from the important city of Kharkov. On the 17th of February new positions were taken up at Tanarowka, *Der Führer* was reattached to *Das Reich* around Krassnograd.

We will now leave *Das Reich* for the moment and briefly cover the advances of *Totenkopf* up to the middle of February 1943.

Totenkopf

This *Division* was still located in France as 1943 opened, being sent there after their near-annihilistic battles at Demjansk that lasted for most of 1942 for them. They had been virtually wiped out after these battles and being in France gave them a chance to rebuild. They arrived there in the second half of October 1942 and began the task of reforming.

This rebuilding and reforming came to an abrupt halt in late January 1943 due to the impending crisis in the southern sector of the Russian Front in the wake of Stalingrad.

Their movement eastwards began on the 1st of February, but took nearly two weeks just for the lead elements to arrive. Those lead elements were thrown into the worsening situation south of Kharkov on the 12th of February 1943. The bulk of the *Division* was not in place as the key city of Kharkov was abandoned a few days later.

It was evident that, although the newly created *SS-Panzer Korps* was a strong formation and contained battle experienced soldiers, it was not quite ready to deal with the huge Russian tidal wave engulfing southern Russia at that time. They needed to draw breath and regroup before taking a second try to regain the initiative on the Russian Front. The importance of this need cannot be underestimated; it really did look as though nothing was capable of stopping the enemy at that time.

Map 5 Army Group South: January - February 1943

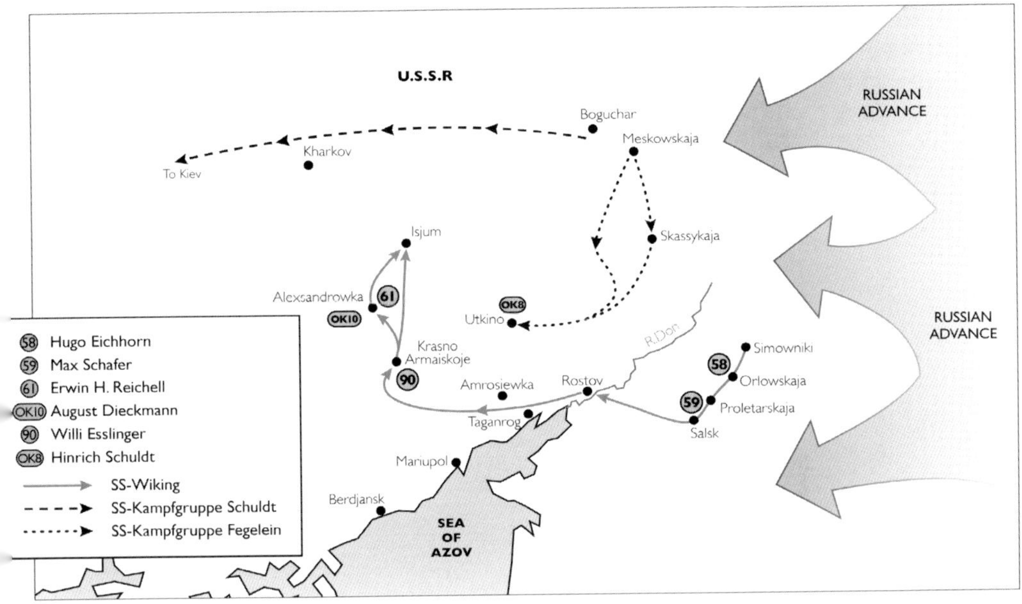

We will leave *Totenkopf* and the rest of the *SS-Panzer Korps* at this stage and cover the situation with *Kampfgruppe Schuldt,* also up to mid-February 1943, as they too got dragged along in this Soviet tidal wave.

SS-Kampfgruppe Schuldt

(SS-Brigade Schuldt/SS-Kampfgruppe Dietrich)

We last covered this *Kampfgruppe* at the end of 1942 whilst they were fighting at Skassyrkaja (*Skasyrskaja).* Hinrich Schuldt himself was sent to Donskoj to take command of a new *Kampfgruppe.* Wilhelm Dietrich took command of the existing *Kampfgruppe,* temporarily named *Kampfgruppe Dietrich.*

In the opening days of 1943 these two units fought in their respective areas; *Kampfgruppe Schuldt* around Kamensk, *Kampfgruppe Dietrich* around Werchre-Obljswkij. By the end of the first week of January 1943 *Kampfgruppe Dietrich* were in Kowytkin and Alexejew. The drastic and fast moving situation forced them to new positions at Krassny Gornjak. In mid-January they moved to Karpowo-Obryskij, were relieved, then moved to Olchowskij, fighting there until mid-February 1943 (as Kharkov was being evacuated). They were moved west to

Ssasonoff, then moved again to Swerdlowsk and finally to Woroschitowa, before finally re-joining Hinrich Schuldt at Utkino on the 19th of February 1943. This was the day that *Wiking* took control of Krasno Armaiskoje.

Back in January, Hinrich Schuldt took his new *Kampfgruppe* from Donskoj and fought eastwards during that month. Millerowo, Matwejewka, Oreschkin, Podgornoje and Alexandrowka all fell under the control of *Kampfgruppe Schuldt*. As January came to a close they were in Woroschiloff. Popowka became the main position as mid-February beckoned. On the 15th of February they were sent to Uspenka and fought in that area for a few days. They moved to Adrianopol, where they joined *Kampfgruppe Dietrich* in readiness for a new threat close to Utkino.

1. SS-Infantry Brigade (mot.) & SS-Freikorps Denmark

These two units were positioned together within Army Group Centre, initially at Velish and then Velikiye Luki. By the start of February 1943 they had moved to Podluschje. There were no major occurrences for these two units in these opening two months of 1943.

SS-Kavallerie Division

We left this unit around the Belij pocket near Rshew at the end of 1942. They remained here as 1943 opened and by the end of the first month were fighting in the forest at Tatianka, Timochino and Nikalinka on the River Vop. This fighting lasted until mid-February and was considered a success for the Germans.

SS-Kampfgruppe Fegelein

This unit was fighting for its' survival at the end of 1942 in the Bocuchar Valley area with Fegelein himself being wounded and evacuated (as well as awarded the Oakleaves!) They managed a break out of an enemy encirclement towards the end of December and headed east. They were encircled for a second time in mid-January 1943 around Kantemirovka. The remnants managed to break out of this encirclement too and headed further east. By the 4th of February 1943 they were reported as being in Kiev, where they were loaded on trains and sent back to Germany.

That brought to an end the existence of that particular *SS* unit.

Now to move further afield to the other extremes of the front line at that time.

Prinz Eugen

This unit was last covered in the final chapter of Volume 1, where they had become involved in their first actions in southern Serbia as 1942 drew to a close.

January 1943 opened with involvement in Operation Weiss, which involved fighting against Tito and his large partisan organization in the western sector of Bosnia. This operation started on the 20th of January. Their initial advance took them to the southeast with Miholjsko, Slunj, Krnjac and Vojnic being taken in the first week of heavy fighting. Bihac was the next target; this was occupied on the 29th of January. The advance continued to Bosanski Petrovac, taken on the 7th of February.

As *Prinz Eugen* pushed to the southeast, the enemy kept moving in the same direction, moving ahead and away from them. This situation continued as mid-February beckoned.

Nord

We had left this unit in northern Finland as 1942 closed. Their situation remained unchanged and was virtually static as 1943 opened. The emphasis for the Russians and Germans was elsewhere on the front lines, so this very extreme northern sector was a low priority for both.

As you read through this volume and see the events that unfolded during 1943, one question to ask yourself is, what difference would an additional *Division* of 20,000 men have made to the overall situation on the Russian front if this unit had been placed at a more critical location?

This ends the coverage of all front-line units in existence at that time, but before covering the initial Knight's Cross awards of 1943, we will provide a brief overview of three new *SS* units that were being raised at that time, before detailing some of the new Knight's Cross holders.

Estonian SS-Legion/Estonian SS-Freiwilligen Brigade

Towards the end of August 1942 this new unit was ordered into existence. The first *Commander* was (future Knight's Cross holder) *SS-Brigadeführer und Generalmajor der Waffen-SS* Franz Augsberger. They focused on formation and training throughout the rest of 1942 in Debica, Poland.

SS-Karstwehr Kompanie/Battalion

The above *Kompanie* was also raised in August 1942 and was placed under the command of *SS-Standartenführer* Dr. Hans Brand. This unit was brought into existence to specifically tackle the growing problem of Partisan activity in the northern Italian/southern Austrian Alps region. This very small unit was positioned in Dachau for their initial training and formation. By the middle of November the same year, they had been increased in size to *Battalion*-strength. They continued with their training throughout the remainder of 1942 and into the first part of 1943.

Hohenstaufen

This unit actually began life in the closing days of 1942, but it was not until January 1943 that things started to take shape. *SS-Brigadeführer* Wilhelm Bittrich – existing Knight's Cross holder – was placed in command. They started their formation near Reims in France. Troops arrived initially in January and February. Experienced officers were sent to this unit. It was raised as a *Panzergrenadier Division,* it had its' own integral *Panzer Abteilung.*

Frundsberg

This unit started formation in Alsace, Saintes, in January 1943. They were initially known as *Karl der Grosse. SS-Brigadeführer* Lothar Debes was their first *Commander* and as with *Hohenstaufen,* experienced officers and NCOs were sent as the foundation. They too were formed as a *Panzergrenadier Division.*

We have covered all of the *SS* units in existence up to mid-February 1943. Now all that is left is to detail the Knight's Cross awards up to the 20th of February 1943 (for actions conducted up to the middle of February), before closing Chapter One.

Hugo Eichhorn

Date of birth: 11.02.1911
SS Number: 44 503
Born in Weilmunster, he entered the *SS* in November 1932, having previously been a member of the *S.A.* from August 1931, and was placed with the *1/78. Sturm* in Wiesbaden. He spent a three-month stint with the *Army* from February to May 1939. As an *SS-Sturmmann* he was sent to Bad Tolz Officer's school from the 27th of March 1940 until the 1st of August 1940, leaving there with the rank of *SS-Oberscharführer.* He was posted to the *2. Kompanie, SS-Pioneer Replacement Battalion* located in Dresden. He gained promotion to *SS-Untersturmführer* on the 9th of November 1940 and followed this by a posting to the *Pioneer Battalion* within the *SS-Division Wiking* at the end of January 1941. He went with *Wiking* as they embarked upon their journey into Russia in mid-1941.

He was initially given the task of commanding a *Kompanie* within *Wiking's Pioneer Battalion,* but this changed in early March when he became the *Battalion Adjutant.* He was awarded the Black Wound Badge on the 14th of September

Hugo Eichorn photographed later in the war, whilst holding the rank of SS-Obersturmbannführer. He was awarded the Knight's Cross as an SS-Hauptsturmführer.

1941 for a shrapnel wound received on the 4th of July, followed six days later by the award of the Second Class Iron Cross. He gained a further promotion to *SS-Obersturmführer* on the 9th of November 1941, the same day that he was awarded the First Class Iron Cross. On the 10th of September 1942 he was presented with the Eastern Front medal. He was then promoted further to *SS-Hauptsturmführer* on the 9th of November 1942.

It was during the difficult fighting around Orlowskaja on the 8th of January 1943 that Hugo Eichhorn was involved in actions that would result in his award of the Knight's Cross. The recommendation document is short and to the point, containing the following overview:

'*SS-Hauptsturmführer* Eichhorn was part of the *Regiment's* fighting at Orlowskaja where he was in command of two weak *Kompanies* and took it upon himself to catch and then destroy the Field Regiment 550.

An example of personal resolute leadership and because of his decision and actions, important streets and a railroad junction were once again firmly in our hands. In the course of the fighting over 700 enemy soldiers were killed, 200 were captured and 5 guns, 3 heavy pak, one heavy flak, 8 anti-tank rifles, 22 MGs and many smaller weapons as well as 30 vehicles were also captured.

The *Generalkommando* recommends the award of the Knight's Cross to the Iron Cross.

Signed: *Generalfeldmarschall* von Manstein.'

This recommendation was quickly approved on the 15th of January 1943, as *Wiking* were conducting their fighting withdrawal towards Rostov. The recommendation itself came through on the 20th of January 1943.

It is known that he was also awarded the Wound Badge in Silver and the General Assault Badge, although the dates of these awards are not listed. What is known is that he received a heavy head wound on the 4th of September 1943 that removed him from front-line service. He later served with the *SS-Pioneer Training and Replacement Battalion 1* from the 8th of October 1943. From February 1944 until the end of the war, he commanded the *SS-Pioneer Training and Replacement Regiment* based in Dresden. In that time he was promoted to *SS-Sturmbannführer,* on the 20th of July 1944. One source listed him as being promoted to *SS-Obersturmbannführer* one year later, although his file does not show this last promotion. Hugo Eichhorn survived the war and died on the 27th of May 1992.

Max Schafer

Date of birth: 17.01.1907

SS Number: 16 362

Born in Karlsruhe, he entered the *S.A.* at the start of 1931, moving to the *SS* in mid-June the same year. He was promoted on the 30th January 1934 to *SS-Untersturmführer.* By April 1935 he was serving as a *Platoon Commander* in the *SS-Pioneer School* in Reutlingen. On the 9th of November 1936 he was promoted further to *SS-Obersturmführer* and proceded through various courses and postings, as well as the actions in Austria and the Sudetenland prior to the outbreak of the Second World War.

He took part in the battle for Poland with the *SS-Pioneer Battalion.* In early January 1940 he was serving with the *SS V Division.* On the 1st of June 1940 he was promoted to *SS-Hauptsturmführer* and two days later received the Second Class Iron Cross, presumably for actions during the western campaign in May 1940? He then moved to the command of the *2. Kompanie,* within the newly created *SS-Division Wiking's Pioneer Battalion.*

He moved with this *Division* as they went east in June 1941 and on the 13th of July was awarded the First Class Iron Cross. It would appear that he led the *Battalion* from late November, although it was not until the 26th December

An autographed photograph of SS-Obersturmbannführer Max Schafer, pictured after his award of the Knight's Cross in early 1943.

1941 that he was promoted to *SS-Sturmbannführer.* He was awarded the General Assault Badge on the 9th of May 1942 and the Eastern Front Medal on the 15th of September 1942. He found himself with his *Battalion* in the deteriorating situation as 1943 opened. As covered above, they were conducting a fighting withdrawal towards Ssalsk in mid-January 1943. It was during this that he was involved in a difficult battle around Prolekarskaja and Manytsch on the 19th of January 1943. It was for these actions that he was recommended for the Knight's Cross to the Iron Cross on the 10th of February 1943, this highlighted the following:

"*SS-Sturmbannführer* Schafer was with his *Battalion* heading south eastwards towards Prolekarskaja on a broad front on the 19.1.1943. In the night, during a bad blizzard, they were attacked by the enemy. The objective was a bridge at Manytsch on the main Prolekarskaja-Ssalsk road. The *Division* held the bridgehead at Prolekarskaja and they had to prevent the enemy from taking it. *SS-Sturmbannführer* Schafer took the decision to be the base of this defense. He launched an attack against the enemy that had broken into the bridgehead by advancing around it in their vehicles. Hard fighting followed and the fall of Manytsch was prevented long enough for the *Division* to pass through and evade loss or capture. Schafer was at the point of this attack and hard fighting."

This recommendation does not name the person who wrote it or who signed it off. It was however, approved on the 12th of February 1943, only two days after the recommendation was dated! By that stage Schafer had been promoted on the 30th January 1943 to *SS-Obersturmbannführer.* He was presented with the Knight's Cross to the Iron Cross by his *Divisional Commander,* Felix Steiner, after they had taken Krasno Armaiskoje on the 19th of February 1943.

We will leave the activities of Max Schafer at this stage as this would not end his association with the Knight's Cross or its' higher grades, but more of that in later volumes.

Gerardes Mooyman

Date of birth: 23.09.1923

SS Number: Unknown

Born in Appeldorn, Holland, Mooyman volunteered to join the *SS* on the 26th of April 1941, aged 17. Although his native country had been overrun less than one year earlier, he was impressed by the Germans and their military abilities and volunteered to join one of the early *Waffen-SS* foreign volunteer units. He

The Dutch volunteer Gerardes Mooyman, photographed on the day he was presented with the Knight's Cross for his successful actions on the Leningrad front.

was placed with the *SS-Freiwilligen-Legion Niederlande*. This unit fought in Russia from 1941 onwards and Mooyman fought with them in those early battles. They ended up as part of the battle around Leningrad and remained there up to early 1943, when the Russians launched another major attack, aimed at relieving Leningrad. He was serving in the *14. Kompanie* at that stage. In January 1943 he successfully engaged Russian tanks and knocked out four of them. For this, he was promoted to *SS-Sturmmann*.

The fighting was not over and on the 13th of February 1943, engaged in actions that resulted in him knocking out 13 enemy tanks. No formal recommendation document survives on his file, but we do know that the award followed soon after the actions.

An overview of the actions is as follows: Mooyman was crewing a French-made PaK 97/38 when the Russians launched another attack in his area. In the early part of the day he knocked out seven T-34s, but his *Gun Commander* was killed, leaving Mooyman as the main leader. The Russians were not put off by their losses during the morning and their determination to relieve Leningrad continued. They sent more tanks against Mooyman's positions and the surrounding area. Mooyman once more stepped up to the challenge and destroyed a further six tanks, bringing his total to thirteen, not a bad accomplishment for one gunner in one day! His actions forced the Russians to think again and he helped to stop the enemy attempts in this immediate area at that time.

As stated above, no recommendation survives, but after action reports contained the following details:

'The Dutch volunteers played a major part in the failure of the Bolshevik attack south of Lake Ladoga, who protected the flank with their PaK guns, the most successful one of these, with 13 enemy armoured vehicles, was *SS-Mann* Gerardus Mooyman.'

Although the rank may be incorrect at that time, his actions were correct and led to him being awarded the Knight's Cross to the Iron Cross on the 20th of February 1943. He was also promoted to *SS-Rottenführer*. As he was the first non-German volunteer (Austria had been absorbed into the border of greater Germany, so Germany and Austria were classed as one country by the Germans at that time) to be awarded this high honour, he was used extensively by Hitler's propaganda machine. This was aimed at helping the recruitment drive at that time and encouraging further foreign volunteers into the ranks of the *Waffen-SS*.

He was sent to Bad Tolz to train as an officer from the 6th of September 1943 until the 11th of March 1944. He was promoted to *SS-Untersturmführer* on the

21st of June 1944 and is listed as serving with the *2. Kompanie/Panzerjaeger Abteilung 54,* at that time. He is also listed as serving within the *Panzerjaeger Abteilung 11* in the closing stages of World War II.

Besides winning the Knight's Cross, he is also listed as being awarded the Second Class Iron Cross, on the 4th of February 1943 and the First Class Iron Cross on the 10th of February 1943. It could be that these were backdated to before the award of the Knight's Cross, something that was not unique. The Russian Front Medal, Infantry Assault Badge and Black Wound Badge were also awarded to him, although the award dates are not known. He is credited with destroying a total of twenty-three enemy tanks by the end of the war and according to Mooyman himself, a number of these were destroyed by the hand-held *Panzerfaust.*

His high profile award and subsequent media circus made him a recognizable individual and he was quickly arrested and imprisoned in Holland after the war. He died on the 21st of June 1987 from injuries sustained in a car accident.

Now that we have covered the first of 1943's Knight's Cross holders, a quick look back, before seeing what developed next in Chapter 2.

Summary

In this initial chapter we have covered the first six weeks of 1943. This was a period of intense activity on the Russian Front. The *Waffen-SS* units in the north held their ground against further enemy advances and attempts to free Leningrad. However, at the opposite end of the front line, the pressure proved too great. The newly equipped *SS-Panzer Korps* were not in a position to halt the enemy advances at that stage around Kharkov. Further east and south, the units positioned there were advancing rapidly westwards to avoid complete destruction. The only *Waffen-SS* units to make forward advances were those in Yugoslavia.

This was not the sort of start that the *Waffen-SS* had hoped for in 1943. The experience, skills and abilities that they had gained in the previous three-and-a-half years were proving to be no match for the might of the increasingly confident Russians. Would this strong enemy completely overwhelm the Germans?

CHAPTER TWO

STOPPING THE TIDAL WAVE

As covered, the *SS-Panzer Korps* were thrown into the rapidly deteriorating situation in southern Russia in the opening stages of 1943. Delivered in an initial piecemeal fashion, they could not effectively stop the Soviet onslaught to start with. They had to evaucuate the key city of Kharkov to save themselves from suffering the same fate as the *6th Army* at Stalingrad, who only weeks earlier, were left with no option but to surrender.

Hausser took his gamble and withdrew his men out of the city and headed southwest. They turned around and prepared for defense, although Hausser had different ideas. He evacuated the city to save his men, but also to wait until he felt the time was right to strike back. This time was not long in coming, so let us continue coverage of the *Divisions* of the *SS-Panzer Korps* as the next stage of this overall battle for control of Kharkov unfolded. We will start with the *LAH* as the next Knight's Cross came from that *Division.*

LAH

By the 18th of February 1943 new positions had been taken up behind the Berestowaia River. The *LAH* assumed control of an area running from Berestowka through to Ochotschaje and up to Borki. *Der Führer* left their previous area and rejoined *Das Reich,* now positioned south of the *LAH,* close to Krassnograd, with elements of *Totenkopf* next to them. The enemy pressure was continuing at this time north and south of these positions.

This placed the three *Divisions* of Hausser's *Korps* into a unified line of defense and gave them the best chance they had of stemming this enemy tidal wave and hopefully stopping it altogether. To stop an advance of this magnitude could not be done in one step, but would have to be done in stages, hopefully ultimately leading to success. So what were those stages?

The *4. Panzer Armee* was moving up from the south, so orders came for the *SS-Panzer Korps* to push to the southeast and affect a link with the *4. Panzer Armee*. This push began for the *LAH* on the 19th of February, with elements of Peiper's *Battalion* moving into the southern sector. *Totenkopf* and *Das Reich* pushed further southwards; Witt's *1. Regiment* held the northern sector against the enemy. As the advance gathered momentum, some *LAH* soldiers conducted actions on the 20th of February that were significant in relation to this overall project. The first was Alfred Gunther who was involved in fighting between Melechowka and Rjabuchino, whilst supporting the *1. Panzergrenadier Regiment,* that resulted in his award of the Knight's Cross (details to follow). Also, over the 19th and 20th of February, Fritz Witt overseen the actions of his men between Merefa and Taranowka that resulted in his award of the Knight's Cross to the Iron Cross with Oakleaves (details to follow). This was the same day that Gerardes Mooymann's Knight's Cross was approved.

These advances southwards were far from easy, but survival was at stake, so the efforts exerted by the *SS* soldiers was significant. Peiper's men gave assistance, but their positions were taken over by elements of the *Panzer Regiment* and the *Aufklarungs*. On the 21st of February Kurt Meyer smashed into Jeremejewka and destroyed the enemy positioned there, with the help of Max Wunsche and his tanks. This action by Meyer resulted in his award of the Knight's Cross to the Iron Cross with Oakleaves (full details will follow). In fact Meyer's Oakleaves were approved only two days later, on the 23rd of February.

They then pushed on slightly to the east, smashing further enemy units in their path. The advance south of here could not be achieved due to the strength of the enemy in that area at that time. On the 25th of February they started to move northeast from Jeremejewka and at Jefremowka, Wunsche's tanks engaged and destroyed significant enemy forces. This fighting resulted in the award of no less than three Knight's Crosses. These were awarded to Max Wunsche, Wilhelm Beck and Hans Reimling – the other part of Reimling's Knight's Cross recommendation being two weeks earlier (details of all of these will follow shortly).

The position of Jeremewjewka became a focus point for elements of the *LAH* defense and also for the Russian attack over the next couple of days. In addition, the *LAH's* positions, initially running from Krassnograd and directly northeast to Bf. Borki, had to be pulled back to a shorter defensive line running

Map 6 **German Frontline: Mid-February 1943**

from Karlowka, west of Krassnograd, around to Jarotin, north of Krassnograd and on out to Jeremejewka. The enemy pressure was still heavy and the *LAH's* task as February ended was to defend against the enemy and keep them busy as their *I Panzer Korps Kameraden* moved closer to the enemy's rear area from the south. Recognition was coming thick and fast for the men of the *LAH,* as approval was granted for Max Wunsche and Hans Reimling's Knight's Cross on the last day of February. This was the same day that Erwin Reichel's (from *Wiking)* Knight's Cross was also approved.

In the first few days of March 1943, the *LAH* began to extent their area further to the east and northeast. This was around the same time as *Das Reich* was moving north into the same area. On the afternoon of the 2nd of March elements of the *LAH* made contact with elements of *Das Reich* at Paraskoweja and the following day *Totenkopf* met the *LAH* further south at Kegitschewka. These links resulted in the encirclement of enemy troops in this area. The destruction of this enemy pocket began – mainly by *Das Reich* and *Totenkopf.* In these first few days of March, further recommendations were approved; Fritz Witt's Oakleaves were approved on the 1st, with Hermann Dahlke and Albert Frey's Knight's Crosses being approved on the 3rd.

For the *LAH,* they began a move back to Krassnograd and rested for a couple of days before beginning their push north of Krassnograd towards Walki. These moves started on the 6th of March. Joachim Peiper conducted rapid actions between Fedrowka and Hf. Bridlock on this day that resulted in his recommendation for the Knight's Cross. It was also on this day that Hermann Weiser was involved in fighting at Hf. Ssenhkoff-Kut that was part of his recommendation. The other part was around Walki the following day. This was the same date that the *LAH* crossed the Msha River at Bridok, as well as the all-important Walki. Elements of the *Panzer Regiment* and the *Aufklarungs* were having a difficult fight against enemy anti-tank guns.

The attacks towards the northeast continued with Ljubotin being reached on the 8th and consolidated on the 9th. This would be used as a springboard into Kharkov itself, but we will halt the coverage of the *LAH* at this stage. The capture of Ljubotin was not the only high point for the *LAH* on this day, with the approval of Joachim Peiper's Knight's Cross to the Iron Cross taking place also. His actions for this award were only three days earlier!

Before covering the continued advance of the *LAH,* let us cover the actions of *Das Reich* up to this point.

Das Reich

As with the *LAH, Das Reich* had to take up new positions southwest of Kharkov in order to regroup. They found themselves at Tanarowka and Krassnograd on the 17th of February 1943. The tank element was particularly hard hit with 50% losses being suffered in the recent fighting. The headquarters were sent to Kiev for a re-fit, but *SS-Sturmbannführer* Tychsen stayed in Krassnograd. On the following day, *Divisional Commander, SS-Oberführer* Vahl, started actions that would form part of his Knight's Cross recommendation. Christian Tychsen also conducted actions that formed the second part of his Knight's Cross recommendation.

The advance itself began on the 19th of February in a southerly direction towards Nowomoskowsk. Heinz Harmel fought close to this objective on this first day and his actions resulted in him being awarded the Knight's Cross. By the end of day one Pereschtschepino was reached and consolidated the following day, this included the very important river crossing over the Orel – crossed by Gunther Wisliceny's *III Battalion, Regiment Deutschland.* (This was taking place on the same day that Erwin Reichel was conducting his Knight's Cross actions further south with *Wiking* and Fritz Witt was conducting his Oakleaves actions further north). The objective of Nowomoskowsk was reached on the second day of the advance by the *III Battalion, Der Führer,* under Vincenz Kaiser.

From there the advance moved directly eastwards and by the 21st, Pawlograd was captured by *Der Führer* in an intensive fight. These moves had taken them approx seventy-five miles through enemy territory and had cut deep into the advancing enemy forces, trying to move further westwards, as had the advances of *Totenkopf* moving slightly north of *Der Führer's* positions. The decision was then taken for *Der Führer* to move to the north and, along with *Totenkopf,* close up a section of the enemy in a pocket and connect with the *LAH* north and northeast of Krassnograd.

Over the next day the greater area of Pawlograd was secured against a strong and increasingly desperate enemy, who attempted many counter attacks. The attacks north across the Samara River were completed on the 23rd and a link with *Totenkopf* was achieved. Otto Baum conducted actions on this day that formed part of his subsequent Knight's Cross recommendation, the remaining part came later in the year. Werbki was the next objective and the rate of advance slowed down at this stage, due to the strength of the enemy attempting to be overwhelmed. Despite this, Losowaja was reached on the 25th of February, 30 miles north of Werbki. It took two days to consolidate this move and take the rest of this town, which was a testament to the strength of the enemy in this area. Hans Wiess' actions around Losowaja formed part of his successful Knight's Cross recommendation.

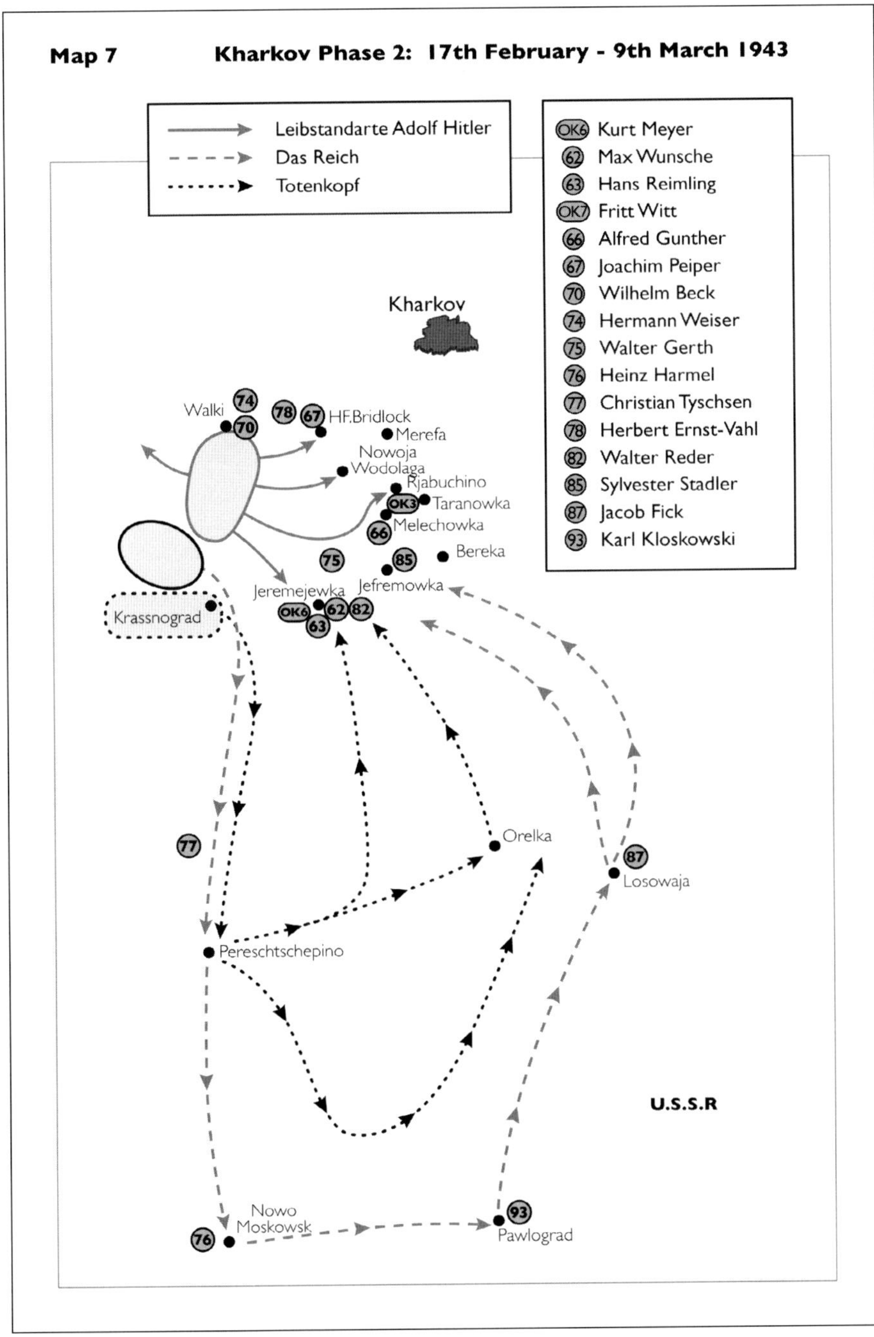

Map 7 **Kharkov Phase 2: 17th February - 9th March 1943**

The last day of February saw Otradono being reached, situated on the Bereka River, around 30 miles north of Losowaja. The start of March witnessed their advance move to the northeast towards the *LAH* and a closing of the enemy pocket. Bereka was reached on this day, two weeks after the *LAH's 3. Kompanie* had fought for their survival there – how the tide was turning! Jefremowka was also reached and *SS-Sturmbannführer* Sylvester Stadler conducted actions that resulted in him being awarded the Knight's Cross (details to follow). This was the same objective that his *Das Reich Kameraden,* Otto Kumm, had fought for back on the 11th of February and would result in him being awarded the Oakleaves. Paraskowaja, situated on the Berestowaja River, was reached on the 2nd of March and this helped to close the noose around the enemy's neck in this area. The enemy was trying to break out at any location. On the following day, Jacob Fick conducted actions around Losowaja that resulted in his award of the Knight's Cross, as his *Kameraden* were fighting further northwest.

Ochotschaje was taken on the 4th of March 1943, as well as a link made with the *LAH.* With this link, the move back towards Kharkov started to take shape. The three *Divisions* of the *SS-Panzer Korps* now began to advance side by side. *Das Reich* attacked Nowoja Wodolaga over the 6th and 7th of March, then over the following two days they crossed the Msha River at Bachmetjewka, punched north to Ljubotin and north east to Korotitsch. The next objective was the prize of Kharkov itself. It was these moves, on the 8th of March, that formed the remainder of *Divisional Commander,* Fritz Vahl's Knight's Cross recommendation.

We will halt the overview of *Das Reich* for now and cover the remaining *Division* of the *SS-Panzer Korps.*

Totenkopf

We last covered this *Division* as their lead elements arrived in the greater Kharkov area, at Krassnograd, towards mid-February 1943. They were initially sent to an area near Ogulzi, west of Kharkov. Due to the on-going worsening situation, they were moved back to Krassnograd by the 20th of February. Two days later they began a push to the south and southeast of Krassnograd; this was an additional element of stopping the enemy tidal wave of enemy troops. *Totenkopf* punched through the 'sea' of advancing Soviet soldiers in this southern sector and took Wasseswjatskoje on the Samara River. They then started to sweep east then northeast, thereby further breaking up the enemy advance; Orelka was taken in the evening of the 24th of February.

Although Orelka was the lead point of the advance, the fighting was raging south and east of there, as other *Totenkopf* elements took on and engaged in bitter fighting with a determined enemy. This fighting was intensive and losses to both sides mounted.

One of the most significant losses was the *Totenkopf Divisional Commander, SS-Obergruppenführer und Generalleutnant der Waffen-SS* Theodore Eicke. He was shot down in his Fiesler Storch near Artelnoje. At that stage he was the highest-ranking *Waffen-SS* soldier to lose his life in battle, as well as being the highest grade of the Knight's Cross to be lost – being an Oakleaves holder. His own troops attacked into the location of the crashed plane to retrieve his body. Max Simon took over command of the *Division* at that point.

Totenkopf's advance had taken them in a wide southeasterly sweep from Krassnograd and back up towards Jeremejewka. The *LAH* had been pushing out and extending their area also, a link between these two units was made on the third day of March 1943. Between the 1st and 3rd of March, Walter Reder was involved in fighting at Schijachowaja and Jeremejewka that resulted in him receiving the Knight's Cross, whilst his *Kameraden,* Walter Gerth, fought around Loswaja and Schijachowaja on the 2nd and 3rd, which also earned him the Knight's Cross.

By this stage the enemy tidal wave had not only been shattered, but had been pushed back, with the enemy streaming north, northeast and eastwards. The push continued and movements north and northeast began. Scenes reminiscent of 1941 came about at this time, in that enemy troops began fleeing eastwards again as the rapidly developing situation became apparent to them. They were attempting to escape destruction and they clashed with the *Waffen-SS* units moving back towards Kharkov. As the end of the first week in March loomed, *Totenkopf* moved in a northerly direction towards Olschany, west of Kharkov.

We will stop covering *Totenkopf* and the rest of the *SS-Panzer Korps* at this stage, highlight what had taken place with the other *SS units* up to the end of this first week of March 1943, before then covering the award of any Knight's Crosses approved up to the 10th of March 1943.

SS-Brigade Schuldt

On the 22nd of February 1943 *SS-Brigade Schuldt* moved to Sselesnewka, then onto Baschtewitsch. Their initial intention was to attack, but due to the strength of the enemy in that area, extreme defensive measures had to be taken over the following days. On the 25th of February they pushed towards Jelisawetowka to try to stop the enemy there. They successfully contributed to the reversing of the situation at that time, in the closing days of February 1942. They were then able to deal with smaller engagements up to mid-March, when the remnants of this unit were moved to Debica for a rest, as well as being able to count the cost of this difficult fighting. It was for his actions leading this *Kampfgruppe* from late December 1942 through to the end of February 1943, that Schuldt was awarded the Knight's Cross to the Iron Cross with Oakleaves.

When this unit was moved to Debica it was actually disbanded, with Schuldt being given a period of rest as a reserve officer.

Now that we have covered the actions of the front-line units until the end of March 1943, let us detail all Knight's Cross awards up to the 10th of March.

Kurt Meyer
Date of birth: 23.12.1910
SS Number: 17 559

We last covered *SS-Sturmbannführer* Kurt Meyer in May 1941, when he was one of the earliest *LAH* recipients of the Knight's Cross to the Iron Cross for actions he conducted in the Greek campaign in April 1941. So what had he been up to since then?

Like his *LAH Kameraden,* he did not have much time to rest as they moved eastwards into Russia a couple of months later. They moved southwards towards the Black Sea with Meyer and his *Aufklarungs Abteilung* leading the way for most of the advance. Cherson, Berdjansk and Mariupol were all successfully taken thanks to the actions of Meyer and his men. After their difficult battles up to the end of 1941, the *LAH* began a relatively quieter time in 1942, initially in Ssambek and further westwards, then in France for their refit. This was a time of further recognition and reward for Kurt Meyer. Back in early February 1942 he was awarded the German Cross in Gold, followed in July with the award of the Royal Bulgarian Bravery Medal IV Class, 1st Grade. September saw him being awarded the Star of Romania Medal with Swords, IV Class and also the Eastern Front Medal. Promotion to *SS-Obersturmbannführer* came on the 9th of November 1942.

Meyer returned to Russia in early 1943 around the Kharkov area with his *Aufklarungs Abteilung*. They played a part in the *LAH's* successful actions in this area during February 1943. It was for these actions and also actions leading all the way back to the first campaign in Russia in 1941 that Meyer was recommended for the award of the Oakleaves to the Knight's Cross. This was written by Sepp Dietrich on the 20th February 1943 and like Fritz Witt's, was a lengthy recommendation covering multiple actions. It read as follows:

'I recommend the *Commander* of the *Aufklarungs Abteilung* of the *Leibstandarte SS Adolf Hitler, SS-Obersturmbannführer* Kurt Meyer, for the award of the Oakleaves to the Knight's Cross of the Iron Cross for:

SS-Obersturmbannführer Meyer has been awarded the Knight's Cross to the Iron Cross on the 18.5.1941 in the Eastern campaign again and again through outstanding personal courage and adept leadership of the *Aufklarungs Abteilung* in their deeds.

On 19.8.1941 Meyer managed to penetrate into the heavily defended Cherson area with a wide flank attack from the east. Thanks to this, the strong enemy defensive front in Cherson collapsed. The city fell into our hands with its' valuable port and industrial installations almost intact. A large number of armed boats were destroyed and, by blocking the road traffic over the Dnjepr River, the withdrawal of enemy forces defending the city were considerably held up.

On 12.9.1941 the *Aufklarungs Abteilung,* after the capture of Nowaja Majatschka, advanced deeply towards the southwest in the middle of the enemy retreat movement, reaching the strongly fortified strong point of Rf. Presbrashenka. With this, considerable enemy forces had to divert their retreat to Perekop and heavy losses in men and equipment were inflicted on the opponent.

Pursuing the westward retreating 9. Red Army, *SS-Obersturmbannführer* Meyer pushed on during 15. and 16.9.1941 with his *Aufklarungs Abteilung* in a daring advance until reaching the isthmus between Ssalkowo and Genitschesk. They took both villages and with it, the last railway and land link of the red forces fighting in the Crimea. A train loaded with abundant war equipment and more than 100 vehicles fell into his hands after smashing the locomotive.

In the defense against the opponent forces that had penetrated in the area of Jelisawetowka, the *Commander* of the *Aufklarungs Abteilung* managed with a mobile defense to prevent any further advance of the enemy. In the following attack, *SS-Obersturmbannführer* Meyer slipped amid the fleeing enemy and, despite a strong enemy resistance, built a bridgehead in Terpenjo. That created the conditions for the ensuing pursuit of the retreating enemy by the main body of the *Standarte*. On 5.10.1941 the staff of the 9. Red Army in Romanowka dispersed.

In the advance towards Berdjansk on 7.10.1941 *SS-Obersturmbannführer* Meyer penetrated into the city against strong enemy columns retreating from the west in the direction of Berdjansk. With these actions he prevented the destruction of important armaments factories. During the mopping up of the city, strong enemy forces were annihilated.

Continuing the pursuit, in spite of the presence of strong enemy forces on his left flank, on 8.10.1941 *SS-Obersturmbannführer* Meyer succeeded in penetrating Mariupol. He pursued the fleeing opponent and, despite the bloody resistance

Kurt Meyer photographed wearing his Knight's Cross with Oakleaves. He is also seen wearing the Italian pattern camouflage, favoured by the Hitler Youth Division.

of the completely surprised forces, managed to take the city. With more than 500,000 inhabitants, after Odessa it was the most important port city in southern Russia. Its' valuable industries were taken before the enemy could carry out any significant destruction.

During the deployment of the *Leibstandarte SS Adolf Hitler* into the area east of Kharkov, *SS-Obersturmbannführer* Meyer and his *Aufklarungs Abteilung* were the first part of the *Division* to reach Tschugujew. They advanced immediately from the disembarkment railway station to the east towards the Donez, taking defensive positions in the area Ossinowka-Kalmyzkoje-Malinowka.

From these positions Meyer carried out several attacks against strong groups of the Russian XII Tank Corps. With his skillful leadership, the fluid enemy advance was held until the main body of the *Division* arrived and took up planned defensive positions. In spite of strong enemy pressure, sections of the *Aufklarungs Abteilung* under the personal leadership of *SS-Obersturmbannführer* Meyer pushed southeast and succeeded in the rescue of the surrounded *298. Infantry Division*.

Thanks to the excellent desire for action of the *Aufklarungs Abteilung* and its' *Commander,* the advance of strong Russian forces towards Kharkov could be stopped, inflicting heavy losses on the opponent.

In the deployment of the *Division* in the area of Norefa, *SS-Obersturmbannführer* Meyer was assigned the task of reaching Jefremowka via Nowaja Wodologa. Despite the resistance of the enemy and the most difficult terrain conditions, he fulfilled the task through his ruthless personal action. Only he and his *Abteilung* accomplished their planned assignment and, although his supply lines were cut off, was able to hold his objective against overwhelming enemy attacks. During this action, the *Aufklarungs Abteilung* tied down strong enemy forces and made possible the annihilation of the VI Russian Guards Cavalry Corps.

When, after the deployment of new units, the opponent tried to rout the south flank of the *Leibstandarte* through massive attacks by the 172. Rifle Division, *SS-Obersturmbannführer* Meyer with his *Abteilung* and the support of a *Panzer Kompanie* were able to repulse all of the enemy attacks against the strongpoint of Jefremowka. During the combat they completely destroyed the 747. Russian Infantry Regiment. The enemy lost, beside numerous hand weapons:

Two batteries of 7.62 long barrel artillery (eight guns)
18 anti-tank guns
A large number of anti-tank rifles, and
Over 1,500 enemy dead

On 21.2.1943, *SS-Obersturmbannführer* Meyer with his *Aufklarungs Abteilung* was assigned the task of pushing south to destroy the parts of the VI Russian Rifle Division gathering in the area Jeremejewka-Krutojarowka; the attack was an immediate success.

SS-Obersturmbannführer Meyer annihilated four strong enemy columns and destroyed, with only light losses of his own (three dead, one of them an officer, and 11 wounded, one of them an officer). Captured were:

17 guns of 7.62 calibre
Four anti-tank guns 4.5cm
Seven heavy grenade launchers
And countless infantry weapons'

The recommendation ends there. The award date appears to be in dispute, as the various documents in his file list two different dates for the award. The dates listed are the 23rd of February 1943 and also the 27th of February. The 23rd appears on two documents, so is probably the most accurate, but whatever the date, it is clear that his recommendation was quickly approved by the end of February 1943, only days after it was written. This award gave the *LAH* their second Oakleaves holder.

The fighting was still taking place around Kharkov as this award was approved, but this would not end Kurt Meyer's association with the Knight's Cross or its' various grades. Further details of that will follow in later volumes.

Erwin Reichell
Date of birth: 11.03.1911
SS Number: 202 925
Born in Vienna, he fought with the *Freikorps Oberland* from 1929 through to 1933. He then joined the *Allgemeine-SS* in early January 1934; by October he had moved to the fledgling *SS-VT*. In April 1935 he was sent to the officer's school at Braunschweig, staying there until February 1936 when he also attended a *Zug Führer's* course. On the 20th of April 1936 he received a promotion to *SS-Untersturmführer*. Just prior to this, in March, he had moved to the Race and Resettlement Main Office, staying there for one year. At the start of March 1937 he moved to the *15. Kompanie,* within *SS-Regiment Deutschland*. In mid-September 1937 he was promoted to *SS-Obersturmführer*. By the start of December 1938 he had moved to the staff of *Deutschland* and followed this exactly six-months later by becoming the *Regimental Adjutant*. On the first day of September 1939 he was

Erwin Reichell seen here with the rank of SS-Hauptsturmführer, sometime in early 1941. He was approved for the Knight's Cross at the end of February 1943, whilst holding the rank of SS-Sturmbannführer. His approval came on the same day that he was killed, so there are no photographs showing him with this award.

promoted further to *SS-Hauptsturmführer*; it was with this rank that he entered the Second World War.

He fought in Poland and the west with *Deutschland*, earning the Second Class Iron Cross on the 1st of October 1939, the First Class Iron Cross on the 29th of May 1940 and the Infantry Assault Badge on the 1st of July 1940. On the first day of January 1941 he moved to service with the staff of *SS-Division Wiking*. From early January until mid-March of that year he attended a *General Staff* training course. He returned to *Wiking*, and on the 9th of November 1941 he gained promotion to *SS-Sturmbannführer*. Almost one year later, on the 26th of October 1942, he assumed command of the *III Battalion, SS-Regiment Nordland*. Just prior to this, in mid-September, he had been awarded the Eastern Front Medal.

Like many of his *Wiking Kameraden*, he found himself rushing northwards through the Caucausus in late 1942 and into early 1943. They became engaged in the difficult fighting that raged in January 1943, as the Russians engulfed the Germans situated in the southern region of the U.S.S.R. Erwin Reichell assumed command of *Westland* as they continued their fighting retreat towards Rostov and on towards Krasno Armaiskoje. In this general area, they fought strong Russian tank forces in a bid to halt their seemingly unstoppable advances. Reichell and his men advanced to the north east of Krasno Armaiskoje up to Alexsandrowka (*Olexsandrivka*). They were fighting elements of the Russian IV Guards Tank Corps. He was heavily wounded and evacuated to Dnjepropetrowsk and a field hospital there.

On the 24th of February 1943 Felix Steiner recommended Erwin Reichell for the Knight's Cross. The details of that recommendation is as follows:

'The *Division* recommends *SS-Sturmbannführer* Reichell, leader of the *SS-Panzer Grenadier Regiment Westland* for the Knight's Cross.

He decided to immediately attack and surround the enemy in the north-east. It was part of the larger fight for Krasno Armaiskoje. The attack successfully divided the strong enemy tank forces there and allowed for their subsequent destruction. Through his coolness and correct decision, he averted an acute crisis that had been started when the enemy armour had pushed deep into their flank.

He was a group leader and fought at Ssalsk and south of Rostov in large battles. His courage was demonstrated during these battles.'

The recommendation was approved only four days later, on the 28th of February 1943. This was the same day that Erwin Reichell died from his severe wounds. As the recommendation had been made earlier than this, this was not a posthumous award of the Knight's Cross. This recent fighting was indeed proving costly for *Wiking!*

Max Wunsche
Date of birth: 20.04.1914
SS Number: 153 508
Born in Kittlitz, he spent time with the *Hitler Youth* from late 1932 until July 1933, when he moved to the *SS*. He spent time at an *NCOs* training course from the start of November 1934, in Jutterbog, until late April 1935. He was then sent to the *SS Officer's School* from that date until the end of January 1936. On the 20th of April 1936 he became an *SS-Untersturmführer* and *Platoon Commander* in the *LAH's, 9. Kompanie*. He also spent time with the *11. Kompanie*. In September 1938 he became an *SS-Obersturmführer* and spent time on the personal staff of Adolf Hitler, often being seen close to the *Führer* in photographs and film footage of that time.

On the 24th of January 1940 he moved back to the *LAH,* serving in their *15. Kompanie*. He went west with them in early May 1940. He received a further promotion to *SS-Hauptsturmführer* on the 25th of May 1940, followed on the next day with the award of the Second Class Iron Cross. The award of the First Class Iron Cross came on the last day of May 1940. He was also awarded the Black Wound Badge for this campaign, although the exact date of the award is not listed. Wunsche is probably best associated with the near fatal action of Sepp Dietrich during this campaign. It was Wunsche who was stuck in the same water ditch alongside his *Divisional Commander,* Sepp Dietrich, during the attacks near the British positions at Esquelbecq. This almost became their last fight, but they managed to survive and fight another day.

After the completion of this campaign, he once again served within the personal staff of Adolf Hitler from June 1940 until early December, when he moved back to the *LAH*. His new role with the *LAH* was *Divisional Adjutant,* a role he held until mid-February 1942. He then moved to service with the *LAH's Sturmgeschutze Abteilung*. From the start of June until the end of August 1942 he attended a *General Staff Officer's* training course. Inbetween this time he was awarded the Royal Bulgarian Bravery Medal IV Class, 1st Grade, the Russian Front Medal and the Infantry Assault Badge.

He returned to the *LAH* once more, as they were stationed in France, and took command of the *Sturmgeschutze Abteilung*; this was on the first day of September 1942, the same day that he was promoted to *SS-Sturmbannführer.* The award of the Star of Romania Medal with Swords, IV Class came two days later. His next

SS-Sturmbannführer Max Wunsche photographed after his award of the Knight's Cross with the Leibstandarte, although he has autographed this picture as Commander of SS-Panzer Regiment 12.

career move came on the 22nd of October 1942, when he moved to command the *I Battalion* of the *LAH's Panzer Regiment.*

The *Panzer Regiment Commander,* Schonberger, recommended Wunsche for the award of the German Cross in Gold on the 14th of February 1943, this being approved and awarded eleven days later. This was for successful actions in the early stages of the Kharkov offensive.

The following day, on the 26th of February 1943, Dietrich signed a recommendation for the award of the Knight's Cross to the Iron Cross for Max Wunsche. It read as follows:

'Knight's Cross recommendation for *SS-Sturmbannführer* Max Wunsche, *Commander, I. Panzer Rgt. 1/LSSAH.*

On 25.2.1943 reports came from the lead elements of the reinforced *Aufklarungs Abteilung/LSSAH,* that a strong enemy column was moving south towards the *LAH's* positions. *SS-Sturmbannführer* Max Wunsche, with the leader of the attached *Kampfgruppe,* took it upon himself, without orders from above, to conduct a comprehensive tank attack out of Jeremejewka towards the north and destroyed the following enemy equipment:

24 guns of 7.62cm long
13 guns of 7.62cm short
10 anti-tank guns 4.5cm
6 guns 12.2cm
1 gun 10.5cm

Numerous mortars, anti-tank rifles, machine guns, also 300-400 horses, ox and covered sleds, also 800-900 dead.

SS-Sturmbannführer Wunsche had not only destroyed this strong enemy column, but also provided the essential relief of the *LSSAH* units in the south. He displayed outstanding courage (his own tank destroyed two 12.2cm guns) and strong leadership (5 dead and 14 wounded as his own losses) the higher award of the Knight's Cross to the Iron Cross for proven worthiness.'

This recommendation also covered the actions of *SS-Oberscharführer* Hans Reimling, who was part of Wunsche's unit and asked that he too, be awarded the Knight's Cross. Both recommendations were approved two days later, on the 28th of February 1943. This made both men the first Knight's Cross holders of the *LAH's Panzer Regiment*, but not the last by far!

Hans Reimling will be covered below, with reference to Max Wunsche specifically, this would not end his association with the Knight's Cross and its' higher grades, but details of that will follow in subsequent volumes.

Hans Reimling
Date of birth: 17.01.1918
SS Number: Unknown
Born in Karlsruhe, there is no information available that details his history up to the 11th of February 1943. It was on this day that he began actions that would result in his award of the Knight's Cross to the Iron Cross.

As detailed above, his recommendation was contained at the bottom of his *Battalion Commander's,* Max Wunsche's, Knight's Cross recommendation. This very short recommendation reads as follows:

(*reading as a continuation of Wunsche's details*)
'Likewise comes *SS-Oberscharführer* Hans Reimling, *2. /Panz. Rgt. 1/LSSAH*

Recommendation for the Knight's Cross to the Iron Cross

Reimling had always placed his tank as the lead vehicle of the *I./Panz. Rgt. 1/LSSAH,* being hit twice himself, but since the 11.2.43, sometimes in short range fire fights has destroyed:

15, 7.62cm long – 10, 7.62cm short – 8, 4.5cm anti-tank guns

Reimling is an example of personal bearing for the whole *Abteilung* and the high award of the Knight's Cross of the Iron Cross is for honour.'

The award was approved on the same day as Max Wunsche's, the 28th of February 1943, adding the second Knight's Cross award to the *LAH's Panzer Regiment.* Hans Reimling did not have much time to enjoy the fact that he was one of the *Ritterkreuztrager,* as he was killed on the 7th of March 1943 near Walki, as the fighting around Kharkov raged on.

He did have time to have himself photographed wearing his new award. No other awards are visible in the photograph. Also, as mentioned above, it is not known when he joined the *Waffen-SS* or when he received his various promotions up to his final rank of *SS-Oberscharführer.*

Reading the award details above, it is clear that the *Panzer* men of the *LAH* feared the anti-tank gun more than the enemy tanks. You will see that this trend of

SS-Oberscharführer Hans Reimling photographed after his approval for the Knight's Cross on the last day of February 1943, but before his death on the 7th of March 1943. The snow / sleet falling at the time add a nice feel to the 'rushed' nature of this picture.

targeting and destroying enemy anti-tank guns continues with many of Reimling's *Kameraden* throughout the rest of the war.

Fritz Witt

Date of birth: 25.05.1908

SS Number: 25 518

We last covered the exploits of Fritz Witt when he became one of the first *Waffen-SS* soldiers to be awarded the Knight's Cross in September 1940. So, what had he been up to since then?

Just over one month after his Knight's Cross award, on the 16th of October 1940, he moved from command of *SS-Regiment Deutschland's, I Battalion* to the command of the *LAH's, III Battalion*. This move took him back to the *LAH,* the same unit that he was a founding member of back in March 1933. In late March 1941 he moved to command of the *I Battalion*. This was just prior to the invasion of Greece and Witt led this *Battalion* in its' successful and swift actions in that area. This campaign was tinged with sadness and joy for Fritz Witt; sadness at the loss of his younger brother, Franz, killed as a *Platoon Commander* in the *I Battalion's, 3. Kompanie* and joy at seeing Gert Pleiss being awarded the Knight's Cross. Pleiss was the leader of Witt's *1. Kompanie* at that time.

He led that *Battalion* as they advanced into southern Russia in mid-1941, reaching the Black Sea, then onto the prize of Rostov in late November. He once again had the pleasure of seeing another one of his young officers, Heinrich Springer, being presented with the Knight's Cross in early 1942. It was also during late November 1941 that he himself received a promotion to *SS-Obersturmbannführer.* Although 1942 was a quieter time for the *LAH,* Witt would see further recognition for his earlier efforts and potential. On the 8th of February 1942 he was awarded the German Cross in Gold, the Infantry Assault Badge on the 23rd of February and the Royal Bulgarian Bravery Medal IV Class, 1st Grade on the 27th. Then on the first day of July he took command of the *LAH's, 1st Infantry Regiment*. This was just prior to the *LAH's* move to France for their much needed rest and refit, as well as expansion. Whilst in France he was awarded the Star of Romania Medal with Swords and the Russian Front Medal, as well as promotion to *SS-Standartenführer* on the last day of January 1943.

He then went back to Russia in early 1943 as the *LAH* were rushed into the southern sector to help stem the flow of enemy troops streaming westwards as part of the worsening situation centered on Stalingrad. Being sent to the Kharkov area, his *Regiment* bore a significant brunt of the enemy pressure in their assigned positions. They dealt with all of this and turned a dangerous situation

A formal portrait photograph of Fritz Witt, after his promotion to SS-Brigadeführer in late April 1944, and a matter of weeks before he was killed during the Normandy fighting. His Knight's Cross with Oakleaves can be clearly seen, along with his other awards.

into a positive one for the Germans. The costs and rewards were high, as detailed previously. For Fritz Witt, recognition came once again, this time in the shape of a recommendation for the award of the Oakleaves to his existing Knight's Cross.

This lengthy and detailed recommendation was written on the 26th of February 1943 by Sepp Dietrich and covered actions all the way back to Greece almost two years previously. To properly convey the significance of his long list of achievements, it is necessary to list the recommendation in full:

'I recommend the *Commander* of the *1st Panzer-Grenadier-Regiment* of the *Leibstandarte SS Adolf Hitler, SS-Standartenführer* Fritz Witt, for the award of the Oakleaves to the Knight's Cross of the Iron Cross for:

1. Klidi Pass:

After the lunge forward of our forces towards the south of Yugoslavia and the crossing of the Greek frontier by Florina, the *Standarte* was assigned the task to open the heavily defended Klidi Pass, enabling with it the further advance of our tank forces towards the south.

Through the courageous intervention of the then *Commander* of the *I Battalion, SS-Standartenführer* Witt, that under difficult conditions personally reconnoitered the assembly area of his *Battalion* and after the arrival of the *Battalion* managed to repel the toughly and bitterly fighting Englishmen in a hard struggle that lasted several hours. The enemy lost numerous dead and considerable amounts of war material.

With this success, that was achieved through the excellent, brave example of the *Commander* that repeatedly rallied on his men to attack, the door for the successful assault into the heart of Greece was blown up. *SS-Standartenführer* Witt has thereby an essential part in the ensuing success of the campaign against Greece.

2. Capture of Nowo Archangelsk:

On 1.8.41 *SS-Standartenführer* Witt received from *General* Kempf the written order to attack Nowo Archangelsk and, as a key position, to take it firmly in our hands. After the appropriate wide deployment of the *Battalion* by Witt, it attacked the far superior enemy at once. In heavy house fighting which lasted for hours, the opponent was expelled and Nowo Archangelsk taken. In spite of the strongest counterattacks of the opponent, Nowo Archangelsk was held. With it was reached another condition for the closing of the cauldron. Witt distinguished himself again through superior leadership and personal bravery.

3. Crossing over the Mius:
The enemy tried to hinder the continuation of the pursuit of the opponent defeated in Mariupol, building a strong bridgehead over the Mius west of Taganrog. Despite the strongest enemy defense from strong well-built positions on the east bank of the Mius the *Commander,* initially only with weak forces, managed to win a crossing over the Mius. In spite of the strongest enemy counterattacks, the enemy was not able to pierce this bridgehead. *SS-Standartenführer* Witt created with it the conditions for resuming the pursuit that drove the capture of Taganrog on 17.10.41.

4. Rostow:
The attack on Rostow was brought to a standstill because of the extraordinarily bad weather conditions and the *III Panzer Korps* switched over to the defense. *SS-Standartenführer* Witt created, through the tireless, planned use of his reconnaissance, the favorable conditions for the later attack on Rostow. When this attack began on 17.11.41 it was also Witt who, at the head of his *Battalion,* rallied forward his men against the hardest enemy resistance.

When the outskirts of Rostow were reached on 20.11.41 after heavy house-to-house fighting, Witt penetrated at good pace at the head of his considerably weakened *Battalion* as far as the Don, and with his few men destroyed strong enemy columns. Crowning this success, especially great in the light of the far superior enemy, his *3. Kompanie* managed to build a bridgehead over the Don the very same day.

5. Defensive fighting eastwards Kharkov:
In the defensive fighting near Tschugujew eastwards of Kharkov, Witt and his *Regiment* performed extremely well. The *Kompanies* and *Battalions* were immediately thrown into the battle from the unloading stations. The skillful leadership, combined with the ruthless action of his own person, is to be thanked that the march forward of the very strong, superior opponent into the defensive sector, 32 kilometres wide, assigned to the *Regiment,* with two *Battalions,* was ready for action. Through counterthrusts from the defensive positions were inflicted bloody losses on the enemy, and finished off the enemy infiltrated into the main fighting line.

6. Merefa:
The *Kampfgruppe Witt* moved forward from the area eastwards of Merefa with the task to shield the left flank of the reinforced *SS-Regiment "Der Führer",* operating in the north flank of the Russian 6. Guards-Cavalry-Corps. The very

An autographed photograph of Fritz Witt dated April 1943, after he was presented with the Oakleaves to his existing Knight's Cross.

first day Witt achieved good successes with his *Kampfgruppe,* and in the course of the attack on Taranowka smashed

3 tanks
2 armoured scout cars
and inflicted on the Russians
600 soldiers killed

In the continuation of the attack Taranowka was cleared, strongly occupied by the enemy, and the opponent thrown back to the north part of Bereka. Together with the *Reconnaisance Detachment,* advancing from the area of Jefremowka towards the east, *SS-Standartenführer* Witt shares an essential part in the annihilation of the 6. Guards-Cavalry-Corps, whose rear communications were severely threatened by the advance on Bereka.

As on 20.2.43 the Russians tried with strong forces to break through the defensive front of *SS-Infantry-Regiment 1* of the *LSSAH,* and through the capture of Wodolaga to reach the rear of the *Army's* north flank. It was the merit of *SS-Standartenführer* Witt, who had to defend a sector 20 kilometers wide with only very small fighting forces, that all the massive attacks of the opponent, partially supported with tanks, were repelled.

When the opponent managed to penetrate the strongpoint Hf. Bulachi eastwards Nowaja Wodolaga, Witt gathered together the last reserves of his *Regiment,* and in a counterattack, succeeded in destroying completely the opponent that had penetrated there (strong parts of the three Regiments of the 1. Russian Cavalry Division).

Through the skillful leadership of his *Regiment* and special bravery before the enemy, Witt has distinguished himself in every fight.

I consider the *SS-Standartenführer* Witt, owing to his evident excellent feats described in the preceeding report, worthy of the high award of the Oakleaves to the Knight's Cross of the Iron Cross.

(signed) Dietrich, *SS-Obergruppenführer und General der Waffen-SS.*'

This recommendation was approved on the 1st of March 1943 and gave the *LAH* their third set of Oakleaves since the start of the war.

Following the successful conclusion of the fighting around Kharkov in early 1943, the *Waffen-SS* continued its' expansion. One of these expansions came in the form of a new *Division* that would consist of *Hitler Youth* members. It was decided that

Fritz Witt would lead this new unit. He therefore left Russia along with a number of his *LAH Kameraden* and went west to begin the formation.

On the first of July 1943 he was promoted to *SS-Oberführer* (still being listed as serving with the *LAH*!). He led the formation of his new *Division* throughout the remainder of 1943 and then 1944, initially in Belgium and then in France, within the Normandy region. He was promoted further to *SS-Brigadeführer und Generalmajor der Waffen-SS* on the 20th of April 1944. His *Division* completed its' training as the *Allies* were sailing towards France from England in early June. It was during the opening phases of the *Allied* campaign that Fritz Witt was killed by offshore naval gunfire. This gunfire was directed upon his headquarters and he was killed before being able to reach the relative safety of the slit trenches.

This brought to and end the life of, what can arguably be, one of the *Waffen-SS's* most effective *Commanders*. He had been with the *SS* from an early stage and moved to various units, seeing action in all of the major campaigns and being recognized for his actions at the highest level. It could also be argued that he was worthy of higher grades of the Knight's Cross, but this was not to be. His career and life came to an end on the 14th of June 1944.

Hermann Dahlke

Date of birth: 11.02.1917

SS Number: 265 202

Born in Greifswald, Pomerania, he entered service with the *LAH* from the 30th of July 1934 until the 31st of October 1938, when he then took up a civilian role. By that stage he had taken part in the march into Austria in March 1938 and also the Sudetenland in October 1938, being awarded both medals for these and also the 4-year long service medal.

He was recalled to active service in mid-August 1939 as the political situation worsened. He was placed in the *3. Kompanie* of the *LAH,* staying there for the remainder of his career and life!

He fought in Poland as a messenger, as well as going west in 1940 where he won the Second Class Iron Cross on the 8th of July 1940. He also went south into the Balkans, where he is listed as being an *NCO* at this stage. He won the Bulgarian Soldiers Bravery Medal III Class. His next campaign took him into Russia from the 28th of June 1941 through to the 31st of May 1942. He had command of a small group of men, but is also listed as being a *Platoon Commander* during this time, although his exact rank is not known. He was awarded the Black Wound Badge on the 3rd of August 1941, the First Class Iron Cross on the 3rd of December 1941 and the Infantry Assault Badge on the 23rd of February 1942. Whilst in France in the second half of 1942 he was also presented with the Russian Front Medal on the 17th of September. He then returned to Russia in early 1943 with his *LAH Kameraden*.

They were sent to the Kharkov area and found themselves in the worsening situation around this city. Dahlke himself was situated around Bereka on the 14th of February 1943, serving as part of *Kampfgruppe Witt*. The fighting was hard and Dahlke's *3. Kompanie* suffered the death of all of its' three officers within the space of two days. Dahlke was an experienced and brave soldier and he took temporary command during this difficult situation. It was for his actions at that time that he was awarded the Knight's Cross. The recommendation was written on the 2nd of March 1943 by his *Regimental Commander*, Fritz Witt and countersigned by his *Divisional Commander*, Sepp Dietrich. It contained the following details:

'I recommend for *SS-Oberscharführer d. Res.* Hermann Dahlke *3./1. Panz. Gren. Rgt./Leibstandarte SS Adolf Hitler* the award of the Knight's Cross to the Iron Cross for:

SS-Oberscharführer d. Res. Dahlke was back again as a messenger in Poland and also during the campaign in France. He also participated in the Balkans campaign as a *Troop Leader*. When the *Leibstandarte SS Adolf Hitler* were used in Russia from the 28. 6.1941 to the 31.5.1942 Dahlke was first a *Group Leader* then a *Platoon Commander*.

In all actions, Dahlke would appear as an exemplary soldier with high soldiery virtues and would complete all tasks with high courage, being awarded the First Class Iron Cross for his repeated bravery. On the 14.2.1943 Dahlke was there for the battle of the *I. Btl./1. Panz. Gren. Rgt.*,also *3./Pioneer Btl.* ,a *Sturm-geschutz-Batterie* and an *Artillery Group*, all part of *'Kampfgruppe Witt'* in the place Bereka (55 km south of Kharkov) for their decisive battle.

The '*Kampfgruppe Witt'* had the order to attack a number of strong positions occupied heavily by the enemy in and around Bereka. The attack objectives for the *I Battalion* were the hills 163, 189.2 and 134.8 at the south west part of the village. The *3. Kompanie* that *SS-Oberscharführer* Dahlke belonged to were ordered to cover the open right flank. To fulfill this order, the *3. Kompanie* crossed the first attack goal (hill 163). The enemy was dug in on hill 197.7 and here Dahlke led the successful advance to the left. They threw their energy and their fire as a brave example in a spirited attack with his men into the enemy positions. They engaged the enemy, who was in the strength of a Company and who had heavy machine guns, in close combat. We owe the quick capture of hill 197.7 to the brave actions of *SS-Oberscharführer* Dahlke. It influenced the attack of

Hermann Dahlke photographed after his promotion to SS-Untersturmführer and award of the Knight's Cross to the Iron Cross. He was killed two months after this approval.

'*Kampfgruppe Witt*' decisively in its' first phase as the threat to the flank was removed from hill 197.7.

In the further course of the attack, they came across difficult terrain and also deep snow that they were only able to pass after delays in time. The artillery and the *Rifle Kompanie* also had to swing through steep hollows and move to the southwest in an extraordinarily difficult situation. The enemy outnumbered them heavily and they held the edge of the area with well-aimed guns, mortars and machine guns. The ground cover was not good and the *Kompanies* had to lie down as best they could. This was especially true for the hard pressed *3. Kompanie,* in which the *Chef* and *Kompanie Officers* all fell. Dahlke lay with his decimated train, far out to the front, when the enemy on their flank prepared a counterattack. Of that, the leader of the *Kompanie,* Dahlke recognized that he had to take control of the *Kompanie.* He took his own decision to hold the *Kompanie* against this attack without moving back. They defended themselves against this enemy even when the machine-guns ran out of ammunition. Dahlke inspired his men further to resist the enemy attacks until the enemy withdrew.

They once again took possession of hill 197.7 and thereby had the dominant position. Out of here, the enemy fire could control the advance of the *3. Kompanie* and also cause difficulties for the *Battalion.* Their heavy fire could reach the *Kampfgruppe.* That this did not happen, is alone down to the bravery we owe *SS-Oberscharführer* Dahlke.

Dahlke, who on the 17.2.1943 became wounded for the third time, is an example of a brave and determined fighter. The honour of the award of the Knight's Cross to the Iron Cross would give him full recognition.

(signed) Witt
SS-Standertenführer and Regiment's Commander

<u>Opinion of the *Divisional Commander*</u>
I agree with the suggestion that, Dahlke, for being the hero of the hour, and his unusual courage and skills that the Knight's Cross to the Iron Cross is awarded to reward him.

(signed) Dietrich
SS-Obergruppenführer und General der Waffen-SS

This award was approved on the following day along with two of his *Kameraden* from the *LAH.* He was also given a field promotion to *SS-Untersturmführer,* back dated to the 1st of March 1943.

The first indication of these awards came via a radio message, taken by then then *SS-Sturmmann* Gerhard Dilling (later to command the remnants of the *3. Kompanie* in the final days of the war, as an *SS-Untersturmführer)*. The radio message came through asking to speak to *SS-Untersturmführer* Dahlke. Dahlke was summoned and took the message. This informed him of his award of the Knight's Cross! Dilling was there as this all took place and he recalled everyone's joy, within what was left of the *3. Kompanie*, with this news.

Dahlke was given command of the *3. Kompanie* and led this unit until the first day of the Kursk offensive on the 5th of July 1943, when he was wounded by an enemy shell fragment. Once again, Gerhard Dilling was nearby and he stopped to try and give first aid to Dahlke. However, the need to continue the advance was critical and Dilling was ordered to move forward. The question is, what difference would have been made to Dahlke if he had been given this first aid. The wounds he was suffering from resulted in his death the same day.

To bring the career and life of this *SS Officer* to an end, there is a document on his file, dating from mid-September 1943 that lists Dahlke moving from the officer reserve list to the active officer list, as well as a posthumous promotion to *SS-Obersturmführer*. This could have been done to help Dahlke's family and their widow's payments? All other sources list Dahlke's final rank as *SS-Untersturmführer*.

Albert Frey
Date of birth: 16.02.1913
SS Number: 111 913
Born in Heidelberg, he entered service with the *SS* in mid-June 1933, serving with the *SS-Regiment Deutschland*. He stayed with them until the end of March 1937, moving up the ranks inbetween. Promoted to *SS-Sturmmann* on the 6th of January 1935, *SS-Rottenführer* on the 20th of April the same year, *SS-Unterscharführer* on the 10th of May 1936 and finally *SS-Scharführer* on the 20th of December 1936. He then moved to the *SS Officers school* at Braunschweig from March 1937 until the start of March 1938, leaving there with the rank of *SS-Standartenoberjunker*. This was quickly followed on the 12th of March 1938 with promotion to *SS-Untersturmführer* and a move to the *LAH*. On the 20th of April 1939 he received a further promotion to *SS-Obersturmführer*; he then entered the Second World War.

He saw service in Poland earning the Second Class Iron Cross on the 25th of September 1939. He also moved west in 1940 and won the First Class Iron Cross on the 30th of June, followed by the Infantry Assault Badge on the 3rd of October

SS-Sturmbannführer Albert Frey photographed after his award of the Knight's Cross in March 1943

the same year. He had been given command of the *LAH's, 11. Kompanie* back at the start of August and this was followed by a promotion to *SS-Hauptsturmführer* on the 9th of November 1940. He also fought in the Balkans and then moved into Russia in mid-1941. On the 16th of October that year he was given command of the *LAH's III Battalion.* The award of the German Cross in Gold came just over one month later, on the 17th of November 1941.

Back on the 25th of October 1941, Dietrich had recommended Frey for the award of the Knight's Cross for the bridgehead his unit had established over the Mius River, north of Taganrog. It highlights his courage and cold-blooded determination and attributes the fast advance and capture of Taganrog to Frey's actions at the Mius River. This recommendation was not approved at that time. It could be for these actions that he received the German Cross in Gold, as no recommendation for that medal is contained within his file?

Towards the end of their first stint in Russia, on the 20th of April 1942, Frey was promoted to *SS-Sturmbannführer.* Ten days later he assumed command of the *I Battalion* within the *LAH.* He moved with his men to France in the second half of 1942 and whilst there received further awards. The Royal Bulgarian Bravey Medal IV Class, 1st Grade came on the 6th of July, the Royal Romanian Medal with Swords followed on the 3rd of September, as well as the Russian Front Medal. It was then time to return to Russia.

The actions of his *I Battalion* are contained in the preceding pages and give a good overview of the intensity of the fighting. Many of his men lost their lives in this difficult struggle and one of his men, Hermann Dahlke, received the Knight's Cross for his part in the fighting. Albert Frey himself was also re-recommended for the Knight's Cross by Sepp Dietrich on the 2nd of March 1943. This recommendation was short and to the point, reading as follows:

'Recommendation for the award of the Knight's Cross for *SS-Sturmbannführer* Albert Frey. (the document then lists existing awards and personal details)

I propose that the *Commander* of the *I./1. Panzer-Grenadier-Regiment/ Leibstandarte SS Adolf Hitler, SS-Sturmbannführer* Albert Frey, under the again adjoining duplicate of the Knight's Cross recommendation from the 25.10.1941 because in it and the recent heavy fighting and attacks, displayed personal courage and outstanding leadership of his *Battalion* and their higher preservation.

(signed) Dietrich
SS-Obergruppenführer und General der Waffen-SS.

(approved) Schmundt.

This second recommendation was approved the following day, the 3rd of March 1943. This award would not end Albert Frey's association with the Knight's Cross to the Iron Cross or its' higher grades, but details of that will follow in later volumes.

Alfred Gunther
Date of birth: 25.04.1917
SS Number: 392 402
Born in Magdeburg, he entered the *SS* at the start of April 1937, serving initially with *SS-Regiment Germania*. He fought with this unit in Poland in 1939 before moving to the *LAH* in early 1940. He was one of the early members of the *LAH's Sturmgeschutze Abteilung,* serving alongside Michael Wittman. He fought in the west in 1940 and in January 1941 is listed as holding the rank of *SS-Unterscharführer* and serving in the *LAH's, V Battalion*. This was the *LAH's Wach Battalion* stationed in Berlin and it was common for soldiers to be attached to this unit during times of recuperation. This could have been the case with Alfred Gunther at that time? He was back with the *LAH's Sturmgeschutze Abteilung* in time for the invasion of Greece in April 1941.

His next campaign took him into Russia in mid-1941 and he is listed as serving as part of Wittmann's crew in August. On the 5th of November he was awarded the Second Class Iron Cross. Whilst in France with the rest of the *LAH* in 1942, he was awarded the First Class Iron Cross on the 12th of September. He would have no doubt been awarded the Russian Front Medal around this time also. By February 1943 he was holding the rank of *SS-Oberscharführer* and engaged in the fighting around Kharkov. It was for this fighting that he would be awarded the Knight's Cross.

The recommendation does not survive, but there are outline details of what he done to be considered worthy of this high award; they are as follows.

In the defensive fighting during February 1943 in the area of Kharkov, he proved to have hunter's courage. With his *Sturmgeschutze* he defended against a heavy enemy attack of 10 tanks and a Soviet Rifle Battalion. He engaged the enemy armour at a range of 200 meters and destroyed 5 of them, as well as dispersing the enemy infantry. He thereby prevented an enemy breakthrough of the thinly held German line at that time. For this decisive action he was awarded the Knight's Cross to the Iron Cross on the 3rd of March 1943. This made him the first recipient of this award for the *LAH's Sturmgeschutze Abteilung*.

In the photographs following his award he is shown as holding the rank of *SS-Hauptscharführer,* although the date of this promotion is not listed. He moved

Alfred Gunther shown after he became the LAH's, Sturmgeschutze Abteilung's first Knight's Cross holder in early March 1943.

to the newly created *101st SS-Heavy Tank Abteilung* in May, moving with them to Italy in the second half of 1943. By November the same year, he was back in Germany with his new unit. A promotion to *SS-Untersturmführer* came at the end of January 1944. At the start of June he was commanding Tiger Tank number 311, within the *3. Kompanie/101st SS-Heavy Tank Abteilung*. It was in this tank that Alfred Gunther lost his life on the 15th of June 1944. He was positioned with some of his *Kameraden* in the town of Evrecy. There were three Tigers in total and they came under *Allied* fighter-bomber attack during the night of the 14th/15th of June. Gunther's tank received a direct hit and burst into flames immediately, with no one surviving this hit. Alfred Gunther was posthumously promoted to *SS-Obersturmführer.*

Joachim Peiper
Date of birth: 30.01.1915
SS Number: 132 496
Born in Berlin, he spent time in the *Jungfolk* from early 1933 and then towards the end of the same year, on the 12th of October, he joined the *Allgemeine-SS*, serving with the *SS-Reiterstandarte 7*. His first promotion came on the 7th of September 1934, when he became an *SS-Sturmmann*. On the 15th of October he was promoted further to *SS-Rottenführer.* In early January 1935 he began service with the *SS-VT* and took part in an officer candidate's course at Juterbog that lasted until late April. He successfully passed that course and left with the rank of *SS-Unterscharführer.* He moved from there to an officer's training course at the Braunschweig officer's school. This course came to a close at the end of March 1936, when he obtained the rank of *SS-Oberjunker.*

At the start of April 1936 he was placed within the *III Battalion* of the *Leibstandarte*. On the 20th of April he received a promotion to *SS-Untersturmführer.* He remained there until early July 1938 and in that time he perfomed the role of *Platoon Leader* and also *Battalion Adjutant*. His next move was to the personal staff of the *Reichsführer-SS,* Heinrich Himmler. This move was at the request of Himmler himself – no doubt a high honour for anyone at that time! He received a further promotion to *SS-Obersturmführer* on the 30th of January 1939. He remained with the staff of the *RF-SS* as the Second World War started, thereby not taking part in the actions in Poland.

As the *German Army* went west in May 1940, Peiper was still on Himmler's staff, but this did not stay so. On the 18th of May 1940, he joined his *LAH Kameraden* once more, serving as a *Platoon Commander* initially in the *9. Kompanie,* but moved quickly, back to his old *11. Kompanie*. Within a week of

Joachim Peiper photographed after he was awarded the Knight's Cross in March 1943.

rejoining the *LAH* he had taken over command of the *11. Kompanie,* due to the wounding of the existing *Commander.* This was during the advance into France and the advance continued as May came to an end and June began. On the last day of May 1940 he was awarded the Iron Cross Second Class. On the 1st of June he was promoted to *SS-Hauptsturmführer.* He continued to fight with his men during the difficult fighting in France until the 24th of June, when he returned to the staff of the *Reichsführer-SS.* He received the First Class Iron Cross for actions during this campaign, on the 13th of June. Later the same year he was also awarded the Infantry Assault Badge (although only fighting in one campaign) on the 3rd of October and a four-year long service medal slightly earlier, on the 7th of September.

He served on Himmler's staff through to early August 1941, missing the campaign in Greece earlier that year. When he rejoined the *LAH* they were embroiled in their advances into southern Russia. He initially served on the staff, but once again took command of the *11. Kompanie* when its' existing *Commander,* Albert Frey, moved up to take command of the *III Battalion.* He remained with them as they fought on until mid-1942. They then moved to France for their re-fit, part of which included an expansion into two *Regiments* and a *Tank Regiment.* In September, Peiper was presented with the Russian Front Medal and followed this by taking over the *III Battalion, SS-Infantry Regiment 2.* Later that same year, this *Battalion* became the *III (gep.)/SS-Panzer Grenadier Regiment 2.* This was due to them being equipped with the new Sd.Kfz.251 armoured personel carrier. At the end of January 1943 Peiper received a promotion to *SS-Sturmbannführer,* a rank more befitting of a *Battalion Commander.* By then he was on route to Russia for the next campaign.

He advanced into the area around Kharkov as the Soviets were in the midst of their steamroller movement in this region. The fighting was very difficult and as detailed above, the advance of the enemy resulted in the temporary loss of Kharkov. It was during this fighting in early March that Peiper conducted actions that resulted in his recommendation for the Knight's Cross to the Iron Cross. The recommendation was not set out in the usual formal recommendation document, but was done via a teletype message, written by Sepp Dietrich on the 7th of March 1943, although a typed version of this is contained within Peiper's file, it read as follows:

'Recommendation for the award of the Knight's Cross for *SS-Sturmbannführer* Joachim Peiper, *Commander III./2.Pz.Gren.Rgt.LSSAH.*

SS-Sturmbannführer Peiper, *Commander* of the *III (gep.)/SS-Panzer-Grenadier-Regiment 2 Leibstandarte SS Adolf Hitler,* was given the mission on

6.3.43 to break enemy resistance along the general line running from the southern edge of Prossjanoje-Hf. Ljaschowa-Gawrilowka and to advance to Hf. Peressel (main objective). Launching the attack at 1145 hours, he reached the southern outskirts of Peressel by 1345 hours. By 1400 hours he had broken through the enemy defensive lines under construction there, and on his own initiative, advanced far beyond the main objective. Moving through enemy columns, he pushed a stronger enemy out of prepared positions in Federowka-Hf. Bridock at 1530 hours and established a bridgehead. He held this bridgehead, in spite of the fact that he was cut-off from all rearward lines of communication and was under attack by strong enemy forces on all sides. Three T-34s were destroyed. By these actions, *SS-Sturmbannführer* Peiper laid the groundwork for the successful attack on Walki on 7.3.1943.

(signed) Dietrich
SS-Obergruppenführer und General der Waffen-SS,
Leibstandarte SS A.H.

F.H.Qu. on 8.3.1943.
Approved
(signed) Schmundt, *Generalmajor*

FH.u. on 9.3.1943
Awarded
The Führer
(signed) Adolf Hitler'

As can be seen from the above translation, the recommendation was quickly approved two days after being sent to the FHQ. Peiper was made aware of the award the same day by radio, but the fighting was still raging, so the focus was very much on the task at hand.

This award would not end Peiper's association with the Knight's Cross to the Iron Cross or its' various grades. Details of those subsequent awards will follow in later volumes.

Wedged in the midst of this recognition for the initial successes of the wider Kharkov campaign was recognition for actions conducted back in late-November 1942 by the *SS* cavalry units.

SS-Kavallerie Division (1942)

They had been moved to an area northwest of Smolensk during October 1942, then moved northeast of there during November, fighting around the Belij pocket. It was during that fighting, that Gustav Lombard and August Zehender conducted their actions detailed below that resulted in both of them becoming Knight's Cross holders.

Gustav Lombard

Date of birth: 10.04.1895

SS Number: 185 023

Born in Spiegelberg, Lombard joined the *SS* at the start of May 1933, initially based with the *SS-Reiterstandarte 6*. He was holding the rank of *SS-Scharführer (SS-Unterscharführer)* just over six months later, followed by *SS-Oberscharführer (SS-Scharführer)* in mid-July 1934, and a further move to *SS-Truppführer (SS-Oberscharführer)* less than two months later. He was with the *1./SS-Reiterstandarte 7* by then. He received his first officer promotion in mid-September 1935, when he became an *SS-Untersturmführer*. At the start of April 1936 he assumed command of the *1./SS-Reiterstandarte 7*. A further promotion came on the 13th of September 1936, by which time he had spent a variety of stints with the *Army*. He was promoted to *SS-Hauptsturmführer* just under two years later.

At the start of March 1940 he moved to the *1. SS-Totenkopf-Reiterstandarte* and is listed as being on the officer reserve list for the *Waffen-SS*. In mid-December the same year he received the Second Class Iron Cross. On this day he also became an *Abteilung Commander* and held this level of command as he moved to the *SS-Kavallerie Regiment 1,* in mid-March 1941. It was with this unit that he went into Russia in June 1941.

On the 21st of June he was promoted to *SS-Sturmbannführer*. He was then given command of *Regiment 1* on the 18th of August and was awarded the First Class Iron Cross on the 3rd of September. Lombard assumed temporary command of the *Brigade* in late 1941, but assumed permanent command in March 1942, the same month that he was promoted to *SS-Obersturmbannführer*. On the 24th of April, he was awarded the General Assault Badge. He returned to command of *Regiment 1* as the newly created *SS-Kavallerie Division* moved to Russia in late 1942. He had a spell as temporary *Divisional Commander* from December and into January 1943. At the end of that month he was promoted to *SS-Standartenführer*. He was awarded the German Cross in Gold on the 11th of February for actions conducted during January and early February.

Gustav Lombard photographed after he received the Knight's Cross in mid-March 1943. He is seen here with the rank of SS-Standartenführer, although the actions that resulted in the award were done whilst holding the rank of SS-Obersturmbannführer.

On the 8th of March 1943 a further award recommendation was penned for Gustav Lombard by Hermann Fegelein. This recommendation was for the Knight's Cross and, unusually, covered actions much earlier, in late-November 1942. This recommendation read as follows:

'*SS-Kavallerie Regiment 1* under the leadership of *SS-Obersturmbannführer* Lombard was positioned in the area of Belousovo-Sergejebka on the evening of 25.11.42 as an *OKH*-Reserve. Lombard was given orders only to deploy by special orders. Just as he arrived in his assigned area, a driver of the *2. Luftwaffe FeldDivision* related that the enemy had broken through near Romanovo with about 100 tanks and 200-300 men. The *2. Luftwaffe FeldDivision* was called, but no confirmation of this message could be obtained. Lombard immediately sent out several reconnaissance patrols, which confirmed that the Russians had indeed broken through with about 25 tanks and 300-400 men in Cholomedina.

Without waiting for the orders to attack, Lombard advanced on his own decision through the forest north of Belousovo. They overran weak enemy security forces on the northern edge of the forest and attacked immediately. The troops used moonlight to see their way through, where necessary, as it was still night and *SS-Obersturmbannführer* Lombard won that advantageous position for the *Regiment*. This enabled him to hold the line before the Russians arrived and to support the right flank of the *2. Luftwaffe FeldDivision*. His position was successful in avoiding a further advance, as it was only a question of hours since our own lines had been penetrated 15 km deep. There had been no noticeable resistance, which would have stopped the advance of the opponent. To fool the Russians about the length of their defensive front, which had no deep penetrations, but which was lengthy on the flanks, Lombard sent out strong patrols strengthened by an anti-tank gun to fool the opponent operating on the right flank. They were successful in holding the positions of the *Regiment* until the next night, when *SS-Kavallerie Regiment 2* lengthened the front to the east and with that, dissolved the threat on the flank.

During the next day the enemy was not very active. With carefully planned artillery fire, Lombard was able to spoil any enemy attack preparations. The positions of the *Regiment* had to be improved in order to be able to carry out a larger defensive action successfully. Again, Lombard decided to give the order to attack and took Okuliza and Knjashe. At the same time, the cornerstone of Medvodevo was cleverly taken by an advance *Squadron* component. As statements by prisoners confirmed, the opponent intended on attacking, the goal of which could not be carried out due to the *Regiment's* artillery preparation and the attack followed. Lombard's command could not report these happenings because the signals units had not yet arrived due to a lack of fuel. In the following defensive battles, the *Regiment* suffered heavy casualties for men, *NCOs* as well as officers.

During the decisive moments, *SS-Obersturmbannführer* Lombard was always to be found at the most dangerous positions. He rallied his subordinates with his composure. Through these two decisive measures, which he decided upon himself, the breakthrough was decisively stopped.

SS-Obersturmbannführer Lombard is especially worthy of this honour because he had distinguished himself through his own decisions and enthusiasm already in the winter of 1941/42 repeatedly.'

This award was approved on the 10th of March 1943, making Lombard the third *Waffen-SS* cavalry Knight's Cross to the Iron Cross holder.

He had obtained valuable experience in the field, especially against the increasing menace of the Partisans in the rear lines. He spent time with other units during 1943, passing on his experience in this area. He remained attached to the cavalry and once again commanded a *Kampfgruppe* in early 1944. In March the same year, he was promoted to *SS-Oberführer* and then left the field the following month. He spent time in training and also on reserve. In late September 1944 he was given the task of raising and commanding the newly created *31st SS-Freiwilligen-Grenadier-Division,* remaining in this command until the end of the war. On Hitler's birthday 1945, he was promoted to *SS-Brigadeführer und Generalmajor der Waffen-SS.* He was taken captive by the Russians at the end of the war and, like many of his *Kameraden,* he spent ten years in captivity. He died on the 18th of September 1992.

August Zehender

Date of birth: 28.04.1903

SS Number: 224 219

Born in Aalen, his military service began in early April 1918, as the First World War was in its' final death throws. He had joined the *Army* at that point and remained with them throughout the difficult post-war years, right up to early August 1932. In that time he had reached the rank of *Feldwebel.* He then followed this with a stint in the *S.A.* from the start of May 1933 until the start of September 1934.

He is listed as serving as a *Platoon Leader* in *Deutschland's 12. Kompanie* on the 9th of November 1935, holding the rank of *SS-Obersturmführer*, although it does not list the actual date he moved to the *SS.* His next promotion came on the 20th of April 1937, moving to *SS-Hauptsturmführer,* he was commanding the *12. Kompanie* by then. At the start of May 1938 he was with the *8. Kompanie,*

August Zehender shown in a formal portrait after his award of the Knight's Cross.

followed in mid-1939 by moving to the *4. Kompanie,* the unit he entered the Second World War with.

He fought in Poland and earned the Second Class Iron Cross on the 14th of September 1939. He then went west in 1940 and earned the First Class Iron Cross on the 18th of June, followed by the Infantry Assault Badge on the 10th of August. A few weeks later, at the start of September, he moved to serve with the *SS-VT's Flak Battalion.* He did not stay there long, as by late December, he had assumed command of the *I Battalion, SS-Regiment 11.* He had been promoted to *SS-Sturmbannführer* one week prior to this move. He fought in Yugoslavia and Greece in early 1941, before moving east into Russia in mid-1941. Whilst with *SS-Division Reich* during the early stage of Barbarossa, he was wounded twice. The second wound removed him from front line service and also resulted in him receiving the Wound Badge in Silver on the 6th of October.

His next posting came in mid-March 1942, this time serving with the *SS-Kavallerie-Brigade.* This unit was in the midst of heavy fighting in Russia at that time. The cost was high and resulted in most of the *Brigade* being sent back to Poland for a re-fit. The elements that remained came under Zehender's command, forming *Kampfgruppe Zehender.* He then rejoined his *Kameraden* in Poland in mid-1942 as the *Brigade* was being expanded into a *Division.* He was placed in command of the *Division's Regiment 2.*

This *Division* returned to Russia in October and on the 16th, Zehender was awarded the German Cross in Gold. This was followed on the 9th of November with a promotion to *SS-Obersturmbannführer.* He conducted actions during late November and early December 1942 that would result in his recommendation for the Knight's Cross. This recommendation would not be written until January 1943, being penned by his *Commander,* Fritz Freitag. It read as follows:

'On the 26.11.42, *SS-Kav. Rgt. 2* was put into action to block the breakthrough south of Belyj. In a forced march the unit reached Baturino with the task of standing by ready for action on orders of the *Division.* The immediate reconnaissance showed that the opponent stood in Cholomedina with about 25 tanks and 3-400 men, having reached with it the rear of the *1. Rgt.* and the deep flanks. Recognising this heavy danger that threatened the flanks of the then marching *Division* and questioned the carrying out of the tasks assigned by the *Division* to block the breakthrough, *SS-Obersturmbannführer* Zehender, against the divisional order, at his own decision and under good moon light attacked at 24:00 hours supported by one *Battery* of light field guns and one 8.8cm anti-aircraft gun. He threw the opponent out of Cholomedina after a difficult fight.

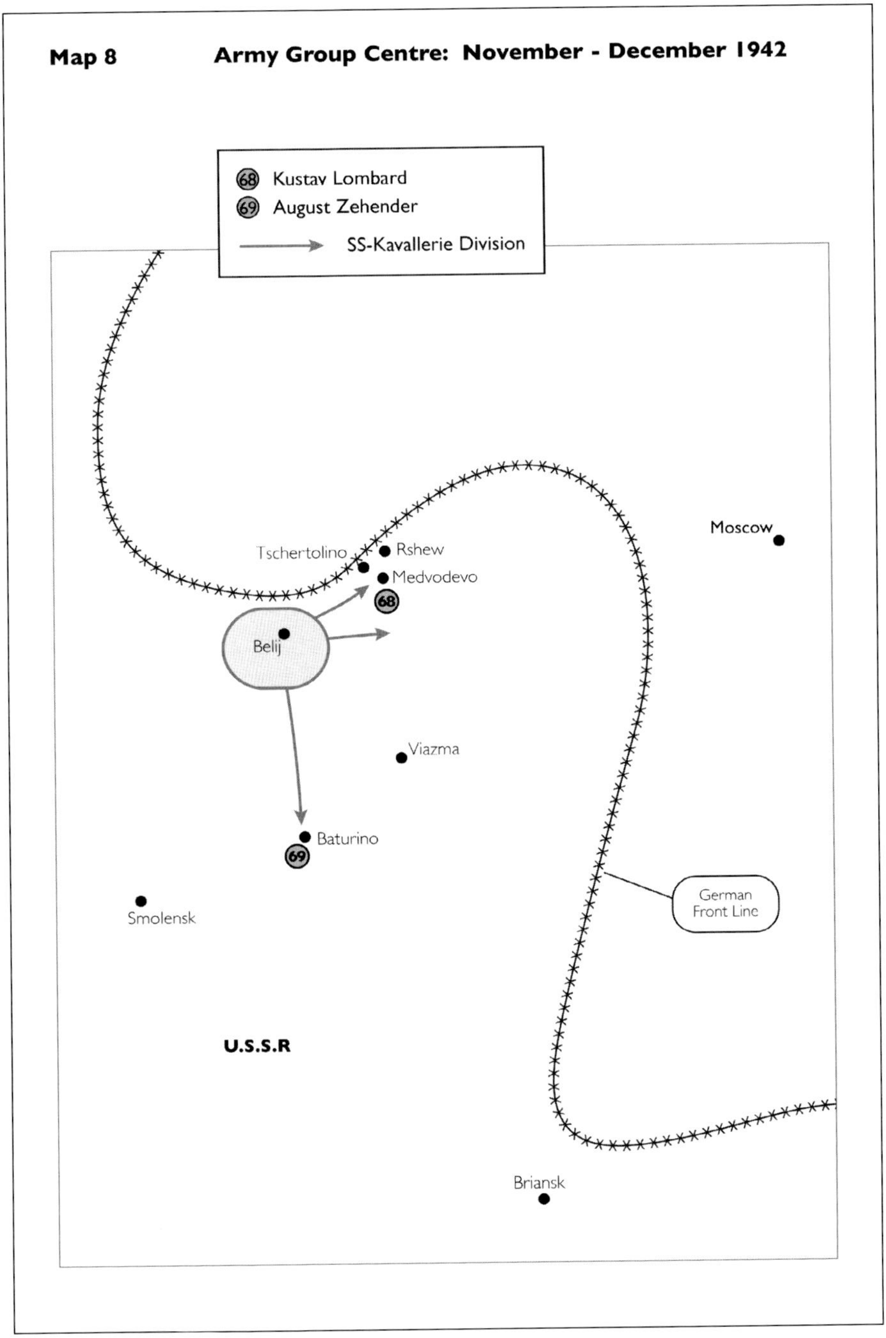
Map 8
Army Group Centre: November - December 1942
68 Kustav Lombard
69 August Zehender
SS-Kavallerie Division
Tschertolino
Rshew
Medvodevo
68
Belij
Moscow
Viazma
Baturino
69
Smolensk
German Front Line
U.S.S.R
Briansk

The following day the enemy tried with larger forces to win back Cholomedina and the road that crossed this village, which was of a great importance for his motorized elements as a march and supply road. In spite of the heavy losses suffered by his *Regiment*, *SS-Obersturmbannführer* Zehender was able to hold the line for the next two days through his personal intervention, giving his men a permanent example of how to fight on. Through this deed, the move forward of the opponent was definitely stopped and a roll-up of our front, and with it a widening of the penetration point, soundly prevented.

As on 2.12.42, *SS-Obersturmbannführer* Zehender verified, through reconnaissance and the statements of deserters, that an attack from the forests was going to take place. At his own decision he attacked with the *Ski Battalion* subordinated to him, outflanked with a *Kompanie* the enemy wing units and pounced on the supplies of the opponent. Numerous field kitchens, ration supply depots and vehicles with fuel and ammunition were blown up.

For 24 hours the *Battalion* was encircled, but thanks to the good leadership and model behaviour of *SS-Obersturmbannführer* Zehender, they destroyed the enemy encirclement. Through this attack, was prevented the advance of the opponent, that had the objective of trying, for the last time, to break through, due to high losses, the thinly occupied position on the road. Through the employment of the *Regiment* for the capture of Cholomedina and the road going through this village, and the attack at his own decision against the rear of the positions of the enemy, Zehender earned a considerable credit in this successful operation. It led to the encirclement and annihilation of the enemy forces that had broken through south of Belyj.

SS-Obersturmbannführer Zehender is especially worthy of the award of the Knight's Cross to the Iron Cross. He has repeatedly distinguished himself through his decisiveness in the campaigns in Poland, France, Serbia, Greece and the East Campaign in 1941 with *SS-Regiment "Deutschland"*. Zehender is a bearer of the German Cross in Gold and was already wounded three times.'

This recommendation was approved on the same day as Gustav Lombard's, the 10th of March 1943. He was still fighting with his *Division* at the time. This award of the Knight's Cross would not end August Zehender's connection to the various grades of this medal. Details of his later actions will follow in subsequent volumes of this project.

Summary

In this chapter we have seen how the initial attack wave back towards Kharkov got underway. The 'withdrawal and wait' tactics of Hausser had proved to be the right thing to do and the initiative had started to pass back into the hands of the Germans. They had blunted the advance of the Russians and were making good advances back towards the strategic goal of Kharkov.

This initial counter-attack was witness to further acts of bravery, as detailed in this Chapter, but the question was – would this continued bravery be enough to re-take the prize?

CHAPTER THREE

RETAKING THE PRIZE

The focus for Hitler and Stalin was without a doubt, the prize of Kharkov. We have seen how the *SS Panzer Korps* were sent to this area to win control.

Although it had not gone well in the first, arrival phase, of this new plan, the counter-attack phase was making good headway. Strong forces had been built up and placed into this southern region of the Russian Front. The Germans had cut through this strong force of enemy troops and blunted their seemingly unstoppable advance. Now they had to continue this advance and hope that they would continue to meet with the successes they had over the preceding three weeks.

Now we need to focus on what took place next – would all this recent effort result in achieving the intended goal?

The next award connected to the Knight's Cross was approved for a soldier within the *LAH,* so let us continue our overview with the further advances of that unit.

LAH

Whilst the various awards already listed in the preceding pages were being approved back in Berlin, the men at the front line had no time for halting their advance. Dergatschi was the next target for the *LAH* and this was taken on the 10th of March in a combined assault with the men of *Totenkopf.* Zirkuny was also reached the same day, thereby taking the advance to the north of Kharkov.

The *LAH* regrouped around Dergatschi and then began their moves into the city of Kharkov itself from the north and northeast. On the 11th of March Alexejewka was one of the main targets on route and it was there that Hugo Kraas led his unit into this objective and secured it, despite difficult fighting. (This resulted in Kraas being awarded the Knight's Cross – to be detailed shortly). *SS-Hauptsturmführer* Hans Becker was fighting around this area on the same day, at Ssewerny, with his *2. Kompanie/2. Regiment.* His successful battle there resulted in him also being awarded the Knight's Cross (to be covered shortly). Losowenka and the airstrip north of Kharkov were also targeted. Kharkov itself was penetrated in the north (with Red Square, Lisa Gora, Pawliwka, the park, the zoo, Sumskaja Street, Stara-Moskowska Street all being reached).

The 12th of March saw a push deeper into the northern sector of the city. It was during these particular advances that *SS-Sturmbannführer* Rudolf Sandig led his *II Battalion/2. Regiment* against the enemy, which resulted in his later award of the Knight's Cross. It was also on this day that Rudolf von Ribbentrop started actions in Kharkov that formed part of his Knight's Cross recommendation. The *LAH* pushed hard all day and elements of the *II Battalion/1. Regiment,* under Max Hansen, made it to the edge of Red Square. The *I Battalion* also fought towards Red Square and the fighting did not relent as this day came to a close.

The following day saw the *2. Regiment* push to the southeast as the *I & II Battalion/1. Regiment* pushed further into the city. The enemy offered very stiff resistance at every turn using tanks, anti-tank guns and all other available weapons. The fighting in the city centre for control of this objective continued on into the 14th. It was on this day that German radio announced the re-capture of this city. The fighting itself raged for a further two days as the *LAH* cleared up any remaining pockets of enemy resistance.

One of our previous photographers – Gerhard Dilling – was involved in these final pushes into the city centre. He took the photograph featured below that shows recent Kinght's Cross holder Albert Frey and Oakleaves holder Kurt Meyer. Other officers and men are present too and the interesting focus of the photo is that it was taken whilst the fighting was still taking place. Albert Frey is on the extreme left of the picture and is seen looking up the street to the left. Next to him is Kurt Meyer, followed by two more officers from the *1. Regiment.* Further men are positioned behind a wall to the right. What Albert Frey is watching is Russians further up this street, who are still shooting at the *Waffen-SS* soldiers. This is why all of the men, including Kurt Meyer, are taking cover behind the thick walls of the building. That is, of course, except Albert Frey, who is standing out in the open. Gerhard Dilling took the photo from the opposite side of this street and he made particular mention of Frey's known bravery, very evident in this photo and also his recent award.

It was on this day, the 16th of March, that Sepp Dietrich was approved for the award of the Swords to his existing Knight's Cross with Oakleaves and full details of this will follow at the end of the chapter.

The need to control the wider area around Kharkov was paramount for the *SS-Panzer Korps,* so the men within this formation were ordered north to Bjelgorod.

The advance to this objective began on the 16th and during this day, and the next, the objectives of Mal. Prochody and Dementejewka were taken against difficult resistance. Ribbentrop fought against enemy anti-tank guns on this second day and this also formed part of his Knight's Cross recommendation. The push towards Bjelgorod continued and by midday the objective was in the hands of Joachim Peiper and his *III/2. Regiment.* They held this objective despite counter-attack attempts by the Russians. It is of interest to note, within the context of this project, that various sources list the capture of Bjelgorod as the reason why Peiper received the Knight's Cross – one of these sources includes the *LAH's* official history. As we already know, he had been approved for this award over one week earlier for actions west of Kharkov!

It is worth adding the recollections of one of the *Waffen-SS* soldiers who led the advance into Bjelgorod in those critical days. His name was Werner Wendt and at that stage, he was a gunner in one the *LAH's* handful of Tiger tanks. Wendt was in one of two Tiger tanks that were advancing with Peiper's unit. Their rapid advance caught the enemy unawares and as they approached Bjelgorod, they came across an enemy anti-tank gun. The enemy crew were not expecting Germans this far forward, so were not even manning their gun. Without hesitation, the Tiger tank rolled straight over the top of the gun and crushed it under their tracks, carrying on with their advance, safe in the knowledge that this enemy gun would not give their following *Kameraden* any trouble.

The tank that Wendt was in was the first German vehicle into Bjelgorod and it steamed across the bridge that led into this objective. Although they had managed to remove the threat of the enemy anti-tank gun, there was no shortage of additional enemy threats in the area. No sooner had they crossed the bridge, than they were informed of the fact that two enemy T-34 tanks had moved into the advance road behind them and were engaging the remaining Germans also advancing towards Bjelgorod. The Tiger that Wendt was in quickly traversed its turret into the 6-o'clock position. They took on one of the T-34s and fired two shells into it – taking it out of action. The second Tiger in the area engaged the remaining enemy tank and destroyed it.

This advance was reminiscent of the *Blitzkrieg* advances in the 1939/40 period. Rapid advance towards the objective at all costs, without halting to engage

Albert Frey (first left), Kurt Meyer (second left) and other Kameraden photographed as the fighting was still taking place in the city of Kharkov. Frey is watching the enemy up the street as bullets are still being fired at them!

the enemy on the flanks. The men of the *LAH* were certainly using their new equipment to good effect!

Werner Wendt had previously been a PaK gunner prior to his move to tanks. Later in the war he would get command of his own Tiger and Tiger II tank and fought during the Normandy and Ardennes battles. He survived the war and died in early 2007.

The remainder of March was spent in defensive fighting within the area surrounding Bjelgorod, before the *LAH* were relieved by *Totenkopf*. On the 21st of March Dietrich left for Berlin to receive his recently approved Swords. When he returned he brought news of the formation of a new *SS-Panzer Korps* and a new *SS-Division*. This occurrence will be covered in the next chapter, alongside the general expansion of the *Waffen-SS*, at this time, in the wake of the Kharkov victory.

Back on the 28th of March the following *LAH* soldiers were approved for the award of the Knight's Cross – Wilhelm Beck, Hans Becker, Max Hansen, Hugo Kraas and Hermann Weiser. These will all be detailed at the end of the chapter.

The next Knight's Cross approval was given to a soldier from *Totenkopf*, so our coverage will move to that unit.

Our photographer from Bereka and also Kharkov centre, Gerhard Dilling, seen here as an SS-Unterscharführer, who finished the war as an SS-Untersturmführer.

Totenkopf

We left them in the previous chapter, as they were moving west of Kharkov, heading towards Olschany. As they continued in this direction, Karlovka and Krassnokutsk, north of there, were reached on the 10th of March. It was in Krassnokutsk that Georg Bochmann started actions that contributed to his later award of the Oakleaves to his existing Knight's Cross.

The advance around the west and northern part of Kharkov continued with *Totenkopf* advancing alongside the *LAH*. They both moved into Dergatschi, then *Totenkopf* moved off in an easterly and south-easterly direction around the outskirts of this all-important city. By the 12th of March Zirkuny was reached and by the following day they were as far as Rogan, southeast of Kharkov on the main Kharkov to Tschugujew road. This situation was improved even further by the middle of March, as Tschugujew itself was reached. This gave *Totenkopf* a line running from there back north as far as Lipzy. Between the 12th and 14th of March Joachim Schubach was engaged in actions between Ssorokowka and Tschugujew that resulted in his later award of the Knight's Cross. Further north, Arzelino Masarie was fighting in Lipzy on the 14th of March and his successful actions also resulted in him being awarded the Knight's Cross – both of these will be covered in detail later.

It was around this time that *Totenkopf* began to move in towards the city itself and engaged retreating enemy troops moving out of the city eastwards. This was whilst the *LAH* were engaged in heavy fighting in the city centre. Additional elements of *Totenkopf* pushed further around the southern outskirts of Kharkov and by the 16th of March had reached Ossnowna. Waldemar Riefkogel conducted actions on this day in Tschugujew that would result in his award of the Knight's Cross – details to follow.

As highlighted above, they reached Tschugujew, situated on the Donez River. Part of the objective now was to extent the northern sector out to the Donez at Woltschansk. This took place up to the 18th of March and during those intervening two days, Georg Bochmann fought at Tetlega and Saroshnje on the 17th that formed the remaining part of his Oakleaves recommendation. The southern elements of this *Division* consolidated their hold and took control of Murow and Ternowaja. This brought their advances to a halt for the time being.

Their advances over the preceding weeks had been difficult and costly. The enemy put up very stiff resistance and the terrain was very unfavourable for the advances of a modern equipped *Panzer Division*. The emphasis now shifted to a defensive posture, with specific focus on rest, repair and replacement. On the final day of this month, Walter Gerth was approved for the award of the Knight's Cross and this will be detailed at the end of this chapter.

So, whilst *Totenkopf* and the *LAH* were moving around to the north and into the city, as well as sweeping around the easterly edge of Kharkov, what was *Das Reich* up to?

Das Reich

We left this unit in the previous chapter as they took Ljubotin and Korotitsch around the 9th of March. They drew breath here and closed up as they prepared to move against Kharkov over the following two days. The actual push towards the city began on the 11th with *Das Reich* moving round the south and southeast – the aim here was a full encirclement of the city. They ran into well-fortified enemy positions and their advance did not get off to a good start. During the early hours of day two, a *Pioneer Kompanie* under Heinz Macher punched through tough enemy defenses at Saljutino (Knight's Cross actions covered in detail later). This small breakthrough developed into an advance route further into the city. Whilst elements fought in the city, other lead elements moved through the city and onto Lossewo, reached on the 13th. Otto Baum led his men to the north and round the eastern outskirts of Rogan. During this fighting in the city on the 12th, Vincenz Kaiser conducted actions that resulted in him being awarded the Knight's Cross. Hans Weiss' Knight's Cross recommendation also covered his actions on this day fighting within Kharkov.

As the *Totenkopf* and *LAH Divisions* fought in the north and northern part of the city, *Das Reich* continued their fight in the south and southeast. By the 15th of March the city was reported to be under the control of the Germans once again. *Das Reich's* successes included the capture of the large tractor works/tank factory southeast of Kharkov at Lossewo.

With the city under German control once more, those enemy units still outside the city were trying to move eastwards. Some of these advances ran into the men of *Das Reich,* especially at Ternowoje, Lossewo and Lipzy.

On the 17th of March *Deutschland* moved to Lipzy as part of the orders to move on Bjelgorod. *Der Führer* took Michailowka on this day as well as Nepokrytoje and Petrowskoje. On the following day they cleared the road leading to Bjelgorod, then moved closer to that objective – taken by the *LAH* later that day. Over the remainder of that day and the next *Das Reich* moved through Netschajewka, Brodok and north Bjelgorod. Acting *Divisional Commander* Herbert Vahl was wounded and evacuated.

The remainder of March was spent securing the area between Kharkov and the Donez River. There was a slight move to the southeast in the closing days of that month. On the 26th of March Karl Kloskowski conducted actions at Pawlograd that resulted in his later award of the Knight's Cross – details to follow in later chapters.

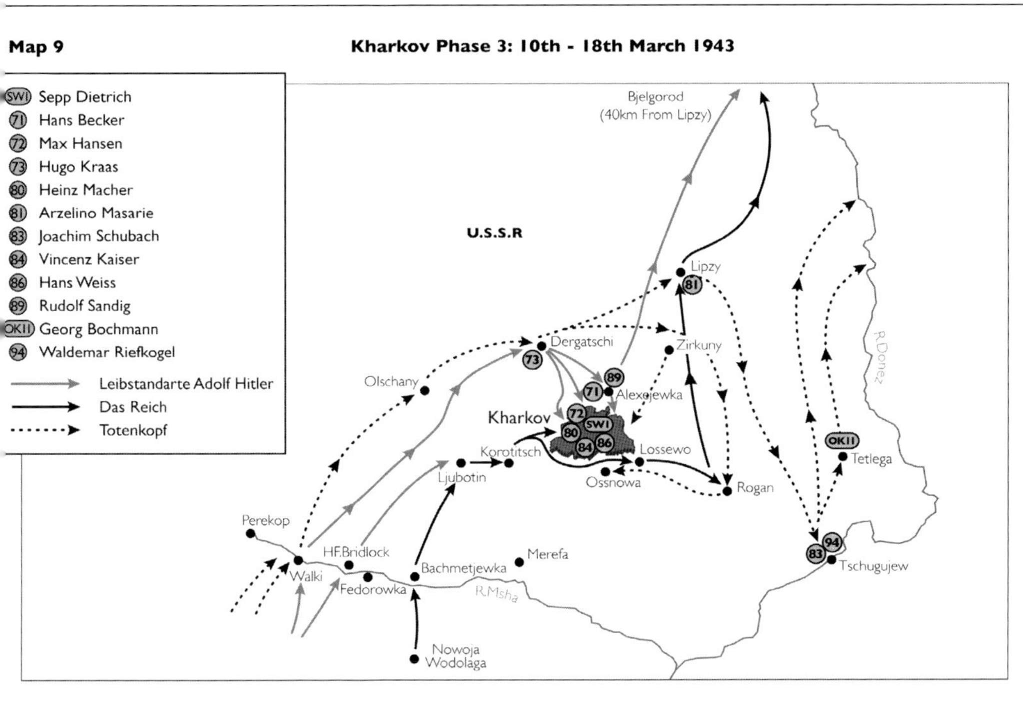

The first official recognition for *Das Reich* with regards to the recent successful Kharkov campaign came on the final day of March 1943. Heinz Harmel, Christian Tychsen, Herbert Vahl and Karl-Heinz Worthmann were all approved for the award of the Knight's Cross to the Iron Cross and will be detailed shortly.

Wiking

We last covered this unit in chapter one as they had taken Krasno Armaiskoje. With that objective taken, the advance continued. They expected to encounter more strong Russian forces in their way, but instead they came across towns and other locations empty of the enemy. It was known that enemy troops had been in the immediate path of *Wiking,* but elements of the enemy had been hurridley moved northwards towards Kharkov.

By the 22nd of February, *Wiking* were in the Byk sector. Over the following two days they advanced to, and engaged, the enemy around Barwenkowo, both sides taking heavy losses. On the 24th February Dieckmann completed actions at Alexsandrowka that formed the final part of his Oakleaves recommendation.

The Suchoj-Torez area was next on the list and advances were made to Boydanowka and Ssemenowka. It was during these advances that *SS-*

Sturmbannführer Erwin Reichell was severely wounded, dying on the 28th of February – the same day that Helmut Pfortner died. The pressure upon the enemy continued with the intended target of the Suchoj-Torez sector being reached at the end of February/first few days of March. The advance stopped at the Donez River around Wjel. Kamyschewicha and Isjum.

Once the Donez was reached, they assumed defensive positions and took stock of the recent fighting. In the opening two months of 1943 they had zig-zagged northwards from the Caucausus and helped to stabilize the front line in the critical southern sector, as their *SS-Panzer Korps Kameraden* were advancing back towards Kharkov. The fighting for *Wiking* was heavy, difficult and costly. In the space of six weeks – within the context of this overall project – *Wiking* lost the *Nordland Regimental Commander* and Knight's Cross holder, *SS-Obersturmbannführer* Harry Polewacz back in January, together with the *Westland Regimental Commander, SS-Sturmbannführer* Erwin Reichell who died on the 28th of February – the same day that his Knight's Cross was approved. Last but not least was *SS-Hauptsturmführer* Helmut Pfortner from *Germania,* who had been awarded his Knight's Cross back in 1942.

Wiking adapted their defensive posture as March progressed and as Kharkov and Bjelgorod were falling to the *SS-Panzer Korps* further north. This situation remained for *Wiking* for the rest of this month.

We will now cover the other *Waffen-SS* units up to the end of March 1943, these units were last covered in Chapter 1. Following close behind will be details all of the Knight's Crosses approved between mid-March and the end of March.

SS-Polizei

In the second half of February they moved to an area west of Kolpino. The Russian pressure in this area was intense and during this part of February the Demjansk salient was finally abandoned and a new line of defense was established on the Lowat River. It would seem that *Totenkopf's* efforts in 1942 had been in vain as the Germans accepted the inevitable.

Staraja-Russa became the new focus of attack for the Russians and this was subjected to repeated attacks during March, although the Germans held it. The Russians also attacked in the southern Lake Ladoga area, but again the Germans prevailed.

Friederick-Wilhelm Bock's Knight's Cross recommendation was penned in the second half of February by his *Regimental Commander* and was approved at the end of March, details of this will follow shortly.

2. SS-Infantry-Brigade (mot.) & SS-Legion Niederlande
They were kept busy for the remainder of February and all of March in their existing positions around the Leningrad sector.

SS-Legion Norwegian
As previously covered, their ranks were low in number and during March 1943 they were sent home on leave. They never actually returned to the front line, as during late May, they were disbanded. This ended the existence of a second *SS* unit during the early part of 1943.

SS-Legion-Flanderen
Due to the increasing pressure in the area surrounding Leningrad, *Flanderen* were moved to Krasny-Bor and placed under the command of the *Heer's 254. Division* during the second half of February. This was followed by a quieter phase in the early part of March, but during the new enemy offensive in late March, they were committed once again. They managed to make advances and captured some of the Russian positions, before fending off repeated counter-attacks. They held their line, but due to 85% casualties, they were withdrawn at the end of March back to Krasny-Bor.

SS-Kavallerie Division
Their situation remained unchanged during February and March 1943.

SS-Kampfgruppe 'Z'
This new unit was created from the existing *SS-Reiter Regiment 2* and placed under the command of August Zehender. They were moved to the Orel salient at Komarichi, north of Svesk. They fought the enemy there until early March before being moved back to Karachev.

1. SS-Infantry Brigade (mot.) & SS-Freikorps Denmark
These two units fought in the Vitebsk – Gurki area from the last week of February until the end of the first week in March, *Denmark* fought in Taidy. Due to losses incurred during this fighting *SS-Freikorps Denmark* were moved to Germany in late March – they too were officially disbanded in early May – another *SS* unit ceased to exist.

Prinz Eugen
Last covered in mid-February as they moved further southeast into Bosnia. They were in pursuit of the enemy Partisans and also had to contend with Partisans who were active in their rear areas.

Drvar was reached on the 27th of February 1943 and this action formed the first part of Artur Phleps' subsequent Knight's Cross recommendation. In the first week of March the advance reached Livno. It was in the first half of March that Operation Weiss was concluded and considered successful. Although they had occupied large parts of Bosnia, the majority of the enemy had escaped. *Prinz Eugen* moved to an area near Mostar. This is how they seen out the rest of March. It was also during this month that Artur Phleps was being tasked with setting up a new *Division,* details to follow later in this volume.

Now that we have detailed all of the units up to this point, let us cover all Knight's Cross related awards between mid-March and the end of March 1943. The first of these would give the *Waffen-SS* their first set of Swords!

Josef 'Sepp' Dietrich

Date of birth: 28.05.1892

SS Number: 1 177

This experienced *Alte Kampfer* was last covered at the end of 1941 when he became the first *Waffen-SS* soldier to be awarded the Knight's Cross to the Iron Cross with Oakleaves for his unit's accomplishments up to the end of 1941, most notably Rostov. Since then they had endured a relatively quieter phase in the first half of 1942, then moved to France for their much-needed refit and expansion. Coming under Hausser's *SS-Panzer Korps,* he led his men as they re-entered Russia at the start of 1943. It was the actions and successes of his men during the fighting around Kharkov that Dietrich was awarded the Knight's Cross with Oakleaves and Swords.

It is not clear who made the recommendation, or when, and it could have come from Hitler himself? The details of the document, dated the 17th of March 1943, are as follows and are compehensive:

'Berlin, 16.3.43

The *Führer* has awarded *SS-Obergruppenführer und General der Waffen-SS* Sepp Dietrich, *Commander* of the *SS-Panzergrenadier-Division Leibstandarte SS Adolf Hitler,* the Oakleaves with Swords to the Knight's Cross to the Iron Cross and sends the following telegram:

"In recognition of proven heroism I award you, the 26. Soldier of the *German Army* the Oakleaves with Swords to the Knight's Cross to the Iron Cross.

(signed) Adolf Hitler"

The unmistakable Joseph 'Sepp' Dietrich pictured after his award of the Swords to his existing Knight's Cross with Oakleaves; the first Waffen-SS soldier to receive this award.

The Swords for *Obergruppenführer* Sepp Dietrich.

How the *Leibstandarte* conquered Kharkov.
Berlin – In the heaviest of struggles that lasted for days, the *Divisions* of the *SS-Panzerkorps* conquered the city of Kharkov in a comprehensive recapturing attack from the north and east. This was a huge result by our troops, an outstanding part of this was from the "*Leibstandarte Adolf Hitler*" under *SS-Obergruppenführer und General der Waffen-SS* Sepp Dietrich. The award of the Oakleaves with Swords to the Knight's Cross to the Iron Cross to Sepp Dietrich, that was announced yesterday evening gives thanks to, and recognition by the *Führer,* for the brave men of the *Standarte* and it's *Commander,* the conquerer of Kharkov.

The *Leibstandarte* opened the attack against the city, expanded by the Soviets to one overall fortress, in the early morning hours of the 10th of March from the north, using several attack columns. In bitter fighting the *SS* men won ground slowly by overcoming the defending opponent. In violent street fighting, the first large break-in successfully brought them into the Soviet positions, through which they were able to get into the centre of the city. The Red Square, the symbol of Soviet domination, and the headquarters at the railway station, were taken with hand-to-hand fighting. Street after street, house after house, factory after factory were snatched from the strongly defending Bolsheviks, that defended the ruins of the city and fields using fast defensive fire. Simultaneously other groups of the *Waffen-SS* gained a hold in the city from the west and east. With that, on the 13th of March, the enemy became divided and the *Leibstandarte* began the annihilation of the remaining enemy groups and in the west part of the city came a group from the *SS-Division "Reich"*. The Soviets in the south east quarter carried out the last embittered resistance, that however on Sunday 14th of March, was broken in the evening. Around 18:50 hours, the entire city was occupied, for the 17th of February was in the past and the Industrial metropolis of the Ukraine was once again in German hands.

There the *Leibstandarte SS Adolf Hitler* was involved, in the decisive conquest of Kharkov, attached a new honour to their flag. In the operations that preceded this significant success, the *Leibstandarte* was engaged for weeks in outstanding heavy fighting between the Donez and Dnjepr. In this fighting, the successes joined the *Heer* and the *Waffen-SS,* within them at the point was the *Leibstandarte,* caught up in the onset of the winter offensive, prepared the way, engaging the enemy in powerful defensive fighting for the recovery of the lost ground and annilhilation of the Soviet attack armies, and as part of that the masterly taking of Kharkov. Two new holders of the Oakleaves (*SS-Standartenführer* Fritz Witt and *SS-Obersturmbannführer* Kurt Meyer) and six new Knight's Cross holders for the *Leibstandarte* are witness to the incredible actions of the *SS* men in the first few weeks. With the award of the Swords to its' *Commander* however, the *Standarte* received its' most beautiful and most valuable honour, an honour that every individual man of this leader places death and life sworn allegiance with enormous fulfilled pride.

In Poland and in France, in Greece and above all in the endless east stood the *Leibstandarte Adolf Hitler* in the fighting, intervening the same men with their weapons for the National Socialist Greater Germany. Before 1933 he fought already in the black-shirted *Schutzstaffeln* for the National Socialist movement. That the *Obergruppenführer,* the soldier of the world war, the fighter of the 9. November 1923, the faithful companion of the *Führer*, the old *SS Leader* and current *General* of the *Waffen-SS,* who started exactly 10 years before as the leader of the *Leibstandarte* at first a *Regiment* and now as a *Division,* into the field. Today the *Führer,* through the Oakleaves with Swords has huge joy and huge pride.'

This award, on the 16th of March 1943, made Dietrich the first *Waffen-SS* soldier to become a holder of the Oakleaves with Swords to the Knight's Cross. As you may recall from Volume 1, he was the first *Waffen-SS* recipient of the Knight's Cross in 1940, followed by the first to receive the Oakleaves to the Knight's Cross. Being the first recipient of the Oakleaves with Swords would not end this soldier's connection to the Knight's Cross or its' various grades. Details of that will follow in later volumes.

Friedrick-Wilhelm Bock

Date of birth: 06.05.1897

SS Number: 405 821

Born in Wreschen, West Prussia, he joined the *Army* in the first few days of August 1914, just prior to the outbreak of World War I. He was posted to the artillery and served with various artillery *Regiments* throughout the war. He was promoted to the rank of *Leutnant* in February 1918. He stayed with the artillery until February 1919, after hostilies ceased. He was awarded the Second Class Iron Cross and also the Black Wound Badge, being wounded in September 1918.

After leaving the *Army*, he then spent time with the *Freikorps* in the northern coastal area during 1919. He then spent a three-year stint in a civilian role, before joining the Police in 1922. He moved around various areas within Germany in the inter-war years and also moved up through the ranks. Prior to the outbreak of World War II, he had reached the rank of *Major der Schutzpolizei*.

A very happy-looking SS-Obersturmbannführer Friedrick-Wilhelm Bock, photographed on the day that he was presented with the Knight's Cross to the Iron Cross.

He took command of *Polizei Battalion 3,* within the *Ordnungspolizei,* from the start of September 1939, staying there until April 1940. He then transferred to the *Polizei Division* at the start of May 1940, just in time for their advance westwards. His first position with his new unit placed him back with his familiar territory of artillery, where he took over the *Artillery Regiment's, II Battalion.* He remained with this unit as they moved east in 1941, where he was awarded the Clasp to the Second Class Iron Cross on the 21st of August and the First Class Iron Cross on the 16th of September. He was officially taken into the *Waffen-SS* on the first day of November the same year and given the corresponding rank of *SS-Sturmbannführer.*

His next promotion came on the 5th of January 1942, with a move to *SS-Obersturmbannführer.* He added the Russian Front Medal to his existing awards on the 2nd of August the same year. He was recommended for the German Cross in Gold just over one month later, for various actions throughout 1942. This recommendation was not approved, despite detailed maps showing his successes up to that point. He was positioned with his *II Battalion* around the Leningrad area throughout this time and on into early 1943. On the 20th of February 1943, his *Regimental Commander,* Fritz Schmedes, wrote a recommendation for the award of the Knight's Cross, which read as follows:

'*SS-Obersturmbannführer* Bock has excellently proven himself as a detached *Commander* of the *SS-Polizei-Artillery-Regiment* since the beginning of the operations in the east, during all attacks and defensive battles. During the difficult winter fighting of the previous year, he led a *Kampfgruppe* on the Volchov and beat off many attacks by a superior enemy through quick accurate firing by his detachment. He was able to do the same at the end of January of this year on the Sinjavino Hills.

During the course of the local battles in the Neva, the Russians attacked at dawn on the 2nd of February 1943, with forces far superior in number and material. The Russians came from the area Kolpino on both sides of the 'October Highway' and broke through during their first attacks on the positions of the *250th (Spanish) Infantry Division.* Without encountering any notable resistance, the Russians pushed to the south, crossed over the October highway and carried out an attack against the hill street Stepanovk-Mischkino, the base of which was reached at 11:00 hours. Before it was too late, *SS-Obersturmbannführer* Bock recognized the danger, which would threaten the left flank of the *SS-Polizei-Division* should the Russians advance further, and he gave his observation posts (which were located in Feklistovo and Mischkino) the order to engage in defensive close combat and also to defend the important hills and to hold at all costs. Under the leadership of the *Battery Chiefs* of the *4th, 6th, 12th Batteries* and the *Staff Battery*, as well as the arriving units of the *Army Artillery* observation posts, the artillery protection positions were occupied. From the beginning on, these positions were defended with dash and determination. To secure the left flank, *SS-Obersturmbannführer* Bock ordered his own defensive line near Feklistovo were mopped up during immediate counter attacks. As the first reinforcements in the form of a *Cannon Platoon* arrived at 14:00 hours, they were thrown immediately into battle in Feklistovo to protect the left flank at all costs. *SS-Obersturmbannführer* Bock personally made sure that the battle was taking place correctly by remaining on the front lines and along the defensive lines. Only his presence here made it possible for him to engage the arriving reinforcements correctly.

New reinforcements continued arriving until almost 17:00 hours, A *Pioneer* and *Mounted Kompanie* of the *SS-Polizei-Division,* which were brought up to plug a hole that was open in the positions of the neighbouring units on the left, were put into action on the left flank. In the meantime, the Russians were advancing along the hilly streets in the direction of Mischkino with strong tank forces. The defensive front, the building of which *SS-Obersturmbannführer* Bock had personally overseen, began to fall apart. Since no available tank-destroying-weapons were available, Feklistovo could no longer be held. *SS-Obersturmbannführer* Bock was also able to master this situation, since, during his own personally ruthless action, during which he displayed decisiveness and calmness in the presence of enemy tanks, he saw to it that his weakening units remained organized and during which they built a new defensive line on the western edge of Mischkino and the northern edge of Porkusi. In the meantime, some tank-breaking weapons had arrived in Mischkino, and his men were able to smash two enemy tanks on the village's main street and hold the newly built defensive positions.

Through his independent decision-making, and also having barely any forces for future defensive actions, which were important to hold the hilly road, *SS-Obersturmbannführer* Bock was able to make sure that his *Division* was able to complete their orders to build a new defensive position.

Because of his excellent performances in the defensive fighting around this important strong point and because of his ruthless personal action in the most difficult of situations, I recommend that *SS-Obersturmbannführer* Bock be awarded the Knight's Cross to the Iron Cross.

Signed: Fritz Schmedes
SS-Standartenführer und Regimental Commander'

This recommendation was also endorsed by his *Divisional Commander,* Alfred Wunnenberg and read as follows:

'*SS-Obersturmbannführer* Bock, at his own decision, beat off the Russians with his weak artillery forces during their break through of the open left flank south of Kolpino. His units also successfully defended the very important positions atop the hills between Mischkino and Feklistovo in bitter close combat against masses of Russian soldiers. By always displaying bravery during these actions he enabled his troops to hold out. It is only his personal action that brought the Russian break through on the left flank of the neighbouring *Division* to a standstill before they were able to complete their goal. Through this action, the goal of the Russians to break the surrounding Front around Leningrad was reduced to nothing. *SS-Obersturmbannführer* Bock is worthy of being decorated with the Knight's Cross to the Iron Cross.

Signed: Alfred Wunnenberg
SS-Gruppenführer und Divisional Commander'

This recommendation was approved just over one month later, on the 28th of March 1943 and was the only such award to a soldier from *Polizei* for the whole of 1943! This award would not end Bock's association with this medal and its' various grades. Details of that will follow in subsequent volumes.

Wilhelm Beck
Date of birth: 22.12.1919
SS Number: 382 517
Born in Bitz, he spent almost five years with the *Hitler Youth* from April 1933 until March 1938, he then moved to a stint with the *R.A.D.* His next move came at the start of November 1938, when he entered the *SS,* being placed with the *16. Kompanie* of the *SS-Regiment Deutschland.* It was with this unit that he entered World War II.

He fought with them in Poland as part of a machine-gun crew. He was wounded there and awarded the Black Wound Badge on the 9th of November 1939. He displayed enough bravery and promise to be sent to Braunschweig from the start of February until early May 1940. It is not known what rank he held as that move took place. He is not listed as taking part in the campaign in the west during 1940, but he is listed as taking part in courses, after this, for *Armoured Car Platoon Leaders,* gun training school with the *Heer* and *Kompanie Leaders* school.

SS-Obersturmführer Wilhelm Beck photographed wearing his Knight's Cross

It can be assumed that he attended all of these as his *SS Kameraden* were fighting in the west. He is listed as serving with the *LAH* as part of their *Sturmgeschutze Abteilung* from the 6th of May 1940, which only adds to the confusion. He was promoted to *SS-Untersturmführer* at the start of September 1940.

He did go into Greece with the *LAH* in April 1941 and was awarded the Second Class Iron Cross on the 2nd of May for actions around the Klidi Pass, still serving with the *Sturmgeschutze Abteilung*. This would have been alongside Michael Wittmann and Alfred Gunther and it would seem that this small unit within the *LAH* was indeed a breeding ground for future Knight's Cross holders. He then went east in Russia in mid-1941. He was noted for his bravery many times and on the 14th of September he was awarded the First Class Iron Cross. This was for actions in August. This was followed by the award of the Tank Assault Badge on the 21st of February 1942. He then went to France with the *LAH* in mid-1942.

He received additional recognition for his efforts whilst there in the shape of a promotion to *SS-Obersturmführer* on the 21st of June, then the Bulgarian Bravery Medal IV Class, 2nd Grade on the 10th of July and the Russian Front Medal on the 26th of August 1942. It can be presumed that he moved from the *Sturmgeschutze Abteilung* to the newly forming *Panzer Regiment* of the *LAH* during this spell in France. He is listed as attending the *Panzer* training school from early November to early December 1942. He then went back to Russia in early 1943, now serving as the *2. Kompanie Commander* within the *LAH's Panzer Regiment*. It was with this unit that he conducted actions that would result in his recommendation for the German Cross in Gold in late February 1943 and also the Knight's Cross on the 17th of March 1943. By then, he had been awarded the Wound Badge is Silver on the 15th of March.

The recommendation for the Knight's Cross to the Iron Cross, written by Kurt Meyer on the 17th of March 1943, contained the following. It starts by listing his existing awards and covering his current rank and position. The second page then covers his existing recommendation for the German Cross in Gold for his decisive share of the success of the *Standarte's Kampfgruppe's* recent operations. It mentions that he is held in high regard and goes on to cover his fighting leadership securing the right flank of the *Division*. It also highlights his constant leadership at the head of the lead *Kompanie* and during 19 days of fighting destroyed:

'7 guns of 12.2cm
59 guns of 7.62cm (long)
14 guns of 7.62cm (short)
43 PaK guns of 4.5cm

Also a higher number of mortars, anti-tank rifles, heavy machines guns and light machine guns. It also lists that he had previously shot down 9 T-34s, he himself shot up 3.'

During this, he was shot three times and wounded twice. It follows by covering the further heavy tank attacks and his *Kompanie* attacking through Walki under his personal leadership. These deeds would lay the foundation that would allow the *Division* their breakthrough on Ljubotin and thereby Kharkov itself.

In the further advance and attack on Kharkov it was owed to his personal energy that the tanks advanced and in a decisive push placed them in the northeast outskirts of the city. His *Kompanie* was the most successful during this, destroying 8 T-34s.

In the subsequent street and house fighting that followed, he was wounded further. His men shot up a further 2 T-34s. Through his leadership and personal courage the *Kampfgruppe* was able to quickly reach the bridge and block the enemy's further advance to the east. He was at the lead with his tanks and was able to make a link with *Battalion* Peiper at that point.

This was signed by Kurt Meyer, the *Kampfgruppe Leader,* but also countersigned by Dietrich, with the following overview:

'A recommendation for the German Cross in Gold has already been sent for the enthusiastic fighting of *SS-Obersturmführer* Beck. His leadership of his *Panzer Kompanie* in the attack on Kharkov and the capturing of the city was a large part of the success. The award of the Knight's Cross to the Iron Cross would give higher recognition.'

This recommendation was approved on the 28th of March 1943. He was one of the men that moved from the *LAH* to the newly forming *Hitler Youth Division* later in 1943. He was promoted to *SS-Hauptsturmführer* on the 9th of November the same year. He was killed in La Cain, France on the 10th of June 1944, in the early stages of the *Allied* Normandy invasion. He did have command of the *2. Kompanie* initially, but then moved to teach the officer candidates course. This course was brought to an abrupt end as the invasion began.

Beck's role then moved to the *Liaison Officer* for the *I SS-Panzer Korps*. This role meant that he would alternate between his own *Korps* and the *Panzergruppe West* Headquarters. It was whilst at these Headquarters that he was killed on the evening of the 10th of June 1944. This position came under fighter-bomber attack that resulted in 16 other people being killed, as well as many wounded. This brought to an end the life of a very brave and respected officer.

Hans Becker
Date of birth: 05.11.1911
SS Number: 247 838
Born in Peenemunde, he entered the *S.A.* in December 1932 and stayed there until mid-March 1933, he then moved to the *SS*. He served with the *LAH* from early July that year within their *1. Kompanie*. Prior to the war he took part in actions in Austria, the Sudetenland, and Czechoslovakia, earning the campaign medals for each of these.

He fought in Poland in September 1939, holding the rank of *SS-Oberscharführer*. He quickly became noted for his bravery and a field promotion to *SS-Untersturmführer* came on the 26th of September, followed by the award of the Second Class Iron Cross on the 1st of October.

Following this campaign, he attended a course at Bad Tolz from the start of November 1939 until the end of February 1940. He is listed as serving with the *LAH's IV Battalion* at the start of March. His next promotion followed at the start of September, taking him to *SS-Obersturmführer*. He was serving with the *5. Kompanie* at the start of May 1941 as their *Kompanie Commander*. He moved with the *LAH* back to France in mid-1942 and whilst there was awarded the Russian Front Medal on the 25th of August. On the 9th of November he was promoted to *SS-Hauptsturmführer*.

He was placed as the *2. Kompanie Commander*, within the *2. Panzer Grenadier Regiment* and went with this unit back into Russia in early 1943.

For actions there he was awarded the First Class Iron Cross on the 27th of February. On the 21st of March his *Regimental Commander*, Theodore Wisch, recommended him for the Knight's Cross to the Iron Cross. This recommendation read as follows:

'On the 11.3.1943 the *I./2. Panz.Gren.Rgt./LSSAH* at 03:10 hours were around Alexejewka, in the front defensive positions of Kharkov with the *3.* and *1. Kompanies* in the front line beginning the attack.

The *2. Kompanie*, under the leadership of *SS-Hauptsturmführer* Becker, were the reserve-*Kompanie* and followed behind on the right, behind the *3. Kompanie*.

The attack on Alexejewka did not succeed. The attack of the *Battalion* stopped in front of the enemy positions. The *3. Kompanie* came under attack by the Soviets with 3 tanks out of the Alexejewka area. In the following firefight the heavy weapons and artillery did not succeed either. The enemy pushed the troops of the *1.* and *3. Kompanies* back and no-one was able to get into the strong positions at the edge of this place. In the course of the morning the *Kompanie Commander*, all *Platoon Leaders, NCOs* and men of the *3. Kompanie* all fell.

The *2. Kompanie* came out of reserve and into the attack. The combat strength amounted to 2 *Officers*, 8 *NCOs* and 56 men. Around 15:00 hours the *2. Kompanie* were given command during this difficult situation. With the support of 4 Sturmgeschutze and 3, 3.7cm Flak guns the *3. Kompanie* planned to move to the high ground and force a break-in.

At 13:25 hours there was a strong attack using all weapons and under this cover, the *2. Kompanie* slowly advanced towards the enemy. They moved along the flank of the positions held by the *3. Kompanie*. At the same time 2 Sturmgeschutze and 2 Flak guns of 3.7cm advanced with the *3. Kompanie* towards this position on the southern ring and the vital hill. Once again the attack was halted. One Sturmgeschutze and one Flak gun were shot up at the point of the break in by a T-34. The attacking troops were thrown back.

In this critical situation, the *2. Kompanie Commander, SS-Hauptsturmführer* Becker, made a lightning quick independent decision. He would not attack the enemy in a frontal move, but would use his own men and combining it with the men of the *3. Kompanie* move west of the hill.

During violent enemy firing, they outflanked the enemy positions to the rear and penetrated the main route on the way to Kharkov. In an example of self-courage *SS-Hauptsturmführer* Becker himself was at the lead of the attack with a

Hans Becker photographed on the day of his Knight's Cross presentation

A different image of Hans Becker taken on the same day

few men. They attacked the main enemy position in two sudden lightning attacks that moved over the main march route and to the south of this also. They snatched this important position from the enemy and held it. *SS-Hauptsturmführer* Becker made sure his men were ready for further attacks. *SS-Hauptsturmführer* Becker created the basis for the further attack by the *Battalion* on the 12.3.1943 on Alexejewka and even the actual storming of the city of Kharkov.

Herewith the fight carried by the *2. Kompanie,* under the leadership of *SS-Hauptsturmführer* Becker, reaped the best result, their penetrating attack of the area around Alexejewka and the close combat breaking the enemy resistance.

The *Battalion,* with the *2. Kompanie* in the lead, attacked the Soviet artillery and flak with their heavy weapons. They increased their positions and out of these positions moved into the enemy positions on the outskirts of the city's southern ring, forcing the enemy to move back.

SS-Hauptsturmführer Becker correctly assessed the enemy situation and made the decision to attack again. His *Kompanie* pressed forward and in their attack, moved to the edge of the city, parralell to the enemy positions and penetrated into the city.

In close quarter fighting they engaged the enemy. The lead troops fought in close combat and pushed further against the enemy. With this the *Battalion* was able to smash the enemy.

They completely wore down a Soviet Regiment and weapons, guns, ammunition and many vehicles fell into the hands of the *Battalion.* This success is as a result of the *2. Kompanie* and its' *Commander, SS-Hauptsturmführer* Becker.

On the way into Kharkov the enemy lost:

5 Officers, with one Regimental Commander, 150 men
Over 300 dead

1 T-34 destroyed, 1 T-34 and 2 small English tanks captured, 7 guns of 7.62cm, 12 Flak, 26 anti-tank rifles, 3 heavy mortars, 27 medium mortars, 5 light mortars, 15 heavy machine-guns, 21 light machine-guns (as well as many other smaller weapons).'

This recommendation was backed up by Dietrich who mentions Becker's bravery as far back as Poland and his subsequent move to officer. He also highlights his successes in all of his fighting and goes on to approve this overall recommendation.

The award of Becker's Knight's Cross to the Iron Cross was approved on the 28th of March 1943.

He served with the *SS-Panzer Grenadier Training and Replacement Battalion* from the 5th of December 1943 until the 23rd of May 1944, he then moved back to the *LAH.* He had been promoted to *SS-Sturmbannführer* back on the 20th of April. He was given command of the *I Battalion, 2. Panzer Grenadier Regiment.* He was listed as missing on the 18th of August and finally listed as killed on the 20th of August 1944. This would have been during the closing of the Falaise Pocket, which cost so many German lives.

Max Hansen

Date of birth: 31.07.1908

SS Number: 27 813

Born in Niebull, he was an early member of the *SS,* joining at the start of August 1931 and serving initially in the *50. Standarte.* By the start of April 1933 he had risen to the rank of *SS-Scharführer (SS-Unterscharführer).* On the 9th of May he moved to the *LAH.* By the 20th of December 1934 he had risen to *SS-Scharführer,* quickly followed at the start of March 1935 with a further promotion to *SS-Oberscharführer.* It can be presumed that he spent time at one of the officer's schools between 1935 and 1936, although nothing specific is listed on his file. However, by the 9th of November 1936 he had been promoted to *SS-Untersturmführer,* being listed as a *Platoon Leader* in the *12. Kompanie* of the *LAH.* His next promotion came on the 20th of April 1938, when he moved to *SS-Obersturmführer.* He entered action in the Second World with this rank and by then had earned the medals for Austria and the Sudetenland, as well as the Olympics medal for being part of the troops that provided security for the 1936 games.

He fought in Poland and earned the Second Class Iron Cross on the 8th of November 1939. He went west in 1940 and earned the Iron Cross First Class, then on the 19th of November was promoted to *SS-Hauptsturmführer.* He followed this by going to Greece in early 1941 and at the end of April, was given command of the *LAH's III Battalion.* He led this *Battalion* into Russia in the latter half of 1941 and his continued bravery and leadership skills were recognised further on the 29th of December 1941 with the award of the German Cross in Gold. Just prior to this, in November, he had been presented with the Wound Badge in Silver, although the individual dates of the various wounds are not listed. On the 11th of March 1942 he received the Infantry Assault Badge.

SS-Sturmbannführer Max Hansen shown on the day that he was presented with his Knight's Cross, following his successful Kharkov actions.

He moved to France in the second half of 1942 and whilst there received further recognition for his efforts. He was awarded the Royal Bulgarian Bravery Medal on the 6th of July, Russian Front Medal on the 25th of August and the Star of Romania Medal with Swords topped off with a promotion to *SS-Sturmbannführer* on the 9th of November. He then returned to Russia in early 1943, now commanding the *II Battalion, 1st Regiment*. He conducted actions during the fighting around Kharkov that resulted in his recommendation for the Knight's Cross.

This recommendation was written on the 15th of March 1943 by his *Regimental Commander*, Fritz Witt. It details his awards to date and the actions he fought in from the start of the war, highlighting his award of the German Cross in Gold. It then details the following:

'On the 11.3.1943 *Kampfgruppe Witt* were in the area Polewaja-Dertgatschi-Pscherkaskaja-Losswaja. They were ordered to attack along the main Belgorod-Kharkov road, north of Kharkov. On the 10.3.1943 *Battalion Hansen* moved through Dergatschi in difficult house fighting and then in the darkness advanced to the village of Ssekeniki. In the morning of the 11.3.1943 this reinforced *Battalion* of *Kampfgruppe Witt* advanced on both sides of the street. They came under heavy defensive fire north and west of Bypedrem. *Kampgruppe Hansen,* prepared to take Schatiliwka from the west and successfully took possession of it during hard street fighting and to the south of it.

He made the decision, *SS-Sturmbannführer* Hansen with his *Battalion,* to begin the advance against the north edge of Kharkov city centre. At 12:00 noon they reached Red Square (Square der *Wehrmacht*) after hard street and house fighting. They then came under violent counter attack from the south and south-east.

They inflicted heavy losses on the enemy and placed a thin line of defense around Red Square (Square der *Wehrmacht*). Then *SS-Sturmbannführer* Hansen made the decision to take the bulk of his men and move towards the main road to Belgorod, therefore allowing the bulk of the *Regiment* to pentrate into Kharkov. With their *Commander* at the lead, an unusually strong street barrier on the northern edge of Kharkov was taken and the way to the south was open.

Through this decision of *SS-Sturmbannführer* Hansen and through his personal go-getting example to his men during the violent house fighting, the way into the centre of Kharkov was guaranteed for the rest of the *Regiment*. During the close combat, *SS-Sturmbannführer* Hansen became wounded for the fourth time by hand grenade shrapnel to his face.

On the 12.3.43 the northern part of Kharkov was taken and came under our control in hard fighting, with heavy lossess. Here also, *SS-Sturmbannführer* Hansen displayed an excellent personal example of courage.

On the 13.3.43 another *Kampfgruppe* (Author's note: This *Kampfgruppe* was from *Totenkopf* and was led by existing Knight's Cross holder Otto Baum – this action formed a small part of Baum's later Oakleaves recommendation – and also contained existing Knight's Cross holder Wilfred Richter) reached Dergatschi and from here they reached the north and north-west part of Kharkov and struggled for the village of Alexejewka. In order to ease the pressure on this *Kampfgruppe,* Hansen, with his *Kampfgruppe* made the decision to push 1000 metres west of Red Square (Square der *Wehrmacht)* and attacked 8 T-34s situated there, before the positions of the *Kampfgruppe* at Dergatschi. With this, the northwest part of Kharkov was taken.

Both *Kampfgruppes* linked up in the area south of Red Square (Square der *Wehrmacht)* and the prerequisite for the fight for the city centre and the east part of Kharkov was achieved.

Witt
SS-Standartenführer and Regimental Commander'

Dietrich counter signed this, agreeing with the recommendation on the basis of Hansen's heroism and unusual courage. The recommendation was approved on the 28th of March 1943 but would not end Hansen's connection with the Knight's Cross or its' higher grades.

Hugo Kraas
Date of birth: 25.01.1911
SS Number: 289 633
Born in Witten, he began service with the various Third Reich organizations in April 1933, when he joined the *R.A.D.* This was followed by moving to the *S.A.* at the start of October the same year, staying there until the 19th of April 1935. He then had a short stint with the *Heer* from July until the end of September. He then started his service with the *SS-VT.*

This began in mid-October 1935 when he was posted to the *I Battalion, SS-Regiment Germania,* with the rank of *SS-Rottenführer* (a rank he achieved with the *Heer).* At the end of January 1936 he was promoted to *SS-Unterscharführer.* His next move came at the start of April 1937 when he was sent to the *SS* officer's school in Braunschweig, staying there until early 1938. He was promoted to *SS-Untersturmführer* on the 12th of March, whilst attending a *Platoon Leader's* course, which came to a close at the end of March. He then moved to the *LAH,* initially serving in the *7. Kompanie* and later the *14. Kompanie.* His next promotion came on the 20th of April 1939, to *SS-Obersturmführer,* the rank he entered the Second World War with.

He fought in Poland, winning the Second Class Iron Cross on the 16th of October 1939. He moved to the *15. Kompanie* before the end of that year and went with his new unit into action during May 1940 in the west. He won the First Class Iron Cross on the 25th of May. Later the same year, at the start of September, he was promoted to *SS-Hauptsturmführer.* There is no mention on his file as to whether he fought in Greece during early 1941, alongside his *LAH Kameraden,* although it also does not say what he did at that time. He did however, receive the Royal Bulgarian Bravery Medal IV Class, 1st Grade.

He went into Russia in the second half of 1941 and was awarded the Black Wound Badge on the 28th of August, the Infantry Assault Badge on the 3rd of September and the German Cross in Gold on the 29th of December (this recommendation does not survive on his file). He was clearly showing a consistent level of bravery and achievement!

In late February 1942 he moved to command of the *LAH's V Battalion* and took that *Battalion* into the Leningrad area days later. Whilst there, he received a promotion to *SS-Sturmbannführer* in late April. This unit stayed in that area until early June, before moving south to join their *LAH Kameraden.* He went to France in mid-1942 as the *LAH* went through their refit and expansion, his unit became the *I Battalion/SS-Panzer Grenadier Regiment 2.* He was awarded the Russian Front Medal whilst there. It was with this *Battalion* that he went back to Russia in early 1943, around the Kharkov area. During February and March he engaged in actions that would result in his recommendation for the Knight's Cross.

This recommendation was written on the 18th of March 1943 by his *Regimental Commander,* Teddi Wisch, which contained the following information:

'I recommend the *Commander* of the *I./2. Panzer-Grenadier-Regiment/ Leibstandarte SS Adolf Hitler, SS-Sturmbannführer* Hugo Kraas, for the award of the Knight's Cross to the Iron Cross for, *SS-Sturmbannführer* Kraas came from the fighting in the west, because of courage before the enemy, with the Iron Cross First Class and in Russia after the heavy fighting in Rostov, at which he was involved as an outstanding *Stellung Commander,* was awarded the German Cross in Gold.

Kraas, who was in action on the Donez River south of Tschugujev with his *Battalion* during the defensive battles, stood at the focal point of the defensive battles experienced by the *Regiment* between 6.2. - 9.2.1943. Krass personally saw to it that the last reserves of his *Regiment* were gathered in *Battalion* strength on the 8. and 9.2.1943 and after hard fighting, the enemy forces that had penetrated

A formal image of new Knight's Cross holder, SS-Sturmbannführer Hugo Kraas

our lines were thrown back or annihilated. With that, Kraas had avoided a rollover of our front by 2 Russian Regiments, which were positioned in Gliniza.

During the night of 9.2.1943 Krass recognized the difficult situation as the Russians had gathered their units in the strength of two Battalions in front of our positions. While fighting at the lead of his *Kompanies,* he attacked and annihilated them. The success of the attack avoided a situation in which the Russians would have penetrated our rear area, and therefore saved the *Regiment* from suffering severe casualties.

In the attack on the northern section of Kharkov during the night of 11. – 12.3.1943 it was Krass' unit that was sent to Alexejewka as the *Regiment's* forward *Battalion.* He and his men had the task of penetrating through the unusually strong built-up enemy positions located at the city's edge, and to free the way along the street Dergatschi-Kharkov for the planned action of the *III. (armoured) Battalion.* Kraas fought in spite of unusually hard resistance until reaching a position 100 metres from the edge of the village of Alexejewka. He lay there during the whole day in the heaviest fighting and could not advance further due to the climbing terrain, which was littered with high buildings.

Despite the action of the heavy weapons, which were personally led by Kraas, or the attack troops, which he had sent in, a break-in could not be accomplished. The battle was unusually hard.

Kraas, who was fighting along with his troops in the very front lines, rallied his *Kompanies* again and again to attack. In the night of the 11.3.1943 the 2. *Kompanie* was successful in advancing to positions from the west, Kraas forced the frontal break-in of the mass of the *Battalion* into the village. Kraas fully took advantage of the situation and at 11:00 hours on 12.3.1943 he stormed the strong enemy positions on the northern edge of the city and completed the break through. This enabled the *Regiment* to continue the attack into the inner city.

I recommend that *SS-Sturmbannführer* Kraas is worthy of the award of the Knight's Cross to the Iron Cross because of his excellent leadership capabilities, his high sense of responsibility and his unusual personal bravery.'

The recommendation is also backed up by the *Divisional Commander,* Dietrich, who highlights Kraas' highest personal bravery since the start of the war, as well as his exceptional leadership qualities and agreed with the recommendation.

This recommendation was approved on the 28th of March 1943, but his association with this medal and its' higher grades would not end there. Details of that will follow in later volumes.

Hermann Weiser
Date of birth: 22.11.1918
SS Number: 351 242
Born in Ottenau, Baden, he entered the *SS* at the start of November 1937 initially serving with the *12. Kompanie, SS-Regiment Deutschland,* but by the start of May 1938, he had moved to their *8. Kompanie.* By then he had taken part in the march into Austria and followed this by taking part in the campaign in the Sudetenland in October, earning both campaign medals. He was then sent to Bad Tolz from mid-November 1938 until mid-August 1939, leaving with the rank of *SS-Standartenoberjunker.*

He did not take part in the Polish campaign, but by the 22nd of October 1939 he is listed as serving with the *15. Kompanie, LSSAH.* This was quickly followed on the 9th of November by a promotion to *SS-Untersturmführer* and a move the role of *Adjutant* for the *LAH's Aufklarungs Abteilung.* He did take part in the campaign in the west in 1940 and was awarded the following medals during that time; Second Class Iron Cross and the Black Wound Badge on the 14th of May, followed by the First Class Iron Cross on the 12th of June and finally the Infantry Assualt Badge on the 3rd of October 1940.

He then took part in the invasion of the Balkans in early 1941 and soon after this, on the 9th of May, he was promoted to *SS-Obersturmführer.*

He went east into Russia in July 1941 and by the 16th of September the same year he was commanding the *Aufklarung's 2. Kompanie.* He advanced with the *LAH* throughout the rest of 1941 and into the first half of 1942. He then moved to France during the *LAH's* 1942 re-fit and whilst there he was awarded the Bulgarian Bravery Medal IV Class, 2nd Grade on the 10th of July, the Russian Front Medal at the start of September, followed by the Star of Romania Medal with Swords on the 3rd of September 1942. He moved back east to help resolve the worsening situation on the Russian Front at the end of January 1943. He was involved in the fighting that centered on Kharkov and it was during this fighting that he conducted actions, which his commander felt worthy of higher recognition.

On the 16th of March 1943, his *Abteilung Commander,* Kurt Meyer, penned the recommendation for his Knight's Cross. This recommendation covers some of his history up to that point, as covered above, but also mentions his assumption of command of the *2. Kompanie* after the existing commander was wounded. The recommendation then goes onto detail the following:

'The *Kampfgruppe* fighting in the southeast and southwest of Kharkov produced an outstanding result there. His *Kompanie,* always in the focus point of the fighting, inflicted high bloody losses upon the enemy.

An autographed photograph of Hermann Weiser showing him with his Knight's Cross

On the 6.3.1943, the *Kampfgruppe* had the order, to move out of their start positions north of the area Olchowatka, over Blagedatnoje-Laideschewo and venture until after Hf. Ssenhkoff Kut in order to break through. Push through the strong hostile positions south of Walki and therefore, create the prerequisites for a further attack of the *Division* cut-off on the Msha.

All leaders at the point of attack succeeded and *SS-Obersturmführer* Weiser, under his own personal attack, pushed against the enemy defensive-system. This was in spite of strongest enemy resistance and relatively unfavourable route through to the point of break through. Without consideration to the threatened flank, he made it possible through this bold penetration with the *Kampfgruppe* early in the day and aiding therefore the course of the attack of the neighbouring *Kampfgruppen*. By the seizure of Hf. Ssenhkoff-Kut itself, in the dawn, in heavy street fighting, through personal courage at the lead with his men he made possible the advance of the Panzers. This was only made possible through elimination of the heavy enemy weapons, especially the tank defenses.

He took the independent decision, on the same day to stop the venture onto Walki, because of munitions and material shortage.

The enemy losses correspond to the success of the day:

3 guns 12.2cm
20 guns 7.62cm long
9 PaK 4.5cm
5 PaK 3.7cm
20 mortars
35 Machine guns
19 tank guns
49 light vehicles and many light weapons

On the following day, the 7.3.1943, in the attack of the *Kampfgruppe* on the strongly enemy occupied Walki, *SS-Obersturmführer* Weiser, with his *Kompanie* sitting on the Panzers, ruthlessly pushed through the heavy weapons and with personal courage. He pushed through the defensive front and made possible, through speed and thoughtlessness for his own defenses, the rapid advance of the *Kampfgruppe* into Walki. He succeeded through lightning-quick acts to destroy the enemy strength in the west part of the city and to prevent mine-laying by the enemy. Out of his own decision, *SS-Obersturmführer* Weiser with his *Kompanie* pushed again the same afternoon over Walki out to the railway line in Hf. Grinzef and therefore transformed the retreat of the enemy into a wild flight. The remaining enemy in the area through Walki was destroyed.

The day's prey:

32 guns 7.62cm long
3 guns12.2.cm
8 light guns
11 mortors
57 trucks

On the 1st attack day on the city of Kharkov, *SS-Obersturmführer* Weiser with his *Kompanie* penetrated through to the main street Stara-Moskowka. Very strong enemy tank strength prevented the intentional taking of the street leading to Tschugujew. On the 2nd attack day *SS-Obersturmführer* Weiser again pushed towards Stara-Moskowka and the strong enemy tank obstacles on the street. *SS-Obersturmführer* Weiser used his pistol to kill 2 enemy tanks commanders whilst in their turrets. In the following hard street-fighting, Weiser was again the lead fighter and the example to his *Kompanie*. His *Kompanie* destroyed and/or captured over 15 guns and 100 anti-tank guns.

SS-Obersturmführer Weiser, through his circumspect leadership, had complete preservation of the expedition.

I ask that the achievements of this *Kompanie* leader be acknowledged with the award of the Knight's Cross to the Iron Cross.'

This recommendation was also endorsed by Dietrich who testified to his courage since he was a young *Zugführer* fighting in the west. He goes on to highlight Weiser's noticeable enthusiasm and the fact that he was an exemplary, outstanding leader with personal bravery. It finished by pointing out his outstanding actions at the focus point of the heavy fighting, and that he agreed with the award entirely.

This recommendation was approved on the 28th of March 1943, making Weiser's Knight's Cross the fifth to be awarded to the *LAH* that day.

On the 20th of April 1943 he was promoted to *SS-Hauptsturmführer.* At the start of August 1944 he was promoted to *SS-Sturmbannführer.* On the 25th of October he became the *IIa* within the *I SS-Panzer Korps*. He survived the war and died on the 21st of March 1970.

Walter Gerth
Date of birth: 14.12.1914
SS Number: 372 351
Born in Kassel, he joined the *S.A.* in October 1933 and stayed as a member until late 1937. In that time he also served in the *R.A.D.* from mid-September 1934 until the end of March 1935. From September 1935 he spent a two-year stint

with the *Artillery Regiment 27,* within the *Army.* It was then on the first day of September 1939 that he moved to the *SS.*

His records show that he was awarded the *Heimwehr Danzig* medal after fighting in Poland as a *Platoon Commander* within their *4. Kompanie,* whilst holding the rank of *SS-Scharführer.* He was taken into *Totenkopf* as they were formed in October 1939, being promoted to *SS-Oberscharführer* in December. He went west in 1940 and was awarded the Second Class Iron Cross on the 3rd of June. He received a wound from a bullet richochet near La Basee Canal and was moved to a hospital. There is no listing for him attending any of the officer schools, but on the 9th of November 1940 he was promoted to *SS-Untersturmführer.* He followed this promotion by being posted to *Totenkopf's Replacement Battalion* until January 1941. He then moved to the *SS-Artillery Replacement Battalion* until early November. It was then that he re-joined *Totenkopf's Artillery Regiment.*

1942 would be a busy time for Gerth. He was awarded the First Class Iron Cross on the 14th of March, promoted to *SS-Obersturmführer* on the 20th of April, awarded the Infantry Assault Badge on the 17th of June and the Eastern Front Medal on the 12th July. All of this would have happened whilst *Totenkopf* were holled up in the Demjansk Pocket.

1943 would see Gerth positioned near Kharkov with his *Kameraden.* In early March, he conducted actions that would result in his recommendation for the Knight's Cross. This recommendation was written by his *Regimental Commander,* Hermann Priess, on the 5th of March 1943 and covered the following:

'In the afternoon of the 2.3.1943, the *7. Batterie* was on the crossroads 4 km south of Loswaja in position with the order to support the attack of the *Pz. Gren. Rgt. 3.*

The enemy, in the afternoon of the 2.3.1943, during the attack of the *Pz. Gren. Rgt. 1* delivered extremely good resistance in Schljachowaja. It knew that it was cut off and tried to break through in an eastwards direction during the night.

They hereby bumped into the *7. Batterie* in the early morning of the 3.3.1943.

Assisted by strong blizzards the enemy succeeded with strong tank attacks and strong infantry to reach the secure firing positions of the *Batterie.* Here *SS-Obersturmführer* Gerth, *Commander* of the *7. Batterie* threw the enemy out of these positions in close combat with his *Batterie* and the enemy retreated. Repeated attempts by the enemy to attack were always defeated with bloody losses.

SS-Obersturmführer Gerth, after knocking out the enemy attacks, used the pause in the fighting as an opportunity to change his positions over to the attack. He took the decision of permanently blocking, with his *Batterie,* the way east for the enemy.

An autographed image of Totenkopf's Walter Gerth, his Knight's Cross clearly visible

Everyone in the *Batterie* attacked the enemy during strong uninterrupted attacks and rejected the enemy sending them back with bloody losses, so that the *Pz. Gren. Rgt 1* could attack and destroy the mass of the enemy in the afternoon of the 3.3.1943.

SS-Obersturmführer Gerth prevented the enemy breakthrough, through his independent decision, and through his personal attack and leadership, so that the enemy to the east was divided and has a considerable share in the annihilation of the strong enemy.

The *Batterie* destroyed during the fighting:

7 T 34
5 Guns
Numerous trucks and covered vehicles
Many light and heavy infantry weapons
Many hundred of dead Russians lay over the battlefield

I please ask that *SS-Obersturmführer* Gerth be awarded with the Knight's Cross to the Iron Cross for his decisions.'

The *Divisional Commander,* Max Simon, backed up this recommendation by highlighting Gerth's part in the destruction of the 3. Russian Tank Army by holding his position during the fighting.

This recommendation was approved on the 31st of March 1943, giving *Totenkopf* their first Knight's Cross holder for 1943 and the recent battle around Kharkov. He would not be the last.

On the 9th of November 1943 he was promoted to *SS-Hauptsturmführer.* Then on the 11th of August 1944 he is listed as being wounded for the sixth time and once out of hospital, on the 20th of October, he was posted to the *SS-Artillery Training and Replacement Regiment* based in Beneschau. This was one of the units incorporated into the *38th SS-Division 'Nibelungen'* in early 1945. He fought with this unit in the closing days of World War II and entered British captivity. He survived the war and died on 10th of January 1995.

Heinz Harmel
Date of birth: 29.06.1906
SS Number: 278 276
Born in Metz, his first taste of military service came when he was with the *Freikorps* from 1924 until 1926. At the start of May the same year he joined the

Reichswehr but left six months later due to injury. He is listed as being a member of the *Stahlhelm* organization from early 1928 until the end of 1933. He next moved to the *S.A.* from the start of 1934 and remained with them until the end of June 1935. He would therefore have been witness to the effects upon the *S.A.* of the Knight of the Long Knives and it is of interest that he remained with this organization for a full year after the blood purge. Also, from mid-March 1935 he is listed as serving with the *Army* once again, staying there until mid-September when he moved to join the *SS*.

His service with the *SS* began in early October 1935 when he was placed with *Germania,* holding the rank of *SS-Oberscharführer.* He stayed with this unit until the end of August the following year, when he then moved to *Deutschland.* At the end of January 1937 he was promoted to *SS-Untersturmführer,* although it does not list which officer school he attended. Exactly one year later he was promoted to *SS-Obersturmführer.* Two months later he became one of the *SS* men moved to Austria to help form the *Der Führer Regiment.* At the start of May he was given command of their *9. Kompanie.* His next promotion came at the end of January 1939, when he moved to *SS-Hauptsturmführer.*

Staying with *Der Führer* he did not see direct action during the campaign in Poland, but he did fight in the west during 1940. It was here that he earned the Second Class Iron Cross at the end of May, with the First Class Iron Cross coming one day later. The Infantry Assault Badge followed on the 4th of December. He is listed as taking official command of *Der Führer's II Battalion* at the start of 1941, although, according to one source, this would appear to have been the case since mid-November in 1940. On the 20th of April 1941 he was promoted to *SS-Sturmbannführer.*

He took his *Battalion* into Russia in mid-1941 and it was here that he was first recommended for the Knight's Cross to the Iron Cross. This initial lengthy recommendation was written on the 19th of October by Otto Kumm and Wilhelm Bittrich and covers a variety of action stretching from July 1941 through to late September, as they fought from Jelnya to Ssakunowo. This recommendation was not approved but Harmel was awarded the German Cross in Gold on the 29th of November 1941. There is no recommendation for that award on his file, so it could be that the initial Knight's Cross recommendation resulted in his award of the German Cross in Gold?

His next promotion came on the 19th of June 1942, when he moved to *SS-Obersturmbannführer.* He was back in France at this stage as *Das Reich* were being expanded and re-fitted, he had also moved to *Deutschland* by then. Whilst in France he was awarded the Russian Front medal in mid-August. He is then listed as *Deutschland's Commander* from the 20th of October and it was with this unit that he returned to Russia in early 1943.

Heinz Harmel photographed with the rank of SS-Standartenführer and wearing his Knight's Cross. He obtained this award holding the rank of SS-Obersturmbannführer

On the 6th of March 1943, his *Divisional Commander,* Herbert Vahl, penned the second Knight's Cross recommendation for Heinz Harmel. It mentions his existing German Cross in Gold and a very brief overview of some of the key actions he was involved in, including the Grebbe mountains in Holland, Rschew and Oskol in Russia. It went on to mention the following:

'On the 19.2.1943 the *Division* recieved the order to venture south to Nowomoskowsk to help the weak German garrison positioned there. *SS-Pz.Gren. Rgt. "Deutschland"* received the order to attack from Otrada Pereschtschepino and to form a bridgehead, out of which the next day the *SS-Pz.Gren.Rgt. "Der Führer"* should begin their advance on Nowomoskowsk.

Already at the lead of the *Regiment*, the *Regiment Commander* showed an especially responsible coolness. In spite of lasting enemy action on both sides of the march route, knocking into the *Panzer Korps,* the reinforced *Battalion,* under the personal command of the *Regimental Commander,* were in Pereschtschepino the night before. Reconnaissance showed that this place was occupied by the enemy and it was penetrated by the mass of the reinforced motorized *Battalion.* At the end of the fighting there was 1500 enemy dead. Therewith the bridgehead was formed and the order of the *Regiment* was fulfilled. *SS-Obersturmbannführer* Harmel used the favourable situation to immediately expand the bridgehead to the south and destroy the enemy situated there. Out of his own decision, they ventured with the reinforced *Battalion* during the night further south and took Dimitrijewka Golubowka after hard fighting. Also there the enemy in the strength of two Battalions was destroyed.

In this fighting, *SS-Obersturmbannführer* Harmel interfered, leading in a command-armoured car, in spite of anti-tank defense, into the fighting, sowing the seed and made possible the *Panzer Korps'* complete annihilation of the enemy.

Through the bold, rapid taking and the expansion of the bridgehead out of the independent decision of the *Regimental Commander,* made possible the *Division's* rapid advance. It became divided, but after the hard fighting of the *SS-Pz.Gren. Rgt."Der Führer"* around Gumbinicha, the *Division* became reconnected in Nowomoskowsk, thereby fulfilling all of the orders given to the *Division.*

It is the bravery and superior leadership of *SS-Obersturmbannführer* Harmel, his decisions and his resolute enthusiasm, evident to all subordinates, that we owe the prevention of further enemy attacks to the west and made possible the attack of *SS-Pz.Gren.Div. "Das Reich"* on Pawlograd.

I hold that *SS-Obersturmbannführer* Harmel, on the basis of his outstanding fighting personality and for proven courage, especially worthy to carry the Knight's Cross to the Iron Cross.'

This second recommendation was approved on the 31st of March 1943, but would not end Heinz Harmel's connection to this medal and its' various grades. Details of his further awards will follow in later volumes. To finish off for the moment, he was awarded the Black Wound Badge back on the 21st of March as well as the Single-Handed Tank Destruction Badge on the same day his Knight's Cross was approved.

Christian Tychsen
Date of birth: 03.12.1910
SS Number: 23 821
Born in Flensburg, he entered the *SS* on the 19th of December 1931 and initially served with the *50. SS-Standarte*. He received rapid promotion in 1933 starting with a move to *SS-Scharführer (SS-Unterscharführer)* at the start of January, *SS-Oberscharführer (SS-Scharführer)* at the start of October, then *SS-Truppführer (SS-Oberscharführer)* on the 10th of December. At the start of October 1934 he moved to the recently created *Hamburg Political Readiness Unit*, which became *SS-Regiment Germania*. Two years later he moved to *SS-Battalion 'N'* and stayed there until mid-1939. Inbetween these dates he received a promotion to *SS-Untersturmführer* at the end of January 1937, took part in the march into Austria in March 1938, was promoted further to *SS-Obersturmführer* at the start of June the same year and then marched into the Sudetenland during October. In June 1939 he moved to the *Motorcycle Replacement Kompanie*.

He did not take part in the fighting in Poland, but was promoted to *SS-Hauptsturmführer* on the 9th of November 1939. He took command of the *3. Kompanie, Kradschutzen Battalion* within the *SS-VT* in March 1940 and moved westwards with them as they advanced through Holland, Belgium and France. He earned the Second Class Iron Cross on the 28th of May, followed by the First Class on the 18th of July.

In early 1941, Tychsen took command of the *3. Kompanie, Kradschutzen Battalion* within *SS-Division 'Reich'*. He fought with this unit in Greece and then the early stages of Barbarossa. He was awarded the Black Wound Badge at the end of July 1941 for a grenade splinter wound. He was wounded twice further on the 20th of October and also the 20th of November, receiving the Silver Wound Badge four days later and also the Infantry Assault Badge. Wounded for a fourth time in December, he next assumed command of the *Kradschutzen Battalion* in January 1942, the same month he was wounded for the fifth time. A heavier wound in early February temporarily removed him from command, this was the same month he was awarded the Gold Wound Badge. This award was followed

SS-Sturmbannführer Christian Tychsen photographed with his newly acquired Knight's Cross. The heavy facial scarring on his chin, testament to the severity of his wounds

in May 1942 with the presentation of the German Cross in Gold. By the end of that month he was back with *SS-Division 'Reich'* after he had recovered from his wounds.

He went with his *Division* as they moved to France in mid-1942. He was promoted to *SS-Sturmbannführer* at the start of September and followed this by taking command of one of the divisional panzer units. From late October through to early November he attended the panzer school in Wunsdorf. He returned to *Das Reich* and commanded the *II Battalion,* within the *Panzer Regiment.* It was with this unit that he went east in early 1943 and also with this unit that he conducted actions around mid-February that resulted in his nomination for the Knight's Cross to the Iron Cross. The recommendation was written on the 1st of March by his then *Divisional Commander,* Herbert Vahl and contained the following information:

'*SS-Sturmbannführer* Tychsen led a counter attack on 11.2.43 to retake Priwolje, east of Kharkov, with 16 tanks of his unit and a *Battalion* of the *213th Security Division.* Through skillful leadership and electrifying bravery, he destroyed a powerful group of the enemy trying to break through to Kharkov. After his infantry took cover, Tychsen thrust into the oncoming enemy with his tanks. When they retreated, he pursued them until they were destroyed. While leading the attack his tank was hit three times by anti-tank fire and put out of action.

On 18.2.43 Tychsen had the order to move his tanks along the border of Kharkov and with his unit, destroy the enemy armour that had entered the northwest edge of the city. This would protect the *Division* when it fought through to the southwest the following night. Simultaneously, the enemy had broken into the southeast section of Kharkov. When Tychsen learned the enemy was already deep within the city, he decided to push into the western area of the city despite having no infantry support. He accepted the hazards of his decision, which involved street fighting because he could prevent a deeper move by the enemy into the inner city if he attacked immediately. That would prevent the encirclement of the *Division* east of Kharkov.

After silencing numerous anti-tank guns, Tychsen led his unit into the city and smashed the strong enemy columns. During the following night he covered the withdrawal of the *Division* with his unit by sealing off the enemy occupied sectors of the city. His independent decision to engage in this street fighting, without regard for his own safety, allowed the remaining portions of the *Division* to extricate themselves as planned.

SS-Sturmbannführer Tychsen has through his independent decision, with his *Pz. Abt.* in street fighting, without any thoughts of the losses, broke through the enemy and made possible the planned capture of Kharkov by the *Div.* By including the *Division* he thereby prevented heavy losses in weapons and equipment.

SS-Sturmbannführer Tychsen is a hard soldier who demands of his men, and also himself, that they reach to the last. In the year 1942, after being wounded five times and regularly displaying personal courage, he received the German Cross in Gold. It is an especially worthy measure, to wear the Knight's Cross.

Attitude of the *Generalkommandos SS-Panzer-Korps:*
Tychsen belonged to the leaders, which the *SS-Pz.Gren.Div. "Das Reich"* owes her results to.

I warmly approve the suggestion.
Signed. Hausser'

This recommendation was approved on the 31st of March 1943, but this award of the Knight's Cross to the Iron Cross would not end Tychsen's association with this medal. Details of that will follow in later volumes.

Herbert-Ernst Vahl
Date of birth: 09.10.1896
SS Number: 430 349
Born in Posen, Vahl was one of a number of soldiers who transferred to the *Waffen-SS* during the war. We will highlight his achievements prior to his transfer, then focus on what he accomplished after his move.

His military career stretches back to the 8th of August 1914. He fought during the First World War and performed the roles of *Regimental Adjutant* and also *Kompanie Commander,* ending the war with the rank of *Leutnant*. He was awarded the Second Class Iron Cross on the 27th of June 1915 and then the First Class Iron Cross at the end of April 1918. The Black Wound Badge was also awarded prior to the end of that war.

He remained in the small inter-war *German Army* and rose to the rank of *Oberstleutnant*. He commanded various units, but just prior to the start of the Second World War, he assumed command of the *Panzer Abteilung 65*.

He commanded various tank units during the first three years of fighting and amassed an impressive list of further awards. These included both Clasps to the Iron Cross, the Tank Assault Badge and the German Cross in Gold. He had also

A formal portrait of Herbert Vahl, after his recovery from his wounds and presentation of the Knight's Cross to the Iron Cross.

been promoted to *Oberst*. The expansion of the *Waffen-SS* in the second half of 1942, especially in relation to tank units, required experienced tank leaders. The *Waffen-SS* did not have many of these at that stage. Herbert Vahl transferred to the *Waffen-SS* at the start of August 1942, with the rank of *SS-Standartenführer,* and moved to the *Das Reich Division,* assuming command of their fledgling *Panzer Regiment.*

He took this unit into Russia in early 1943 as they moved on the strategic objective of Kharkov. He conducted actions during that fighting that resulted in him being recommended for the Knight's Cross to the Iron Cross. This recommendation was written by Paul Hausser on the 9th of March, by which time, Vahl has assumed command of the whole *Division,* due to the illness of his predecessor. He had also been promoted to the rank of *SS-Oberführer* just over one month earlier. The recommendation read as follows:

'Within the framework of the operations of the *4. Panzer-Armee* from the 18.2 – 6.3.43 *SS-Oberführer* Vahl led his subordinated *SS-Panzer-Grenadier-Division "Das Reich",* in a breathless attack and pursuing battle over 350 km, under the most difficult leadership conditions, where it was repeatedly necessary to redeploy the *Division* in the shortest possible time, he destroyed the opponent wherever he encountered it.

The *Division* was almost always at the focal point of the attack for the entire operation. The result for the *Division* is owed to the energy of *SS-Oberführer* Vahl, through his presence at the head of the attack and through his multiple independent decisions influenced the pace of the attack and outcome decisively.'

This short recommendation was approved on the same day as Harmel's and Tychsen's, the 31st of March 1943, giving *Das Reich* their third Knight's Cross holder on this day alone.

He had been wounded back in mid-March and was recovering when the news of the award came through. In between the actions detailed above and him being wounded just under two weeks later, he found time to pen six successful Knight's Cross recommendations for the men under his command. These recommendations are contained on the surrounding pages.

On the first day of April, he was promoted to *SS-Brigadeführer und Generalmajor der Waffen-SS*. At the start of July 1943 he was given the post of *Inspector der Waffen-SS Panzertruppen* within the *SS Leadership Main Office*. He remained there for one year, then was given command of the *4th SS-Polizei-Grenadier-Division*. They were stationed in Greece at that time and whilst on route to his new command, he was killed in a car accident on the 22nd of July

1944. This brought to an end the life of a very capable and brave officer, who had given the young tank commanders of the *Das Reich Division* much needed experience of tank warfare that stood them well throughout the rest of the war.

Karl-Heinz Worthmann
Date of birth: 18.11.1911
SS Number: 61 115
Born in Hagen, he joined the *SS* in late 1933. He attending an *NCO*'s training course and is listed as serving with *Germania* pre-war. He took part in the campaigns in Poland, holding the rank of *SS-Oberscharführer*, and the west serving as a squad-leader, following this by becoming a *Platoon Leader*. He was awarded the Second Class Iron Cross (award date not listed), the First Class Iron Cross on the 8th of August 1940, as well as the Infantry Assault Badge and Wound Badge in Black (award dates not listed). It is known that a wound he received in Russia during the first year of fighting there, removed him from front line service for a time. When he recovered, he moved to *Das Reich's Panzer Regiment,* serving with the *6. Kompanie*.

It was with this unit that he returned to Russia in early 1943, by that stage holding the rank of *SS-Hauptscharführer*. He conducted actions that resulted in his recommendation for the Knight's Cross. The document was written by Herbert Vahl on the 20th of February and covered the following action on the 11th of February:

'On the 11.2.43, *SS-Hauptscharführer* Worthmann received the order, the enemy, who had broken in with the strength of 1-2 Battalions onto Hill 209.4, from the *Division* for his subordinated *Battalion* to move back with the infantry of the *II./SS-Deutschland* and engage and destroy the enemy and retake Hill 209.4 once again.

The attack, through the leading ground waves, over free, open ground was stopped immediately in strong hostile tank defensive fire. It was determined that around 20 tanks were defending. The *Platoon* immediately opened fire with all weapons and under the leadership of *SS-Hauptscharführer* Worthmann worked its' way up to the enemy through the use of mutual fire support. Already after the first fire exchanges, an amount of defensive weapons were destroyed. The first group, under the leadership of the *Zugführer, SS-Hauptscharführer* Worthmann advanced with the highest speed against the enemy.

The hostile infantry was thrown back and the advance increased and captured some of the defensive weapons. With that, the firefight continued reinforced.

Karl-Heinz Worthmann shown after his award of the Knight's Cross

The dismounted infantry could not follow or support the rapidly advancing tank fighting. Regardless of this, *SS-Hauptscharführer* Worthmann was at the forefront of the attack into the enemy without the security of the infantry. His venture resulted in heavy damage to the frontal armour from an enemy anti-tank hit and also the light wounding of his radio operator. Nevertheless, Worthmann fought on further. Through a second hit the tank was unable to move any further and the driver was wounded. A third hit set the petrol tank ablaze. With this phase of the fighting over and with his tank unusable, Worthmann used the machine pistols, loading and directing the fire against the enemy infantry. He then went with the wounded and transported them back. With the 3 remaining tanks of the *Zug* he set up a defensive position, until they were shot up or made incapable of fighting. However, 2 more were brought up at this time and fought too, until their tank guns were also damaged. *SS-Hauptscharführer* Worthmann led a further attack on the hill and threw the enemy infantry back and destroyed them. After observation, the following enemy weapons were destroyed:

3	7.62cm Pak
22	3.7 and 4.7cm Pak
2	Tank guns
2	Artillery guns

Also many light and heavy infantry weapons,
Bloody losses in the fighting around 100-120 men.

Worthmann is a qualified outstanding, vigorous and purposeful *Zugführer* and is an example of bearing, energy and fighting will to his men. He proved himself to be outstanding in all expeditions since the beginning of the year's fighting actions of the *SS-Div."Das Reich"*, especially on the 5.2., 7.2 and 11.2.43. Referring to these 3 battles he destroyed, through personal courage, several enemy anti-tank guns and gave the enemy high bloody losses.

The result on the 11.2.43 was the clearing up of the enemy break-in into his own lines, was taken with a lack of infantry strength or with his own infantry no longer available for the counterattack. His courageous leadership taught the enemy heavy losses. He had with only 4 tanks, fought a far superior opponent and through his courage, decided the successful outcome of the combat and fulfilled the order. *SS-Hauptscharführer* Worthmann is highly worthy of holding the Knight's Cross to the Iron Cross.'

This recommendation was approved on the 31st of March 1943. His bravery in the field not only resulted in his award of Germany's highest medal, but he received a field promotion to *SS-Untersturmführer* on the same day that Vahl wrote his Knight's Cross recommendation – the 20th of February 1943.

Karl-Heinz Worthmann was killed in the opening stages of the Kursk offensive in July 1943. Sources differ on the actual date, one listing the 6th another listing the 7th as the date of his death. The actual date may not be clear, but it is known that he was killed in his *Panzer IV* when he came under attack from a Russian pak-front.

Kharkov Summary

The first quarter of 1943 had been a very eventful time for the men of the *SS-Panzer Korps*. By the end of March they had obtained the objective they were sent back into to Russia for, that is, to keep Kharkov in German hands. You have read over these first three chapters just what was involved in making this happen, the many feats of bravery and heroism and the initial wave of official recognition.

Up to the end of March, no less than 19 *Waffen-SS* soldiers had been officially recognized for their individual achievements during the fighting that centered around Kharkov – as well as 6 others who were recognized for fighting achievements elsewhere. There would be at least one dozen more who would be officially recognized for this Kharkov fighting – but that will come in the following chapters. One of those recognized was the *LAH Divisional Commander,* Sepp Dietrich. Another one of the initial 19 people recognized was the *Divisional Commander* of *Das Reich*. In the midst of this long list of recognition, there is one notable omission.

You have read how the Germans were facing another catastrophic defeat in the wake of Stalingrad and how the efforts of the *SS-Panzer Korps* were chiefly responsible for turning this impending defeat into a stunning victory that had far-reaching outcomes. The one person who history had deemed as being the chief architect of this stunning victory was the *SS-Panzer Korps Commander,* Paul Hausser. Despite two of his *Divisional Commanders* being recognized, one with the award of the Swords to his existing Knight's Cross and Oakleaves and the other with the Knight's Cross – Paul Hausser himself received no official recognition for what he and his men had achieved. This can only be interpreted as official recognition of the fact that he had ignored a direct order from Hitler in order to turn this situation around. This was indeed a 'snub' from the highest level.

One final aspect to consider; You may recall from Volume 1 when the first *Waffen-SS* soldier was awarded the Knight's Cross to the Iron Cross in 1940. This was of course Sepp Dietrich and you may also recall that he was awarded this high honour and recognition, despite the fact that the actions which, resulted in it, were in direct dis-obedience to an order from Hitler himself. What was the difference in these two acts, identical in their motivation, successful outcome and dis-obedience. You, the reader, can draw your own conclusions.

There was one other notable aspect coming off the back of this spectacular victory. That was the fact that large numbers of the enemy had managed to evade capture and had made it to the relative safety of their own lines further eastwards. The victory at Kharkov helped to stop the Russian advances for the time being, but it had not produced the level of destruction needed at that time to swing things back in Germany's favour.

Last but not least in all of this was the cost to the *Waffen-SS* in this recent fighting. The *SS-Panzer Korps* alone lost 11,500 casualties and this was roughly divided as follows: 40% within the *LAH*, 40% within *Das Reich* and 20% within *Totenkopf*. Add to this the unspecified casualties within the remaining *Waffen-SS* units fighting in Russia and elsewhere in this opening phase of 1943.

Before detailing what came next for the *Waffen-SS* as 1943 progressed in the wake of Kharkov, let us have a quick overview of which units had been given recognition between January and March 1943:

Leibstandarte Adolf Hitler – 1 set of Swords, 2 sets of Oakleaves and 11 Knight's Crosses
Das Reich – 4 Knight's Crosses
Totenkopf – 1 Knight's Cross
Polizei – 1 Knight's Cross
Wiking – 3 Knight's Crosses
SS-Legion Niederlande – 1 Knight's Cross
SS-Kavallerie Division – 2 Knight's Crosses

Now let us continue with the unfolding situation in Russia and what further recognition would follow.

CHAPTER FOUR

BUILD UP STRENGTH - MARCH TO JUNE 1943

Whilst the recognition was coming thick and fast for the soldiers of the *Waffen-SS,* additional decisions were being made at the highest level that would have a significant effect upon the *Waffen-SS,* how it was constructed, controlled, but also what would be expected of it in the future.

No one can argue that Kharkov was a superb victory, spearheaded by the *Waffen-SS*. This was achieved against a backdrop of the enormous German defeat at Stalingrad. Hitler had been furious with the surrender of the *6th Army,* but had to quickly focus his attentions on the seemingly unstoppable enemy advance closer towards Germany. The fact that the *Waffen-SS* produced a victory in such difficult circumstances, helped to elevate their importance. A fresh wave of expansion was ordered in the immediate aftermath – an expansion that was only possible due to the inclusion of foreign volunteers from many countries, a trend that would continue for the rest of the war. It was also the first time that the *Waffen-SS* were ordered to be given preferential treatment with regards to men and material, sometimes in preference to *Army* units. It had only taken three-and-a-half years for the High Command to wake up to the potential of the *Waffen-SS!*

Let us now cover which new units were raised in the months up to the end of June 1943, before detailing what the *SS-Panzer Korps* and other existing units got up to during this time. Some of these new units were grown out of existing smaller units, some of them being amalgamated together.

Estonian SS-Legion/Estonain SS-Freiwilligen Brigade

We last covered this unit in Chapter 1, as they were involved in their initial raising in late-1942.

In March 1943 they numbered one thousand men and the first of these soldiers were sent to join the *SS-Wiking Division* in the Caucuasus, with the name of *Estonian Volunteer Battalion 'Narwa'/SS-Panzergrenadier Battalion 'Narwa',* a unit that fought with distinction. Other elements joined the *1. SS-Infantry Brigade (mot.).*

In May 1943 they were renamed the *Estonian SS-Frewilligen Brigade* and continued with the latter stages of their formation and training, which carried on throughout the remainder of May and June 1943.

SS-Karstwehr Battalion

We also last covered this unit in Chapter 1, as they too were busy with training in Germany. Around May/June 1943 they were considered to have completed their formation and were sent to Arnoldstein in Austria to continue their mountain training.

Sturmbrigade Reichsführer-SS

This new unit was formed on the 1st of February 1943 from Himmler's *Escort Battalion.* They were initially commanded by *SS-Obersturmbannführer* Karl Gesele and they began their formation in France.

They initially had three infantry *Kompanies,* two heavier *Kompanies* and also anti-tank, Flak and *Sturmgeschutze Kompanies.*

In late June 1943 they were sent south into Italy to help the worsening situation unfolding there.

Latvian SS-Freiwilligen Legion/Division

This unit was formed on the 26th of February 1943 by drawing together all of the Latvian nationalist organizations that included police combat units; some of these had seen action with the *2. SS-Infantry-Brigade (mot.). SS-Gruppenführer* Rudolf Bangerskis was placed in command with *SS-Standartenführer* Arthurs Silgalis as his Chief of Staff; both of these men were Latvian nationalists.

The various elements were raised at various locations; from Jelgava – south of Riga, to Paplaka and Vainode – both southwest of Riga, through to Cesis – northeast of Riga.

This formation was plagued by various issues from the outset that included; political arguments, clarifications of demands from the Latvians and changes of command. *SS-Brigadeführer* Peter Hansen then *SS-Brigadeführer* Carl Graf von Puckler-Burghauss had taken over command within the first month of formation.

In May 1943 the *Latvian Legion* was expanded and changed in name to the *Latvian SS-Freiwilligen Division.* It proceeded with its' overall training and formation.

Croat SS-Freiwilligen Division

This unit became the second *Waffen-SS Division* to be raised from within the former Yugoslavia. They began life at the start of March 1943, after much political discussion behind the scenes. It was raised from Bosnian Muslims and was initially overseen by Artur Phleps from *Prinz Eugen.* The *Divisional Commander* was *SS-Standartenführer* Herbert von Obwurzer, with *SS-Sturmbannführer* Erich Braun from *SS-Nord* assisting.

From March until the end of May 1943 recruitment began in earnest. The political 'discussions' continued with lots of interference from the Croat Government. This resulted in the *Division* being removed and sent to France to begin their formation and training. They were to be based in central France, in the Loire Valley and the surrounding areas of Le Puy and Mende.

Nordland (SS-Freikorps Denmark, SS-Legions Norwegian & Niederlande)

Initial plans for this new *Division* began in February/March 1943, with a vision to merge the foreign legions into one combined unit. The pieces of this jigsaw would take time to come together and name changes, along with changes in various integral units took place before finally settling into what became *Nordland.*

One of the components, *SS-Legion Norwegian,* was withdrawn from the Russian Front in March 1943 and disbanded. They reformed in May 1943 as *I Battalion, SS-Regiment 'Norge'.*

In May 1943 *SS-Legion Norwegian, SS-Freikorps-Denmark* & *SS-Legion-Niederlande* were moved to the Grafenwohr training camp to form the main nucleus, along with *SS-Regiment Nordland* from the *SS-Division Wiking.*

Latvian SS-Freiwilligen Brigade (2. SS-Infantry Brigade (mot.))

It was during May 1943 that the existing *2. SS-Infantry Brigade (mot.)* was renamed the *Lettisches SS-Freiwilligen Brigade* with *SS-Brigadeführer* (and existing Knight's Cross holder) Fritz von Scholz being placed in command. As this unit was already employed in the front line, this delayed the actual formation of its' sister, *Latvian Division,* as elements were extracted and sent to the front line to help fill losses within the *Latvian Brigade.* The losses mounted as this renamed unit fought along the Volkhov River from Teremets-Kurlyansk to Spasskaja Polisst. These battles continued through the summer months of 1943.

SS-Sturmbrigade Langemarck (SS-Legion Flanderen)

This unit was formed on the last day of May 1943 when the *SS-Legion Flandern* was withdrawn, expanded and renamed – much to the annoyance of the Belgians! Their formation and training was conducted at a training area in Heidelager near Debica.

SS-Sturmbrigade Wallonien

On the 1st of June 1943 the *Legion Wallonien* was transferred from control of the *Wehrmacht* to the control of the *Waffen-SS,* they would not be the only ones! This *Legion* had already been fighting for the Germans for at least a year in areas such as the Caucausus.

Renamed the *SS-Sturmbrigade Wallonien,* they went to the Wildflecken training area. *SS-Sturmbannführer* Lucien Lippert was placed as the *Commander.*

Hitler Youth

This fresh *Division* was formed on the 1st day of June 1943 and this unit was sent to Beverloo, north west Belgium. It was designated as a *Panzergrenadier Division* and contained 16 and 17 year-old *Hitler Youth* members. This formation was led by experienced officers and NCOs from the *LAH Division.*

SS-Oberführer Fritz Witt, Oakleaves holder, was given command with other notable Knight's Cross holders joining him. Heinrich Springer was the *Divisional Adjutant,* Max Wunsche was given command of the *Panzer Regiment,* Kurt Meyer was placed in command one of the *Regiments,* Gert Bremer was given command of one of the *Battalions,* with Rudolf von Ribbentrop and Wilhelm Beck commanding *Kompanies.* All of these men already held the Knight's Cross, with Kurt Meyer holding the Oakleaves.

Hohenstaufen

We last covered this unit in Chapter 1 as they were engaged in their initial formation in Reims. In March 1943 they were moved from Reims to Flanders, positioned at Kortyk, Mennen, Halvin and Elverdinge. It was around this time that the official name of *Hohenstaufen* was given. This was the second *Waffen-SS Division* to be named after a well-known Germanic historical figure. In May, *SS-Brigadeführer* Bittrich was promoted to *SS-Gruppenführer und Generalleutnant der Waffen-SS.* In June they were moved to Amiens as they needed a larger training area.

Frundsberg

Their situation remained unchanged as they continued with their formation training in the Alsace area.

What about the situation back in southern Russia with the *SS-Panzer Korps* and their *Wiking* neighbours further south?

LAH

In the immediate aftermath of Kharkov the *LAH* went through a period of rest, whilst still positioned in the general Kharkov area. We highlighted in the previous chapter that Dietrich returned from Berlin with the job of raising a new *Division,* that would be incorporated into a new *SS-Panzer Korps.* Dietrich did not leave immediately, but stayed with the *LAH* to oversee the command handover and the arrival of new replacements.

In the third week of April 1943 the *LAH* began a new phase of training and prior to the end of April the *Division* moved to an area west of Kharkov. On the 5th of May, Rudolf Sandig was approved for the award of the Knight's Cross. Later in the month thousands of former *Luftwaffe* men were transferred to the *LAH* to help make up their recent losses.

It was also during May that the transfer of command began. Those who left the *LAH* around that time were Swords holder Sepp Dietrich, Oakleaves holders Fritz Witt and Kurt Meyer and Knight's Cross holders Heinrich Springer, Max Wunsche, Hermann Weiser and Wilhelm Beck. Knight's Cross holder Teddi Wisch took over command of the *LAH,* with fellow Knight's Cross holders Albert Frey and Hugo Kraas taking over the *Regiments,* Hans Becker took over one of the *Battalions.* Those men that left the *LAH* were transported in the first half of June 1943.

As June came to a close the men who remained with the *LAH* readied themselves for their imminent participation in the next push.

Das Reich

They too remained in the Kharkov area and as April began they received further recognition for their recent bravery. On the 3rd, Heinz Macher was approved for the award of the Knight's Cross. This was followed three days later by the award of this medal for Vincenz Kaiser, Sylvester Stadler and Hans Weiss. This was followed on the 8th of April by the award of the Knight's Cross with Oakleaves to Otto Kumm, the first such award to a soldier of *Das Reich.* Five days earlier an existing Knight's Cross holder, *SS-Gruppenführer und Generalleutnant der Waffen-SS* Walter Kruger, assumed command of the *Das Reich Division.* He precided over a well-documented award ceremony for the recent *Das Reich* Knight's Cross and Oakleaves recipients on the 20th of April 1943. Three days after this ceremony Jacob Fick was approved for his Knight's Cross.

The *Division* was resting, incorporating new men and getting combat ready once more as April rolled on. They moved to a new area centered round Peresetschnaja. They conducted intensive training in May and June as they readied themselves for the next objective.

Totenkopf

We last covered this unit at the end of March as Walter Gerth was honoured with the Knight's Cross. They too shifted their emphasis onto defense, rest, repair and replacement.

On the 3rd of April three soldiers from *Totenkopf* were honoured for their recent actions and became Knight's Cross holders. These men were Arzelino Masarie, Walter Reder and Joachim Schubach – this was the same day as Heinz Macher's approval and these will all be detailed shortly. Around mid-April *Totenkopf* took over the area northeast of Kharkov from the *LAH,* as they moved to western Kharkov.

Just before the end of this month one *Totenkopf* man, Hermann Priess, was recognized and rewarded with the Knight's Cross for actions conducted on the 3rd of February 1942 whilst fighting in the Demjansk Pocket.

On the 17th of May Georg Bochmann was awarded the Oakleaves to his existing Knight's Cross – the second such award to a soldier from *Totenkopf* – for his actions two month's earlier and this will be detailed shortly.

The continued defensive posture for the *Totenkopf Division* remained pretty much unchanged during May and June as they also prepared for the next push.

Wiking

Positioned further south of the *SS-Panzer Korps* area, *Wiking* too enjoyed a period of rest after their recent intensive fighting. They too, like the *LAH,* had to contend with experienced men being removed to aid the further expansion of the *Waffen-SS.*

In mid-April they moved to an area between Losowaja and Michailowka and were placed as reserve. Around one month earlier *Regiment Nordland* had started their departure. They were to join the new *Nordland Division* being formed at that time. In addition, *Wiking* lost the *Finnish Battalion* – returned to Finland and disbanded. To replace this *Battalion* a new *Estonian Battalion "Narwa"* was sent to this *Division* around this time. Last, but certainly not least, the *Divisional Commander,* Oakleaves holder Felix Steiner, left the *Division* to assume command of the newly forming *III (Germanisches) SS-Panzer Korps. SS-Brigadeführer und Generalmajor der Waffen-SS* Herbert Gille took over command of *Wiking* at that time.

Herbert Gille (left) and Eberhard Heder (right) photographed during the exercise detailed above in the prelude to the forthcoming Kursk offensive.

On the 20th of April August Dieckmann was approved for the award of the Oakleaves to his existing Knight's Cross, the second such award to *Wiking*. This was the same day that Walter Kruger was holding his large ceremony for the *Das Reich* recipients. Almost two months later, on the 19th of June, Willi Esslinger received the Knight's Cross for his actions earlier in the year.

During this time of 'defensive posture' one future Knight's Cross holder – Eberhard Heder – took part in a large exercise that *Wiking* conducted. Flying overhead was the new *Divisional Commander* Herbert Gille. He observed the actions of the then *SS-Obersturmführer* Heder and his unit. Gille landed his Feisler Storch on the ground near Heder's position, just after the exercise concluded. He made a point of going to Heder and personally congratulating him on a job well done during this exercise. A war correspondent took a photo of this occasion and I have included it in this volume. Highlighted above is the fact that Heder would later become a holder of the Knight's Cross and Gille would become the first *Waffen-SS* holder of the Diamonds grade of the Knight's Cross. This photograph captures both men prior to their later bravery and subsequent recognition coming to the fore.

This exercise was to prepare *Wiking* for their inclusion in the forthcoming campaign. We will cover their part in that campaign in the following chapter, but for now we will leave them and cover the remaining *Waffen-SS* units on the front lines at that point.

Polizei

The situation initially remained unchanged for these men in the spring of 1943. However, before June was ended, the main bulk of this *Division* was sent to the Czecheslovakia area to be re-fitted as a *Panzergrenadier Division*. A smaller *Kampfgruppe* remained behind on the Leningrad front. On the 10th of June 1943, Alfred Wunnenberg handed command of this unit over to *SS-Oberführer* Fritz Schmedes.

SS-Gebirgs-Division Nord

Their situation remained unchanged during this part of 1943.

Prinz Eugen

We left this unit at the end of March 1943 as they were positioned near Mostar and enjoying a period of rest after their fighting in the early part of the year.

During April and the first half of May they went through a re-fit. Then in mid-May Operation Schwarz began. *Prinz Eugen* moved southeast of Mostar to Bileca, then moved onto and occupied Niksic. The taking of this objective formed the second part of Phleps' Knight's Cross recommendation. Savnik was reached in the closing days of May – this formed the final part of Phlep's Knight's Cross recommendation and will be detailed in full shortly. *SS-Sturmbannführer* Bernard Dietsche fought in the area around Krusevice on the 29th of May and this action resulted in his later award of the Knight's Cross, also to be detailed in full later.

With the taking of Savnik, the enemy Partisans changed their direction of advance and began to move to the north and northwest in order to avoid further destruction by the Germans. *Prinz Eugen* moved back through Niksic, then onto Bileca and then Avtovac. Maglic was fought for as May closed and this battle was intense, as it was part of the closing of the pocket, which contained Tito and around 40,000 of his men. For the first few days of June 1943, Tito and his men fought very hard in this area as they were determined not to be defeated there. The *SS* men had to give ground and contend with some heavy losses.

In the first week of June the enemy managed to force a breakthrough and advanced as best they could to the north. *Prinz Eugen* and other German forces initially gave chase; the area around Camerno became the focus of actions. However, there was not a decisive victory delivered as a result of this fighting.

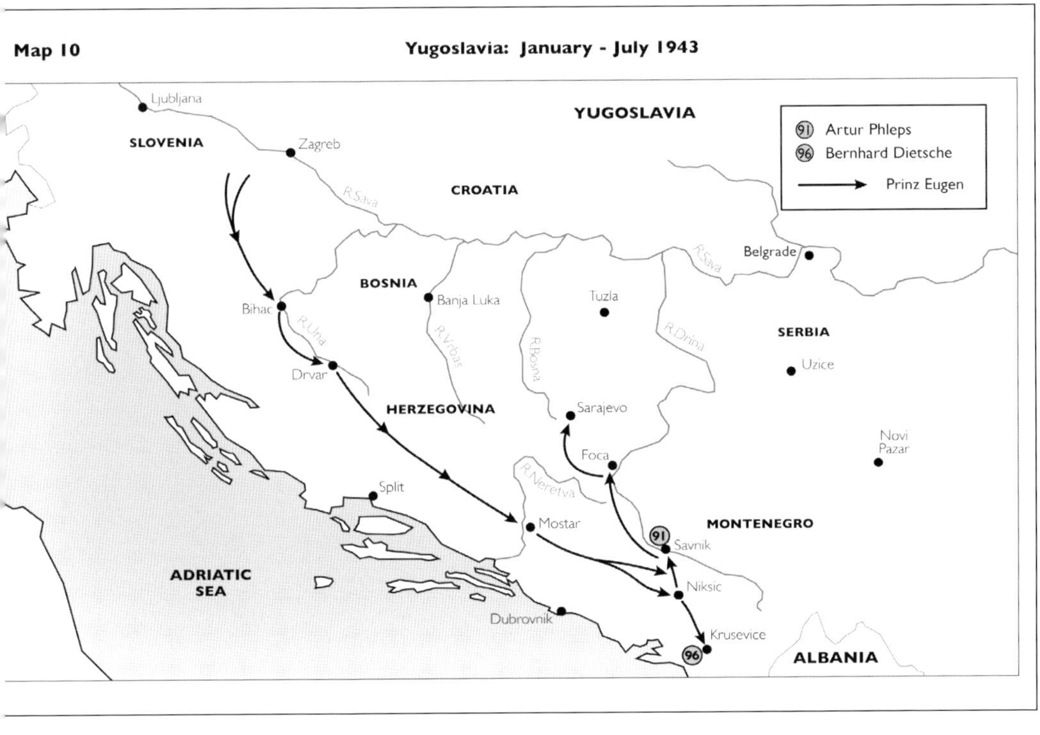

Tito and many of his men managed to evade capture and lived to fight another day – much to the annoyance of Phleps. During mid-June, *Prinz Eugen* were stopped in their further advances and moved back to the area around Sarajevo. Operation Schwarz was concluded at this point. It is also worth noting that Artur Phleps left command of *Prinz Eugen* at this stage and focused on forming a new *SS Korps* – details of this will follow later – *SS-Brigadeführer und Generalmajor der Waffen-SS* Carl (Reichsritter) von Oberkamp took over command of this unit. We will now halt the covering of this unit towards the end of June 1943 and pick up their activities in the next chapter.

1. SS-Infantry Brigade (mot.)

The situation remained unchanged for this unit during the April to June period, whilst they were in the Vitebsk-Gurki area.

SS-Kavallerie Division

This unit was moved to Bobruisk in April for a refit, with Fritz Freitag in command. During May and the first part of June they were involved in anti-partisan warfare around the Khoyniki-Bragin highway, in the Komany-Pertitsk, Ulianovka-Rysnkov areas. In late June they were moved to the Army Group South area of control.

Re-cap

We feel that a quick re-cap at this stage would be worthwhile, before moving ahead with the next occurrences.

This now left twenty-one different *Waffen-SS* units in existence at the end of June 1943. These twenty-one were:

SS-Panzergrenadier Division Leibstandarte Adolf Hitler
SS-Panzergrenadier Division Das Reich
SS-Panzergrenadier Division Totenkopf
SS-Polizei Panzergrenadier Division
SS-Panzergrenadier Division Wiking
SS-Gebirgs Division Nord
SS-Freiwilligen Gebirgs Division Prinz Eugen
SS-Kavallerie Division
SS-Panzergrenadier Division Hohenstaufen
SS-Panzergrenadier Division Frundsberg
SS-Panzergrenadier Division Nordland
SS-Panzergrenadier Division Hitler Youth

Croat SS-Freiwilligen Division
Latvian SS-Freiwilligen Brigade
Sturmbrigade Reichführer-SS
Latvian SS-Freiwilligen Legion
Estonian SS-Freiwilligen Brigade
SS-Karstwehr Battalion
SS-Sturmbrigade Langemarck
SS-Sturmbrigade Wallonie
1. SS-Infantry Brigade (mot.)

Disbanded during the first half of 1943:
SS-Brigade Schuldt
SS-Kampfgruppe Fegelein
SS-Kamgfgruppe 'Z' (returned to parent unit)
SS-Freikorps Denmark (used to help form *Nordland)*
SS-Legion Norwegian (used to help form *Nordland)*
SS-Legion Niederlande (used to help form *Nordland)*
SS-Legion Flanderen (used to form *SS-Sturmbrigade Langemarck)*
2. SS-Infantry Brigade (mot.) (used to form the *Latvian SS-Freiwilligen Brigade)*

Before starting the next major phase of operations on the Russian Front and elsewhere, let us detail the Knight's Crosses that were approved between the start of April and the end of June 1943, for the men of the *Waffen-SS*.

Hinrich Schuldt
Date of birth: 14.06.1901
SS Number: 242 677
We last covered Hinrich Schuldt in April 1942 after his *Regiment's* difficult fighting in Juchnow, Russia in the opening months of 1942 and Schuldt's subsequent award of the Knight's Cross to the Iron Cross in April 1942. If you recall from Volume 1, the remnants of his *SS-Infantry-Regiment 4* were withdrawn in March 1942. So what had taken place after that? The remnants mentioned above were sent to *Das Reich* and Schuldt stayed with them, this *Regiment* had received the title *SS-Regiment 'Langemarck'* by then. At the start of August, Hinrich Schuldt received a promotion to *SS-Standartenführer.* He then left the command of *Langemarck* in October the same year. His next assignment came in early December when he was given command of a new *Brigade*. The actions of this *Brigade* between December 1942 and March 1943 have been detailed in the preceding pages. These actions

This image shows Hinrich Schuldt with his existing Knight's Cross, with the Oakleaves added to the photograph afterwards. He won the Oakleaves as an SS-Standartenführer, although the image above shows him holding the rank of SS-Obersturmbannführer.

would result in his recommendation for the Oakleaves to his existing Knight's Cross during the same month.

This recommendation was unusual due to it being written by one of Schuldt's junior officers. *SS-Hauptsturmführer* Carl-Gunther Molt wrote the recommendation for his *Commander's* Oakleaves to his existing Knight's Cross on the 10th of March 1943. The recommendation covers actions lasting just over two months, reading as follows:

'On 19.12.1942 *SS-Standartenführer* Schuldt with three *Leibstandarte Kompanies* and one-and-a-half *Kompanies* from the *SS-Polizei Division* were moving in the billeting area assigned by the *XXIX Armeekorps* in Meschkoff. On the way they met the Italians from *Armeeoberkommando 8* falling back and rushing in disorder, closely pursued by the Russians. In a quick and bold resolution, *SS-Standartenführer* Schuldt switched over from the march to counter attack and took the high ground east and north east of Meschkoff that dominated the entire area. The Russians were thrown back in the whole area and the high ground held. Then a report about the failure of the Italian defensive front was sent to the *XXIX Armeekorps*.

This was the first report that the German Command received about the collapse of the Italian Front.

Schuldt displayed a clear and widespread knowledge of the tactical situation. With the resolute and energetic leadership of the *Commander* of the *Kampfgruppe* and the bravery of his *SS* men, the majority of the Italian troops could be saved from being completely annihilated.

Under the personal leadership of Schuldt, the positions in Meschkoff were held against strong enemy infantry and tank attacks. Meanwhile two Russian Tank Corps broke through the left flanking unit towards the west and in the course of the following day completely encircled the *XXIX Armeekorps*. The entire *XXIX Armeekorps Staff* with the *Korps Commander*, straggling German troops and Italian units in disorder found themselves in the cauldron. They were harassed by the tanks of the attacking opponent from all sides. The only worth fighting power at disposal were the elements of *SS-Kampfgruppe 'Schuldt'*. Again it must be credited to the energetic and accurate leadership of the *Brigade Commander* that after hard battles, on 29.12.42 the breakout of the *Armeekorps* to reach the lines of *Heeresgruppe Don* could be successful.

On 15.01.43 in spite of the strongest defense, parts of the *SS-Brigade 'Schuldt'* were surrounded at the bridgehead and blocking positions near Nowo-Jerochin and Klitwenezkaja. The order of the *XXX Armeekorps* to disengage and fall back to Kamensk did not reach the *Kampfgruppe* because the radio station was destroyed by a direct hit. In that moment, when the position in Nowo-Jerochin was almost completely surrounded by 15 Russian tanks, the vigorous leadership of the *Commander* of the *SS-Brigade, SS-Standartenführer* Schuldt was proven again. He ordered that all the forces engaged in Nowo-Jerochin should break out towards Kamensk. Schuldt, with a small group of *SS* men and officers attracted the attention of the enemy to facilitate the escape of our troops. The next morning the *Commander* with one officer and five men finally reached Kamensk, after having gone through the Russian units already deployed in front of Kamensk.

In the night from 31.1. to 1.2.43 the enemy attacked *SS-Brigade 'Schuldt'* by surprise with strong forces reinforced with tanks. The area became our defensive front over the Donez. In an extremely hard and, also for the *Kampfgruppe* bloody combat, the positions in Woroschilow and Shiroky were held for two days and two nights. They thwarted a complete breakthrough of the opponent that severely hit the *Brigade's* defensive positions, with the concluded goal of reaching Krassnodon. This must be credited to the energetic and lively leadership of the *Commander* and his individual personal combat performance.

After the withdrawal of the defensive front to Wodjanoj position, it was only thanks to the compelling personality of the *Commander,* often by force, that the newly attached elements of the *304th Infantry Divison* held back the enemy. He forced them to build up the positions so that the massive attacks of the opponent were resisted until the order to withdraw was given. The opponent recognized the *Brigade's* hard defensive willpower and, with the support of tank forces, tried repeatedly to force a breakthrough either by right or by the left flank. That put the *Brigade* in extreme danger and in a serious situation. Only through the bravery of the *Brigade* and attached units under the energetic and prudent leadership of its' *Commander* could the situation be successfully held. In this period, the *Brigade* destroyed 24 tanks and three armoured attack airplanes of the enemy.

To finish off a local opponent break-in to the west of the Olchowaja sector, *SS-Brigade 'Schuldt'* was transferred on 22.2.43 into the area of Nikitowka-Bachtewitsch. On 23.2, after moving into the assembly position, they attacked the opponent in Wassjukowa-Schl. with an assault group under the command of the *SS-Sturmbannführer* Dietrich. They had the objective of enabling the retaking of the main fighting line by *Gruppe 'Hunten'*. With the attack progressing, the battle developed more and more into close combat by assault detachments at short range. After a hard fight under the personal leadership of the *Brigade Commander,* who in the course of the battle was wounded by a shell splinter above the right eye, the old main fighting line could be reached and occupied.

In the meantime, during 24.2.43, the Russians managed to penetrate with strong forces the left flank of *Gruppe 'Hunten'*. At that moment, when the whole defensive front in the right sector of *Gruppe 'Kreysing'* threatened to collapse, this sector was subordinated to *SS-Brigade 'Schuldt'* with the following words of *General* Kreysing, "Herr Schuldt, you must do it, I rely on you". The *Commander* of the *Brigade*, *SS-Standartenführer* Schuldt, recognized quickly that hills 287.4 and 227.4 were essential for the defense and also as a departure point for any counterattack. They had to be held at any price. Schuldt's energy, which he stressed to the officers subordinated to him and at the same time was transmitted to all of the fighting troops, must be thanked. The heights were again snatched away from the opponent in a surprise counterthrust, and with it, the menacing breakthrough could be halted as well.

After a very hard initial battle, on 26.02.43, a counterattack, again under the personal leadership of the *Commander,* destroyed the massive opponent in the Ssereschina-Schl. in two-and-a-half hours. The day's objective and with it the old main fighting line were reached. During the attack the *Commander* was wounded for the second time by mortar splinters in the shoulder and back. After that time the assignment of the *Kampfgruppe* was fulfilled and the disengagement of the *Brigade* began.'

This recommendation for the Oakleaves to Schuldt's existing Knight's Cross was approved on the 2nd of April 1943, but would not end his connection to the various grades of the Knight's Cross. More details of that will follow in later volumes.

Heinz Macher
Date of birth: 31.12.1919
SS Number: 311 752
Born in Chemnitz, he served in the *Hitler Youth* from the start of May 1934 until the 20th of April 1937. This was the same day that he moved to the *SS*. From early November 1938 until late March 1939 he spent a spell with the *R.A.D.* He was posted to the *SS-Pioneer Battalion* and it was with this unit that he entered the Second World War.

He fought in Poland and the west, by which time he had become an *NCO* (although the exact rank at that time is not listed). Inbetween the campaign in the west and the Balkans campaign, he attended the officer's school at Braunschweig and was commissioned an *SS-Untersturmführer* on the 20th of April 1941. He was fighting in the Balkans by then and was covering the role of *Platoon Commander.* His next action was during the invasion of the Soviet Union in mid-1941 and by

Heinz Macher shown after he was awarded the Knight's Cross to the Iron Cross.

the end of that year, he had started to accumulate what would be a long list of awards. The Second Class Iron Cross came on the 24th of September with the General Assault Badge following on the 2nd of October. During the intensive fighting in early 1942, his bravery was put to the test again. He was awarded the First Class Iron Cross on the 15th of March, the Wound Badge in Black on the 1st of April and the Russian Front Medal at the start of August, whilst being stationed in France. He then returned to Russia in early 1943, by this stage he was serving with the *16. (Pioneer) Kompanie,* within *Das Reich's, Deutschland Regiment.*

He was involved in the intensive fighting around Kharkov in March and he conducted actions during the counter-attack phase that would help influence the outcome of the battle decisively. His *Regimental Commander,* Heinz Harmel, wrote a Knight's Cross recommendation on the 18th of March 1943 that read as follows:

'*SS-Untersturmfhurer* Macher has already distinguished himself in the previous fighting in the east during 1941/42 through special courage. The close support of the assembled weapons of the *16. (Pioneer) Kompanie/SS-Pz.Gren. Rgt. "Deutschland"* in February 1943 in the enemy fighting in the Oskol area, contributed substantially to the resulting tactical outcome which the *SS-Pz.Gren. Rgt. "Deutschland"* had.

In the course of the fighting pursuit from Krassnograd to Kharkov, Macher with his *Kompanie* had undertaken themselves in mine clearing activites and also as shock troops, again and again displaying special courage.

In a tank attack on Pawlograd, which the mass of the *SS-Pz.Gren.Rgt."Der Führer"* and the staff of the *SS-Division "Das Reich",* as well as the *16. (Pioneer) Kompanie./SS-Pz.Gren.Rgt."D"* were subjected, Macher took the decision to collect his *Kompanie*, destroyed 2 enemy tanks, forced a retreat of the remaining 10 tanks too and destroyed the mass of two enemy Companies.

On the 11.3.1943, Macher received the order, with his *Kompanie*, without the support of heavy weapons, to take the west of Kharkov, to create with a *Panzer-Pioneer-Zug* a crossing for the attack of our own tanks into the outskirts and then into the city of Kharkov.

Macher penetrated into the enemy tank-ditch position, destroyed the M.G. nests there and took full possession of the tank-ditch, which gave a favourable crossing place.

Out of this, Macher made his own decision to storm over the tank-ditch immediately and move towards the enemy positions in the outskirts of Kharkov in order to take the houses and anti-tank front lying behind it. These, were in a controlling position and included enemy tank weapons, which made the further advance of our own tanks on the 11.3.1943 impossible.

In close combat, Macher took his 32 man-strong *Kompanie* from tank cupola to tank cupola and moving from house to house were able to destroy the enemy weapons in their set positions.

Macher held and defended this first position, in spite of multiple, bitter enemy counter-attacks. Macher distinguished himself through outstanding courage and fearlessness.

The decision of *SS-Untersturmführer* Macher made possible the early opening of the way for the mass of *SS-Panzer-Grenadier-Division "Das Reich"* to pass freely and also for insignificant losses. It was also a prerequisite for the fast capture of the city of Kharkov.

To emphasize, that Macher with the use of his *Kompanie,* in spite of bitter close combat produced low losses from the fighting.'

This recommendation was also endorsed by the acting *Divisional Commander* and also by the *Korps Commander,* Paul Hassuer. The award of the Knight's Cross to the Iron Cross was approved on the 3rd of April 1943. By the time of this award being approved, Macher had been wounded four times. This action and the resulting award would not end Heinz Macher's association with this medal. Details of his future actions and awards will follow in subsequent volumes.

Arzelino Masarie

Date of birth: 10.10.1912

SS Number: 71 687

Born in Nuremburg, he joined the *SS* in early 1933. He became an *SS-Untersturmführer* on the 20th of April 1936 after attending officer's school. He served as a *Platoon Leader* in *Totenkopf's Aufklarungs Abteilung* after their formation. He went west with them in 1940 and earned the Second Class Iron Cross at the start of July. In 1941 he went into Russia with *Totenkopf* and on the 25th of September he was awarded the First Class Iron Cross. In early 1942 he found himself in Demjansk, becoming engaged in difficult fighting with Siberian troops during heavy snow-storms and very low temperatures. He was leading the *1. Kompanie* at that time. In late April 1942, he was promoted to *SS-Hauptsturmführer.* It is not listed as to when he was promoted to *SS-Obersturmführer.* For his successful action during the Demjansk fighting he was awarded the German Cross in Gold at the end of July.

He returned to Russia in early 1943 and found himself involved in the fighting around Kharkov. In late March, Max Simon penned a recommendation for the Knight's Cross to the Iron Cross for Masarie that read as follows:

Arzelino 'Lino' Masarie photographed in 1944 after he was promoted to SS-Sturmbannführer, wearing the Knight's Cross he was awarded in 1943.

'*SS-Hauptsturmführer* Masarie on the afternoon of 14.3.1943, with the *Aufklarungs-Abteilung* were clearing both sides of the main road from Kharkov to Belgorod in the north. The lead troops arrived at Lipzy around 04:30 hours and assessed that there was strong enemy forces blocking the further advance of the *Aufklarungs Abteilung*. *SS-Hauptsturmführer* Masarie took the decision to attack Lipzy with his weak *Aufklarungs*, thereby clearing the way open on the main road and also disperse the enemy between Kharkov, Belgorod and Woltschansk. In the difficult attack *SS-Hauptsturmführer* Masarie penetrated into Lipzy and fought the enemy who were defending well. Despite the difficult and bitter fighting, they threw the enemy out of this town. In this fight they captured or destroyed:

1 tank
4 amoured cars
28 light vehicles
3 tractor
1 ammunition dump with artillery and mortar rounds
8 000 litres of diesel fuel
6 motorcycles
The Bolsheviks also lost over 100 dead.

SS-Hauptsturmführer Masarie through his own decision and successful attack on Lipzy, created the prerequisite for the later advance to the northeast of the *SS-Pz.Gren. Div. "Totenkopf"*.

The hard counterattacks of the Russians proved how much the recovery of this location meant to the enemy.

I please ask that *SS-Hauptsturmführer* Masarie be awarded the Knight's Cross to the Iron Cross in recognition of his heroic deeds and the connected results.'

The *SS-Panzer Korps Commander*, Paul Hausser also endorsed this recommendation.

This recommendation was approved on the 3rd of April 1943. He was promoted to *SS-Sturmbannführer* in July 1944 and given command of *Totenkopf's Aufklarungs Abteilung*. It was whilst leading this unit that he was killed in action on the 9th of August 1944 in Poland. Besides winning the above listed awards, it is known that he won the General Assault Badge, the Black Wound Badge and the Russian Front medal.

Walter Reder
Date of birth: 04.02.1915
SS Number: 58 074
Born in Freiwaldau, Austria, he served with the *Hitler Youth* from June to December 1932. He then joined the *SS* in early February 1933. From the start of October 1934 until late April 1935 he served within the *II Battalion, SS-Regiment Deutschland.* He immediately followed this by moving to the officer school in Braunschweig between that date and the 5th of April 1936. He started service with the *Totenkopf Standarte 'Oberbayern'* from the 20th of April, the same day that he was promoted to *SS-Untersturmführer*. After this, his file has conflicting information. Some documents state he was back with *Deutschland* from the start of April 1937, others state that he remained with *Oberbayern* until the start of the war. He did earn the pre-war campaign medals for 1938 and 1939, which would lean more towards *Deutschland.* What is not in dispute is that he was promoted to *SS-Obersturmführer* at the end of January 1939. There is also mention of him serving on the staff of the *Reichsführer-SS* pre-war.

He is listed as serving with the *14. Kompanie,* within *Totenkopf's 1. Regiment* when they were formed after Poland. By the time that they moved west in 1940, he was on the staff of *Totenkopf's 2. Regiment.* He earned the Second Class Iron Cross at the end of May. In July he moved to the *3. Kompanie* within that *Regiment,* but by early 1941 he was back with *Totenkopf's, II Battalion, 1. Regiment.* He moved with this unit into Russia in mid-1941.

On the 28th of July he was awarded the First Class Iron Cross, promoted to *SS-Hauptsturmführer* at the start of September, awarded the Black Wound Badge on the 20th of September and the Infantry Assault Badge on the 8th of October. Like his *Totenkopf Kameraden* he fought in the Demjansk Pocket throughout the majority of 1942, earning the Russian Front Medal on the 28th of July. He conducted actions there that also resulted in his award of the German Cross in Gold on the 17th of October.

After moving to France in October 1942, he then returned to Russia in February 1943. It was here that he was recommended for the Knight's Cross to the Iron Cross. The recommendation was written by Max Simon on the 17th of March and contained the following:

'*SS-Hauptsturmführer* Reder had orders on the 1.3.1943, with his *Battalion* working together with the *I./SS-T Pz. Rgt. 3* moving eastwards, with Orel to the north and over Par Schljachowaja onto Schjachowaja and west into Jeremejewka.

The *Battalion* bumped into hard resistance in Par Schljachowaja, they penetrated into this village after hard fighting and defended it during the night against 4 violent tank counter attacks by the enemy, with only limited support.

An autographed photograph of Walter Reder showing his Knight's Cross award.

On the 2.3.1943, the *Battalion* smashed strong enemy west of Schljachowaja in the Leninskij factory and defended again with limited support, against violent tank attacks of the enemy. Despite the superhuman exertions of *SS-Hauptsturmführer* Reder, the enemy firmly held Jeremejewka. On the 3.3.1943 the men went forward again towards Jeremejewka and ventured into the western part of the town during hard street fighting. On his own decision they turned to the north and northeast and destroyed and divided the strong enemy, who retreated back.

The bold attack of the *Battalion*, possible only through the last personal attack of *SS-Hauptsturmführer* Reder, created the prerequisite for the dividing and annihilation of the strong Russian 3rd Tank Army.

The *Battalion* Reder itself captured or destroyed in these battles:

13 tanks
82 guns
1 Flak Battery
354 light vehicles
Around 300 panje wagons
25 mortars
53 anti-tank rifles
25 field kitchens
Many machine guns and over 1000 rifles

SS-Hauptsturmführer Reder, who with his *Battalion,* was the highest example of go-getting spirit, was heavily wounded on the 10.3.1943.

I please ask that this brave officer receive recognition for his boldness and the result associated to it with the award of the Knight's Cross to the Iron Cross.

The *Divisional Commander*
Simon

SS-Brigadeführer und Generalmajor der Waffen-SS

<u>Attitude of the *Generalkommando SS-Panzer-Korps*:</u>
SS-Hauptsturmführer Reder had the decisive share in the successful pocket battle around Jeremejewka. I warmly approve the award of the Knight's Cross.

Signed: Hausser.'

This award was approved on the 3rd of April 1943.

Walter Reder officially stayed with *Totenkopf* until the middle of April, when he was moved to the *SS-Panzergrenadier Replacement and Training Battlion 3*. He stayed with that unit until the 20th of December 1943. There is mention of him coming out of hospital a few days earlier, so it can be presumed that the wounds he received back in March near Dergatschi kept him in hospital all of that time? He moved to the *16th SS-Panzergrenadier Division "Reichsführer-SS"* then at the end of January 1944 he was promoted to *SS-Sturmbannführer*. He was given command of the *Aufklarungs Abteilung* within that *Division* and led them as they fought against the Allies and Partisans in 1944.

It was for this fighting that Walter Reder found himself being imprisoned after the war. He was placed in prison and was only released in late January 1985, despite many attempts to have him released. He died on the 26th of April 1991 in his native Austria.

Joachim Schubach
Date of birth: 17.09.1910
SS Number: 17 597
Born in Hannover, he joined the *SS* at the start of October 1931, being placed with the *12. Standarte*. By late March 1933 he had achieved the rank of *SS-Scharführer (SS-Unterscharführer)*, then in early July he moved to the *LAH*, the same day that he was promoted to *SS-Truppführer (SS-Oberscharführer)*. His next promotion came in late December 1934 when he moved to *SS-Hauptscharführer*. He remained with the *LAH* up to the outbreak of war. In that time he was promoted to *SS-Untersturmführer*, on the 30th of January 1937, followed by *SS-Obersturmführer* at the start of June 1938, serving with the *9. Kompanie*. He had also spent a 3-month stint at the pioneer school in Dresden.

He fought in Poland with the *LAH*, but in mid-October 1939 he moved to the newly created *Totenkopf Division*, serving within their *SS-Infantry Regiment 3*. He was promoted to *SS-Hauptsturmführer* at the end of January 1940, now serving with *Totenkopf's 1st Regiment*. He then went west with *Totenkopf* during May the same year where he earned the Second Class Iron Cross on the 30th of May.

His next move was into Russia in mid-1941 where he earned the First Class Iron Cross on the 14th of July, followed by the Infantry Assault Badge on the 8th of October, then the Black Wound Badge on the 17th of October. He received a promotion to *SS-Sturmbannführer* on the 4th of January 1942. He fought in the Demjansk Pocket during 1942 and earned the Russian Front Medal in July and the German Cross in Gold on the 26th of September, the Demjansk Shield was also added to his list of awards.

An autographed image of Joachim Schubach with the Knight's Cross.

He moved to France for *Totenkopf's* refit in October 1942, before moving back to Russia in February 1943. He fought with his *Kameraden,* leading the *III Battalion* in this struggle and during early March he took part in fighting that would result in his award of the Knight's Cross to the Iron Cross. The recommendation for this was written by Max Simon on the 17th of March 1943. It contained the following details:

'*SS-Sturmbannführer* Schubach, *Commander III. /SS-T-Pz.Gren. Rgt. 1,* received the orders on the 12.3.1943 to venture to Tscherkasskaja Losowaja (10km north of Kharkov) over Bolschaja Danilowka, Ssorokowka on the main road from Kharkov to Tschugujew.

As the 12.3.1943 begun, *SS-Sturmbannführer* Schubach already reached Ssorokowka about midnight, where they bumped into strong enemy resistance. In bitter night fighting they threw the enemy back and rolled it up, on the 13.3.1943 with his *Battalion,* the strong enemy positions along the Roschanka stream to the main road into Kharkov; He waited ready at Roganj for orders to assault Tschugujew.

At the beginning of 14.3.1943, *SS-Sturmbannführer* Schubach, in collaboration with the *I./SS-T-Pz. Rgt. 3,* threw the enemy of the western heights of Kamenaja Jaruga and out of the village itself. The road bridge in the southern part of Kamenja Jaruga, over the Studenok stream, was destroyed by the enemy. The *Pioneers* had first to create the possibility for the tanks, vehicles and heavy weapons to cross.

SS-Sturmbannführer Schubach advanced on his own decision without the support of heavy weapons, tanks and without artillery support further onto Tschugujew and penetrated the enemy positions around 18:00 hours, he surprised perfectly, in which the northwest part of the city was fought for through difficult street fighting. In violent fighting onto the Donez, they blocked the streets to the southwestern and north and also the bridge over the Donez River. Then in the city the hidden enemy emerged and the Russian Batteries were taken in hand to hand fighting, then turned and immediately used against the enemy.

SS-Sturmbannführer Schubach has through his own decision and through his personal outstanding courage prevented the escape of strong enemy forces from Kharkov to the southeast, that also took their possibility of escape over the Donez. Through this cool headed push on Tschugujew his *Battalion* captured and/or destroyed:

20 tanks
2 21cm guns

25 guns of between 7.62 and 12.2 caliber
47 light vehicles
14 prime movers
Also many machine and hand held weapons, as well as aircraft bombs and diesel fuel.

SS-Sturmbannführer Schubach became heavily wounded in the house fighting around Tschugujew during the night. However, he remained with his *Battalion* until Tschugujew was taken.

I please ask, that *SS-Sturmbannführer* Schubach receive the Knight's Cross to the Iron Cross in recognition of his heroic courage and in appreciation of his decisive result.'

He was approved for this award on the 3rd of April 1943.

No doubt that his wound received in the fighting resulted in his removal from the frontline, as he is listed as serving with the *SS-Panzergrenadier Training and Replacement Battlion 3* from late April until the 11th of July 1943. He then returned to *Totenkopf* where on the 12th of October he was awarded the Close Combat Clasp in Bronze and Silver. The following month he was badly wounded and left frontline service for the remainder of the war. He is listed as serving with the *SS-Führer Main Office* from the start of December 1943. He received a further promotion to *SS-Obersturmbannführer* on the 20th of April 1944. He was also awarded the Wound Badge in Gold, although the exact date of this award is not listed. He survived the war and died on the 5th of November 1980 in his home city.

Vincenz Kaiser
Date of birth: 28.02.1904
SS Number: 17 127
Born in Judenburg, Steiermark in Austria, he was a member of the *Hitler Youth* from mid-June 1925 until mid-September 1927. He then moved to the *S.A.*, serving with the *26. Sturm,* and stayed there until October 1931. He followed this by a move to the *Allgemeine-SS* and served with the *38. Standarte*. Towards the end of August 1933 he moved to the *SS-Legion Lechfeld* based in Austria. He was promoted rapidly that year and rose from *SS-Schutze* to *SS-Obertruppführer (SS-Hauptscharführer)* by the end of December, by then he was also serving with the *8. Sturme*.

A very pleased looking Vincenz Kaiser photographed on the day of his Knight's Cross presentation. His many acts of bravery are clearly visible on his uniform!

In mid-June 1934 he had moved to the *II Battalion*, within *Deutschland* and was holding the rank of *SS-Sturmführer (SS-Untersturmführer)*. By the start of October 1935 he had moved to *Germania* and seven months later, he was promoted to *SS-Obersturmführer*. He started a stint at Bad Tolz as an instructor and stayed there until early 1938. He moved to the newly created *SS-Regiment "Der Führer"* at this time and shortly after, on the 20th of April, he was promoted to *SS-Hauptsturmführer* and took command of a *Kompanie*. He took part in the annexation of Austria and the actions in the Sudetenland, earning both medals for these pre-war campaigns.

Staying with *Der Führer*, he fought in the west in 1940, the Balkans in 1941 and then moved in Russia in mid-1941. It was in Russia that his bravery came to the fore and before the end of 1941 he had accumulated further awards. The 8-year *SS* Long Service Medal came at the start of July, the Second Class Iron Cross on the 28th of July, the First Class Iron Cross on the 24th of August, the Wound Badge in Black in early November and the Infantry Assault Badge at the start of December. He commanded the *1. Kompanie* during that time. At the start of April 1942 he had moved to the *II Battalion*, then on the 29th of October he was awarded the German Cross in Gold for various actions in this first year of fighting on the eastern front.

He returned to Russia with his *Kameraden* in early 1943 to help halt the Russian advances around Kharkov. He conducted successful actions within this fighting that resulted in his recommendation for the Knight's Cross to the Iron Cross. He was commanding the *III (Armoured) Battalion* at that time. This particular recommendation was written by *SS-Standartenführer* Kurt Brasack on the 22nd of March 1943. Brasack had assumed temporary command of *Das Reich* only four days earlier, following Vahl's wounding. The recommendation contained the following:

'On the 12.3.1943, the *I./SS-Pz.Gren.Rgt."Deutschland"* had threaded over the tank ditch taken by the *16./SS-Pz.Gren.Rgt."Deutschland"* and penetrating into the first lines of houses in Kharkov, forming a bridgehead there. In the early morning the enemy launched violent counter-attacks against this bridgehead. The *Regiment* therefore sent the *III (Armoured)/ SS-Pz.Gren.Rgt."Der Führer"* into the bridgehead. Later, there was the intention to penetrate into the city with the *Panzer Abteilung* and *Armoured Battalion* after being supplied.

SS-Hauptsturmführer Kaiser took the decision to pull out, not using his *Battalion* to reinforce the front held by the *I./Pz.Gren.Rgt. "Deutschland"*, but rather to attack out of the *I./SS-Pz.Gren.Rgt. "Deutschland"* held bridgehead towards the opponent, in order to create relief for the *I Battalion* and if possible to expand the bridgehead. *SS-Hauptsturmführer* Kaiser prepared and personally led the attack to its' full success. He succeeded in not only expanding the bridgehead considerably but, rather he succeeded in forcing the opponent back even further. *SS-Hauptsturmführer* Kaiser had an insight into the situation and his *Battalion* pushed after the yielding opponent. *SS-Hauptsturmführer* Kaiser took the decision not to wait on the tanks. His fast and courageous grab was successful and it is owed to him, with the mass of his *Battalion* they advanced to the railway station on the southern ring and from there with the armoured cars made a connection between the *III/SS-Pz.Gren.Rgt. "Deutschland"* and the *SS-Pz.Gren.Div. "Adolf Hitler"* advancing to "Red Square".

Through his decision, without waiting on the tanks to attack, *SS-Hauptsturmführer* Kaiser created the prerequisite, that already in the morning of the 12.3.1943 the total west part of the city was in our own hands with high bloody losses for the opponent.

Out of a prepared forest position *SS-Hauptsturmführer* Kaiser took a *Kampfgruppe* containing a few armoured cars and advanced against a strong opponent southwest of Kharkov. Advancing over land, they cut-off the enemy and captured 40 guns.'

The recommendation goes on to mention his leadership skills, bravery and personal modesty in all of his actions and the fact that these have been recognized with his existing awards of the German Cross in Gold and his 4 Tank Destruction Badges.

On the 6th of April 1943 he could add the Knight's Cross to the Iron Cross to his long list of existing awards. Slightly earlier than this, he had been promoted to *SS-Sturmbannführer* at the start of April. This award would not end his connection to this medal, but details of that will follow in later volumes.

Sylvester Stadler

Date of birth: 30.12.1910

SS Number: 139 495

Born in Fohnsdorf, Austria, he joined the *SS* on the 2nd of May 1933. He initially served with the *38. SS-Standarte* who were based in Austria, but like many of his *Kameraden,* he left Austria for Germany as the Austrian Government made life difficult for the supporters of Hitler. He was initially a member of the *Austrian Legion,* before moving to the new *SS-VT* in December 1933. He received promotion to *SS-Rottenführer* on the 20th of April 1934, followed by a rapid promotion to *SS-Scharführer (SS-Unterscharführer)* exactly one month later. He moved to the *SS-Standarte 'Deutschland'* in early October 1934.

Above: Sylvester Stadler (on the extreme right) shown here wearing his Knight's Cross, whilst conversing with Walter Kruger (centre) and also Heinz Harmel (left).

Right: Another photograph of Sylvester Stadler showing him after his promotion to SS-Obersturmbannführer, his Knight's Cross is just visible.

He was sent to Bad Tolz from late April 1935 until early February 1936, leaving there with the rank of *SS-Standartenjunker.* He then went straight to Dachau for a platoon leader's course, which ended on the 4th of April. On the 20th of April he was promoted to *SS-Untersturmführer.* He was then assigned to the *SS-VT's Signals Battalion.* Whilst with this unit he attended the Olympic Games in Berlin, was promoted to *SS-Obersturmführer* on the 12th of September 1937, marched into Austria in mid-March 1938, followed by the Sudetentland in October the same year, then rounded this all off with a promotion to *SS-Hauptsturmführer* at the end of June 1939. He then entered the Second World War.

He fought in Poland with *Division Kempf* and earned the Second Class Iron Cross on the 25th of September. Then moving westwards in May 1940, he earned the Black Wound Badge in mid-June, the Infantry Assault Badge on the 21st of June and the First Class Iron Cross on the 26th of June. After this campaign ended, he moved to the *SS-Regiment "Der Führer"* in early August and assumed command of their *5. Kompanie.* He fought in Yugoslavia and entered Russia in mid-1941.

Whilst in Russia he assumed temporary command of the *II Battalion* in the second half of September, but did not stay there long as he was wounded on the 10th of October. This wound removed him from front-line service temporarily. He spent the remainder of 1941 at the *SS* officer's schools, staying there until the end of February 1942. He returned to *Der Führer* and assumed command of the *II Battalion.* A promotion to *SS-Sturmbannführer* came at the start of September the same year.

He returned to Russia in early 1943 and became involved in the bitter fighting around Kharkov, fighting that would result in him being awarded the Knight's Cross to the Iron Cross. The recommendation was written by Herbert Vahl on the 8th of March and it covered the following:

'*SS-Sturmbannführer* Stadler has since the 7.6.42, been the acting *Commander* of the *II/SS-Pz.Gr.Rgt. "Der Führer".*

SS-Sturmbannführer Stadler with his *Battalion*, after breaking weak resistance in two villages, reached the town of Jefremowka on the evening of 1.3.43. Reconnaissance patrols detected strong enemy forces occupying the fortified town.

The intention of the *Regiment* was to attack early on 2.3.43, after a detailed preparation. Then *SS-Sturmbannführer* Stadler decided independently to take advantage of the night and to start the attack with the support of two assault guns. He himself accompanied the leading *Kompanie* through the intense defensive fire until he reached the town, deployed there with his *Kompanies* for the attack and penetrated with them deep into the town. With the first light of the morning, he continued the annihilation, by 08:00 hours the town had fallen. About 250 enemy dead, 12 tanks, 17 artillery guns and 38 anti-tank guns were left on the battle field.

Thanks to Stadler's independent decision of penetrating the town by night without preparation, the first phase of the success was accomplished. An attack in daylight could have been carried out only with heavy losses. Through his resolute performance and personal action, could he push forward his *Kompanies* across the heavy fight into the town to complete the success. With his daring bravery he allowed the *Division* to establish, the very same day, the link with the *SS-Pz.Gr. Div. "Adolf Hitler"*. With it, the isolation and the encirclement of one-and-a-half Russian Tank Corps in the area of Schljaybwaja was closed, making possible their ensuing annihilation by the *Totenkopf-Division*.'

Underneath Vahl's signature was an endorsement of this recommendation by Paul Hausser. The award was granted on the 6th of April 1943, but this award would not end his association to the Knight's Cross. Some details of his further actions will feature in later volumes.

Hans Weiss

Date of birth: 28.08.1911

SS Number: 47 390

Born in Vohringen, Weiss was initially a member of the *S.A.* from late 1931 until August 1932. He then moved to the *SS* the same month and by mid-1935 he was holding the rank of *SS-Hauptscharführer*. He attended an officer's training course, which started that year and on the 9th of November 1936 he had been promoted to *SS-Untersturmführer* and was serving with the *IV Battalion,* within the *Deutschland Regiment*. On the 20th of April 1938 he had risen to the rank of *SS-Obersturmführer*. He spent time with the *Kradschutzen Replacement Battalion* and the *Aufklarungs Abteilung* prior to the outbreak of the war, staying with the *Aufklarungs* as the war started.

He fought in Poland and earned the Second Class Iron Cross and the Black Wound Badge there. He then fought in the west and was presented with the First Class Iron Cross on the 12th of August 1940. Just prior to that, on the 1st of July, he had been promoted to *SS-Hauptsturmführer*. He then moved southeast and fought in the Balkans during the first part of 1941, before moving into Russia in mid-1941. He remained there throughout 1941 and into 1942, conducting actions that would result in his recommendation for the Knight's Cross. This recommendation

SS-Sturmbannführer Hans Weiss photographed after his award of the Knight's Cross.

was written on the 2nd of April 1943, but mentions actions just over one year earlier, between late February and late March 1942; a summary as follows.

It covers actions on the 24.2 and the fighting at Noshkino, west of Rshew, where the *Kradschutzen Battalion* fought strong enemy forces and suffered heavy losses due to enemy artillery fire, loosing 60 men over the course of 5 days. It then highlights further advances between the 6.3 and the 10.3.1942 around Olenin, where heavy and difficult close combat took place. It finishes off by mentioning Weiss' personal bravery during the fighting around Dorogino and the resulting heavy losses upon the enemy.

It is of interest that this Knight's Cross recommendation ends with asking for the German Cross in Gold?

One other source mentions the action of Weiss during the fighting at the end of February 1943 as the source for his resulting Knight's Cross award. This source highlights the fighting around the city of Losowaja and after it fell into German hands, how the pursuit back towards Kharkov could begin. It goes on to cover the *SS-Panzer Aufklarungs Abteilung 2* and its' *Commander* Weiss in this fighting against a strong Soviet group numbering between 5000 and 6000 men. They pursued this group and wore it down along with Heinz Harmel's *Kampfgruppe*. It makes specific mention of Weiss being in the front line of this very bitter fighting, with the result that the enemy lost 6 tanks, 30 heavy guns, a large amount of anti-tank guns and many other weapons and vehicles in the space of a few hours.

Whilst the precise actions that resulted in the recommendation may be in contention, the outcome was the same. Hans Weiss was approved for the award of the Knight's Cross to the Iron Cross on the 6th of April 1943.

One day prior to the recommendation being written, he was promoted to *SS-Sturmbannführer.* By the end of 1943 he had moved to the *I Battalion,* within *Das Reich's Panzer Regiment*. Staying there, he progressed into the *SS (Schwere) Panzer Abteilung 102* and fought with them in Normandy during the summer of 1944. Back on the 23rd of April he was awarded the German Cross in Gold for fighting during 1942 and 1943. He was also awarded the Close Combat Clasp in Silver. On the 21st June 1944 he was promoted to *SS-Obersturmbannführer* and was commanding the whole *Battalion* by then. Heavily wounded in the fighting around the Falaise Pocket on the 19th of August 1944, near Trun, he fell into the hands of the advancing British. After having his head and lung wounds attended to, he spent time as a prisoner of war. He survived the war and died on the 2nd of August 1978.

Otto Kumm
Date of birth: 01.10.1909
SS Number: 18 727
This officer's actions were last highlighted in mid-February 1942 as he led the remnants of *SS-Regiment "Der Führer"* back to Model's headquarters. It was there on the 17th of February that Model presented him with the Knight's Cross to the Iron Cross. After that he gained permission personally from Adolf Hitler to remove *Der Führer* from the Russian front and take them back to Germany for rebuilding. This was after Walter Model and Heinrich Himmler had refused this request. Kumm stayed with his *Regiment* as they initially went to Germany and then onto France, where they were joined by the rest of *Das Reich* in mid-1942. He overseen the reforming of *Der Führer* during the second half of 1942 and then once again led them as they returned to Russia in early 1943. During this re-fit he was awarded the Russian Front Medal at the end of August 1942.

The overview of what his *Regiment* achieved has already been listed and it was for these achievements that *SS-Obersturmbannführer* Kumm himself would be recommended for the Oakleaves to his existing Knight's Cross. This recommendation was written by his *Divisional Commander, SS-Oberführer* Herbert Vahl on the 10th of March 1943 and read as follows:

'On the 11.2.43 *SS-Regiment "Der Führer"* received the order to attack the enemy whose excellent positions where in the hill and gorge filled area south of Merefa. The enemy had numerous heavy weapons, mainly anti-tank guns, in his positions. Our reconnaissance estimated his strength at seven Battalions. The *Panzer Regiment* of the *Leibstandarte* was attached to *Der Führer*. The order was: Push back the enemy along the rail line and village of Borki with tank support. After wining the first attack targets, Hills 172.3, 161.8 and 160.3, the *Panzer Regiment* would attack from a wide bow into the enemy's left flank to enable, with close cooperation, the removal of the enemy from its' strong positions. The *Regiment* reached its' first target and was ready in the advance positions to attack the rail line and Borki. The enemy fired heavy barrages so a further advance seemed ill advised. Here the tank attack had to force a decision. That didn't work when the enemy could not be forced from Dahgun and they were forced to withdraw. The *Regimental Commander*, observing from a most advanced position, recognized that action was an immediate must and decided to attack without tank support. This he managed with utmost clever use of his *Battalions* that ejected, pursued and destroyed the enemy. The railway was taken and the enemy lost his retreat and supply line. With that, the cut off parts of the enemy could be destroyed. Through his own decision to attack a superior strength enemy, Kumm prepared the basis for the destruction of the cut-off enemy units.

An autographed formal portrait of Otto Kumm after he was presented with the Oakleaves to his existing Knight's Cross to the Iron Cross.

On the 16.2.43 *SS-Regiment "Der Führer"*, received the order to reach Jefremowka and make contact with *Kampfgruppe 'Meier'*. The enemy was to be encircled in a pincer movement and defeated. The *III Battalion* of *Der Führer* attacked, but soon realized only a portion of the enemy was withdrawing towards Jefremowka with the bulk of their units moving southeast. The *Regimental Commander* decided to diverge from his original order and to attack both Jefremowka and follow the other units to destroy them as well. The result appeared a day later when the *III Battalion* reported the destruction of an enemy Regiment. The capture of 20 guns, 30 anti-tank guns, numerous mortars, machine-guns and other equipment as well as enemy casualties was reported; Statistics that verified the original order that was diverged from and brought success from the subsequent pursuit. Additionally, during the entire attack there was a continuous struggle against snow and terrain. During the tough advance, the *Regimental Commander,* always to be found with the most exposed spearhead, applied his own personal energy in the quick recognition of the units' situation and in his own decisions in employing units. Consequently, the *Division* has to thank him that all operations were successful. The performance of both leadership and troops was extraordinary.'

This recommendation was also counter-signed by Hausser who approved of the recommendation and made reference to his personal bravery.

The recommendation was approved on the 6th of April 1943, giving *Das Reich* their first Oakleaves holder, but would not end Kumm's association with the Knight's Cross and its' grades. Like with his *Kameraden,* details of that will follow in later volumes.

August Dieckmann

Date of birth: 29.05.1912

SS Number: 183 917

We last covered the actions of, the then *SS-Sturmbannführer,* August Dieckmann in Volume 1, as he became a holder of the Knight's Cross on the 23rd of April 1942. So what had he been up to since then?

The document that resulted in his award of the Oakleaves to his existing Knight's Cross, reads more like a German Cross in Gold recommendation, as it covers a series of actions from July 1942 through to late February 1943. An overview of these actions is as follows.

It highlights the hard fighting in the north of Rostov from the 21st to the 23rd of July 1942 and covers Dieckmann's part in the successful outcome of the attack of the *Panzer-Gefechts-Gruppe,* advancing through enemy artillery, mortar and rifle fire. They reached the southwest part of the city by the evening of the 23rd of July, after advancing over the river, with Dieckmann being singled out as a shining example of bravery for his men.

It follows by covering the actions around Grigoripoliskaja on the 3rd of August 1942, where Dieckmann's *Kampfgruppe* were fighting in the bridgehead there. They endured hard street fighting with house to house clearances being the order of the day. It mentions Dieckmann leading his men through heavy enemy fire and conducting reconnaissance through the bridgehead, then always being at the forefront of the fighting and spurning his men onto further successes, always with calmness and cold-blooded effectiveness during this time of emergency.

The next actions came a few days later on the night of the 10th of August, around Woronzowo-Daschkoff. Here, Dieckmann led a rapid attack through the enemy held positions. He directed the fire of a battery of light artillery weapons, shooting over open sights, against the enemy who were moving 100 metres ahead. The result of this attack was enormous losses to the enemy. Dieckmann's personal example and leadership prevented the enemy from cutting the supply route of the *Division*, which in turn allowed the *Division* to move up.

His personal courage was further demonstrated during the advances into the area around Chadyshenskaja, where significant heavy losses were inflicted upon the enemy by his *Kampfgruppe* as they advanced towards the Maikop area.

On the 5th of October 1942, they were fighting in the hills west of Malgobek and his *Battalion* came under heavy enemy fire from all weapons from two surrounding hills. He recognized the immediate danger and advanced with the lead *Kompanie* and stormed these enemy positions. The personal example of this *Battalion Commander* encouraged the whole *Battalion* and in a short space of time, threw the enemy off the objectives and they took possession of them. An immediate Russian counter-attack was defeated with heavy losses to the enemy.

His leadership skills came to fore once more on the following day as they continued their advance through this hilly terrain, and in particular, around an objective known as the 'White House'. They had suffered heavy losses, but Dieckmann led his men against this objective over the next couple of days, as they came under enemy tank and artillery fire. He was once again in the lead of the attack and spurned every single man onto the highest state of readiness.

He continued to display his abilities on the 17th of that month during the fighting for Hill 701. The difficulty of the fighting had not lessened and Dieckmann was in the midst of the attack using machine-pistol and hand grenades to help clear the enemy and place it within the possession of the *Division*.

August Dieckemann photographed after he was awarded the Oakleaves to his Knight's Cross and also after his promotion to SS-Obersturmbannführer.

All of these significant and successful actions were an excellent example of *SS-Sturmbannführer* August Dieckmann's abilities, but it was not until early 1943 that his continued display of ability would result in the recommendation being written.

On the 12th of February 1943 *SS-Sturmbannführer* Dieckmann with his *Battalion,* took the village of Grischino in one cool-handed stroke, from the stretched out defending enemy and cut off the supply route and advance of Army Group Popow. The enemy launched repeated heavy counter-attacks against Grischino, but these were halted through adept defense.

In the attack against the Donez, the *Regiment* was given the order on the 24.2.1943 to take the village of Alexandrowka on the Ssamara River. The enemy defended this village with several thousand men, over 20 tanks and heavy artillery. The *I Battalion* were the lead *Battalion* and led a comprehensive attack to the east of Alexandrowka, with the *II Battalion* being ordered to hold the enemy in a frontal attack to the south. Around 13:00 hours the *I Battalion* attack initially went well, but then a violent enemy attack on the edge of the village threatened to force the advance to halt. Advancing with the middle *Kompanie, SS-Sturmbannführer* Dieckmann, who was at the head of that *Kompanie,* encouraged the men forward and he went with them into the violent enemy fire.

The break-in into the city succeeded thanks to his courage. The city of Alexandrowka became a fight for each house and man against man, due to the violent resistance of the enemy.

The enemy left over 100 dead and following equipment behind:

7	Tanks
12	7.62cm anti-tank guns
4	7.5cm rifles
6	Anti-tank rifles
14	Heavy machine-guns
16	Light machine-guns
55	Rapid-firing rifles

And a large amount of hand weapons and grenades

This recommendation was signed by his *Regimental Commander.* There was also a further document dating from the 27th of March 1943 written by the *Divisional Commander, SS-Gruppenführer und Generalleutnant der Waffen-SS* Felix Steiner that highlighted Dieckmann's actions over the preceding year, since his award of his Knight's Cross. It testified to his courage, energy, cool-headedness and personal cold-bloodedness.

The recommendation was approved on the 20th of April 1943, but even this further award for August Dieckmann did not end his association with this award. Further details of what he did next will be covered in volume three.

Jacob Fick
Date of birth: 17.01.1912
SS Number: 3 247
Born in Ulm, he spent time in the *Hitler Youth* from the start of June 1929 until early October 1930. The exact date of his move to the fledgling *SS* is not listed, but his low four-digit *SS* number would indicate this was very early 1930s. What is known is that he was holding the rank of *SS-Untersturmführer* by the 25th of March 1934 and serving in the machine-gun unit within the *Ellwangen Battalion*. He had moved to the *12. Kompanie* within *Deutschland* by mid-May 1935, then on the 20th of April 1936, he had moved to the rank of *SS-Obersturmführer*. In March 1938 he took part in the action in Austria, followed by the Sudetenland in October. The following month, on the 9th of November, he was promoted to *SS-Hauptsturmführer*. In January 1939 he took part in a heavy mortar course in Doberitz then in mid-1939 he had moved to *Deutschland's, 19. Kompanie*. He spent a brief spell in the *4. Kompanie, SS-Kradschutzen Battalion,* before moving to the *SS-Flak Abteilung*. This is the unit that he entered the Second World War with.

He fought in Poland and earned the Second Class Iron Cross on the 7th of October 1939. He then fought in the west and was awarded the Black Wound Badge on the 3rd of June, followed by the First Class Iron Cross on the 20th of July in 1940. He had taken command of the *Flak Abteilung* by then. Following the fighting in the west he spent time at Bad Tolz and also Braunschweig as an instructor, thereby missing the fighting in the Balkans. He was awarded the General Assault Badge on the 26th of April 1941. By mid-September he had moved to the *SS-Freiwilligen Norwegian Legion*. He was promoted further to *SS-Sturmbannführer* on the 20th of April 1942 and by this stage he was back at Braunschweig, but not for long. At the start of May, he was placed with the *Kradschutzen,* in command of the *I Battalion,* within *Langemarck* and fought with them in the latter stages of 1942.

He remained with the *Kradschutzen,* but moved to the *II Kradschutzen Battalion, Das Reich* in late 1942 or early 1943. He found himself in the Kharkov area as the Germans fought their titanic struggle around that city in early 1943. On the 3rd of March he conducted actions that resulted in his award of the Knight's Cross to the Iron Cross. He was recommended by his *Divisional Commander,*

SS-Oberführer Vahl, on the 10th of March 1943. This recommendation covered the following:

'The *SS-Kradschutzen Battalion 2* were ordered on the 3.3.43, to take from the enemy the Berestowaja valley, eastwards to Paraskoweja, the forest that was to the northeast of that and west of Ochotschake and connect with the hard attack of the *Aufklarungs Abteilung* of the *SS-Panzer-Grenadier-Division "Adolf Hitler"*. The *Battalion* was shielding the left flank of the *SS-Panzer-Grenadier-Division "Adolf Hitler"* in the night of the 2. to 3.3.43 in Losowaja and began to pull out in the morning over Perstowaja. It would advance after the work of the *Pioneers* on the large destroyed bridge in Berestowaja, that in the night had divided the *Division,* some of who stood assembled in several columns in the high-lying streets in the east of Losowaja. The *Commander* of the *SS-Kradschutzen Battalion 2, SS-Sturmbannführer* Fick carried out reconnaissance near the bridge and expected a *Battalion* to be there, but they had suddenly pulled out as a southern alarm group. The *Commander* observed a 2km gap on the western heights of Losowaja. The *Commander* observed distances of about 2 km unfold between the advancing infantry on the western heights at Losowaja - Berestowaja. He quickly recognized the dangerous situation for the *Division* and it's vehicles, he gathered everyone that was standing around to use them in the defense and also prepared them for a counter-attack. He immediately controlled the high ground south of Berestowaja through the use of the available infantry and occupied the bridge, not letting the Soviets take this yet. The enemy opened fire with artillery, flak and anti-tank gun fire in open firing positions into the first houses on the western area and their advance proceeded. Without regard to the enemy fire the *Battalion* went into the counter attack against the advancing enemy. The counter attack became divided through the enemy fire from all weapons but the unexpected momentum of the counter attack destroyed the enemy, penetrated into Losowaja and sent the remainder back in a wild retreat, at the same time the enemy losses in men and material were high.

The opponent lost a minimum of a regiment in in this desperate breach attempt:

13 guns	12.2cm
4 guns	7.62cm
1 anti-tank gun	3.5cm
1 17 cm mortar	
1 anti-tank rifle	
28 light vehicles	

An autographed formal photograph of Jacob Fick showing his Knight's Cross award

30 sleds
120 horses
A large amount of hand weapons and artillery ammunition
200 men captured and around 650 dead

Through his quick reaction decision and the complete use of all strength, *SS-Sturmbannführer* Fick in 30 minutes, completely prevented a threatening break-in to the flank of the *SS-Panzer-Grenadier-Division "Adolf Hitler"*, without exception every man of the troop was involved in the fighting.

Through his personal interference prevented a retreat of his own troops in the fore most lines, through the sudden threat to the flank.

Through this, out of his own decision and personal employment penetrating through the attack, created the further prerequisites for the *Aufklarungs Abteilung* of the *SS-Panzer-Grenadier-Division "Adolf Hitler"* for their hard attack upon Ochotschaje.

<u>Attitude of the *Generalkommandos SS-Panzer-Korps:*</u>
I approve the recommendation:
(signed) Hausser"

He was approved for the award of the Knight's Cross to the Iron Cross on the 23rd of April 1943. It is of note that he was also recommended for the award of the German Cross in Gold for actions in February 1943, but this was not approved.

He remained with this unit until late August 1943, when he moved to the *SS-Panzer-Aufklarungs Ausbildungs und Erzatz Abteilung 1*. He stayed there until late November the same year. His next move took him to the newly created *17th SS-Panzer Grenadier-Division 'Gotz von Berlichingen'* as *Commander* of their *SS-Pz.Gren. Rgt. 37.*

At the end of January 1944 he was promoted to *SS-Obersturmbannführer.* He fought during the tough Normandy battles and following this, took over the *SS-Pz.Gren.Rgt. 38.* He is listed as being promoted to *SS-Standartenführer* at the end of March 1945, but just prior to that, he had taken short-term temporary command of the *Division*. He survived the war and died on 23rd October 1978.

Hermann Priess
Date of birth: 24.05.1901
SS Number: 113 258
Born in Marnitz, his military service began in late January 1919, when he joined the *Army*. The same year he spent just over four months serving with the *Freikorps*. He remained with the *Army* until 1932.

He joined the *SS* on the 3rd of March 1933 and served with the *4./II/22. Standarte*. He then moved to the *6./22. Standarte* in mid-October the same year, staying with them until the 7th of April the following year. By this stage he had shown sufficient capabilities to receive promotion to *SS-Hauptscharführer*. His next posting was with the *I Battalion* of *SS-Regiment Germania*. He was a *Platoon Commander* within the *3.* and *4. Kompanies*. He was then promoted to *SS-Untersturmführer* in late February 1935, although he is not listed as attending any of the officer training schools. He was promoted just over six months later to *SS-Obersturmführer* in mid-September. He remained with the *I Battalion* throughout 1935 and also attended the infantry school at Doberitz. At the start of 1936 he moved to the *13. Kompanie,* within *Germania,* staying with them until April 1939. Back on the 13th of September 1936, he had received promotion to *SS-Hauptsturmführer*. From April 1939 he began training with the artillery, receiving promotion to *SS-Sturmbannführer* at the start of June. He was given command of the *II Battalion* with the *SS-VT's Artillerie Abteilung* at the same time, and it was with this unit that he entered the Second World War.

He fought in Poland and was awarded the Second Class Iron Cross on the 22nd of September, followed by the First Class Iron Cross on the 15th of October 1939. He then moved to the newly created *SS-Totenkopf Division* in October. It can be assumed that he fought in the west during 1940, although there is little mention of this on his file. He was promoted to *SS-Obersturmbannführer* at the start of August 1940 and later the same month, was given command of *Totenkopf's Artillery Regiment*. He went with this unit into Russia in June 1941, the same month that he received a promotion to *SS-Standartenführer*. For his leadership of this unit, he was awarded the German Cross in Gold on the 6th of January 1942. He fought in the Demjansk Pocket during 1942 and whilst there, received a further promotion to *SS-Oberführer,* in mid-July.

It was for his actions in Demjansk that was recommended for the award of the Knight's Cross to the Iron Cross. This recommendation was written on the 10th of March 1943 by Max Simon and refers to actions in early February 1942, over one year earlier! It contained the following information:

SS-Oberführer Hermann Priess photographed in 1943 after he was awarded the Knight's Cross, for actions he conducted over one year earlier as an SS-Standartenführer.

Map 11 Army Group North: January - December 1942

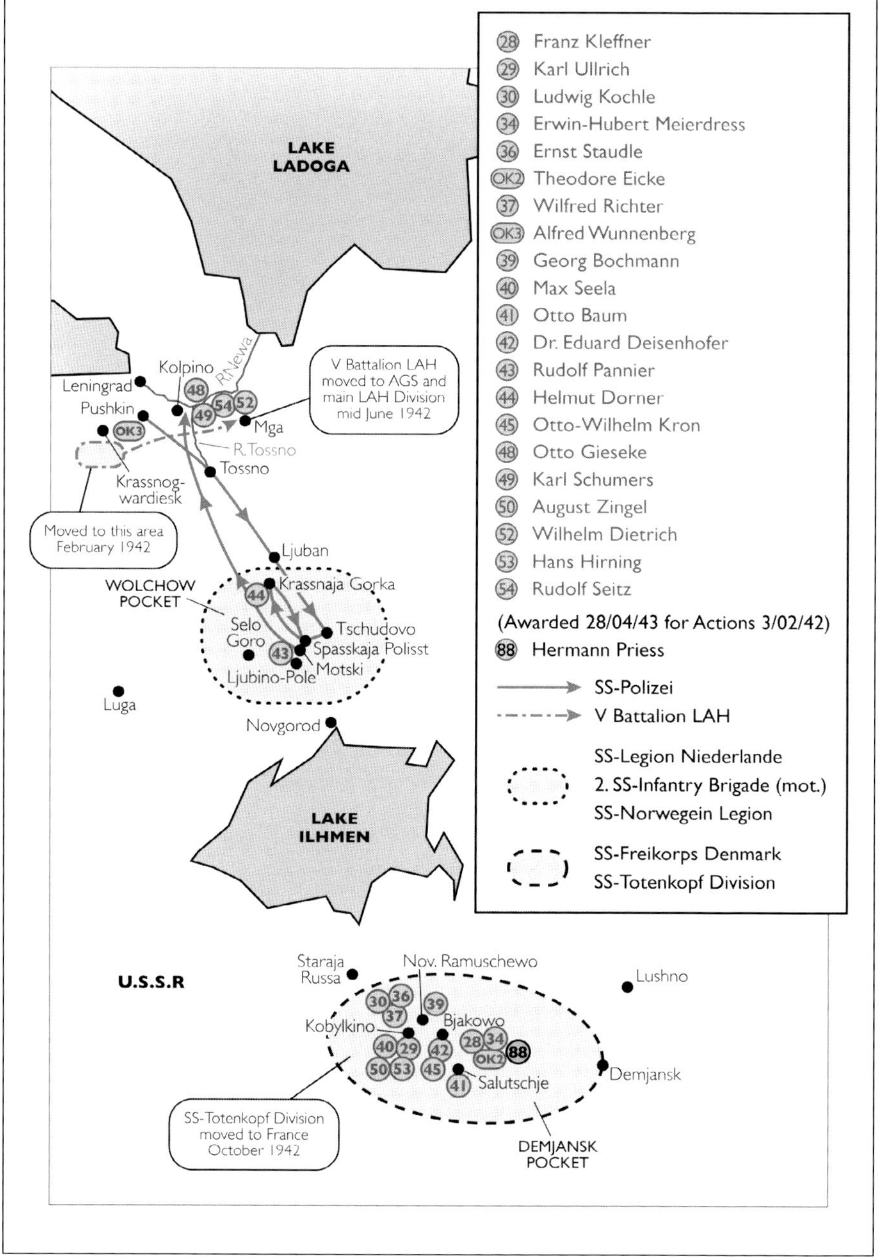

'In the closing of the ring around Demjansk by the Russians on the 3.2.42 *SS-Oberführer* Priess stood as the artillery *Commander* with the *Gruppe Eicke* and had at his disposal all of the standing assembled *Batteries.*

SS-Oberführer Priess attacked again and again in the most-bitter cold against enormous Russian superiority in men and material. With his few *Batteries* and through his nimble leadership, and his quick personal reactions, smashed the enemy.

In the fight with enemy tanks, they had to use the artillery in direct gunfire, because they were lacking other defensive weapons, they broke and annihilated the enemy infantry, *SS-Oberführer Priess* was always to be found at the most dangerous places, through his highest personal achievements he was an example to his men.

It is certain that without the aid of the always-reliable artillery, together with the combination of the infantry, that the overpowering of the enemy would have been impossible to produce.

In the 41km long positions of the cut-off *Gruppe Eicke,* they did not loose one foot wide of ground to the Russian. The fight ended successfully and the 'Fortress Demjansk' was held under the heaviest of conditions, this was a success of decisive importance, that we alone owe to the artful leadership and heroic, exemplary will of *SS-Oberführer* Priess. Through this success was the certain basis for the exit and later explosion of the ring around Demjansk.

I please ask for the award of the Knight's Cross to the Iron Cross for *SS-Oberführer* Priess, in recognition of his decisive result.'

The recommendation was approved on the 28th of April 1943, thereby providing further recognition of the heroic and difficult fighting that *Totenkopf* had endured in the Demjansk Pocket. This award would not end Priess' connection to the Knight's Cross and its' higher grades. More details of that can be found within this volume and will also be covered in the next volume.

Rudolf Sandig
Date of birth: 11.09.1911
SS Number: 10 676
Born in Eppendorf, he was an early entrant to the *SS.* The exact date of joining is not listed, but was holding the rank of *SS-Scharführer (SS-Unterscharführer)* by mid-May 1933. This same document lists him as serving with the *6. Kompanie* at that stage, but the very youthful *LAH* did not contain that many *Kompanies* at that stage! Within six months he had risen to the rank of *SS-Oberscharführer*

SS-Sturmbannführer Rudolf Sandig pictured in the early summer of 1943, after he had been awarded his Knight's Cross.

(SS-Scharführer). He was promoted twice more in 1934, holding the rank of *SS-Obertruppführer (SS-Hauptscharführer)* by late December. He held the appointment of *Spiess* in early 1935, with a move to *SS-Untersturmführer* coming in mid-September 1936. It is not listed whether he attended officer school to achieve this, or which school he attended. By the end of January 1938 he has risen to *SS-Obersturmführer*. Prior to the outbreak of World War II, he took part in the actions in Austria, the Sudetenland and also Bohemia-Moravia, earning the awards for those campaigns.

He took part in the campaigns that opened and defined this new war and new ways of fighting. Whilst in Poland he earned the Second Class Iron Cross on the 9th of October 1939. He followed this by fighting in the west the following summer and earned the Black Wound Badge at the end of May 1940. When the campaign ended, he was awarded the First Class Iron Cross and the Infantry Assault Badge on the 3rd of October the same year. Just prior to this, at the start of September, he had moved to serve within the *7. Kompanie*. He served in the Balkans in early 1941 and was promoted to *SS-Hauptsturmführer* on the 20th of April. He then crossed Russia's border a few months later and for the fighting in this first Russian campaign he was awarded the German Cross in Gold on the 25th of January 1942, followed by the Russian Front Medal later the same year. His capability in leading men was being further recognized and he was given command of the *II Battalion, SS-Regiment 2*, within the *LAH*. A promotion to *SS-Sturmbannführer* came in early November 1942, whilst the *LAH* were in France for their much-needed re-fit.

He returned to Russia in 1943 and was involved in the heavy fighting in and around Kharkov. He conducted actions in February and March that resulted in his recommendation for the Knight's Cross to the Iron Cross. The recommendation was written by his *Regimental Commander*, Teddi Wisch, on the 1st of April 1943. The original documents have not stood the test of time very well and are incredibly difficult to read, due to their general deterioration over the past 65 years. The following overview may not be exact, but will aim to give the main points that resulted in Sandig's award.

It begins on the 15th of February 1943 and mentions Sandig personally leading the men of his *Battalion* as they fought around the airfield at Ossnovo, directly south of Kharkov. It highlights the heavy frontal attacks that they had to contend with from Russians in at least Regimental strength and that, although they were forced to finally give up their positions due to the level of enemy pressure, they managed to inflict heavy losses on the enemy in and around this airfield.

The next event mentioned is the attack on Ogulzy on the 8th of March, as the push back towards Kharkov got underway. Sandig's *Battalion* entered this town in the early morning and spent the entire day fighting through this objective, finally securing it in the evening. It makes note of the loss to the enemy of 3 tanks, 6 anti-tank weapons, 3 heavy mortars and 12 heavy machine-guns. It once again draws attention to Sandig being at the front of the attack and the co-operation between his unit and Peiper's *Battalion*.

The recommendation continues by covering another difficult assault by Sandig and his survivors as they advanced closer to Kharkov and began to assault the city from the north. They attacked the village of Ssewerny and Alexejevka on the northern ring and penetrated into the main rail station. This was all done under strong attack by the defending Russians, who had no intention of giving up this area. The recommendation mentions the speed of the attack by Sandig and the fact that this speed resulted in the success. This particular attack was conducted over the 11th and 12th of March 1943. It did result in success and once again, Peiper's men fought close by.

The document finishes off by summing up *SS-Sturmbannführer* Rudolf Sandig's overall qualities. His *Regimental Commander* assesses that he is an outstanding natural fighter and leader. That he is resolute, and masters all situations without consideration for himself and that he is always in the focal point of the fighting. He finishes by asking for these abilities to be honoured with the high award of the Knight's Cross to the Iron Cross.

In addition to this main award recommendation, there is an additional short document written by Dietrich. It supports the assessment of Sandig as a brave fighter since the start of the war, but in particular the hard winter fighting in and around Kharkov. It mentions his leadership of his *Battalion* and also asks for the award of the Knight's Cross.

The dual recommendation was approved on the 5th of May 1943. Details of Rudolf Sandig's career are very limited after this point. He was promoted further to the rank of *SS-Obersturmbannführer* by late 1944, although the exact date of that promotion is not listed. He survived the war and died on the 11th of July 1994.

Georg Bochmann

Date of birth: 18.09.1913

SS Number: 122 362

We last covered this soldier in Volume 1 of this project, when he was awarded the Knight's Cross, on the 3rd of May 1942 for his actions in the Demjansk Pocket. He had conducted these actions whilst holding the rank of *SS-Hauptsturmführer*, although by the date of the award he had been promoted to *SS-Sturmbannführer*.

A smiling Georg Bochmann seen here wearing his Oakleaves and Knight's Cross.

So, what had he done since May 1942?

He is listed as being in command of the *I Battalion* within *Totenkopf's Panzer Regiment* on the 21st of October 1942, whilst they were in France for their re-fit and expansion. However, he is also listed as being in command of the *II Battalion, SS-Regiment 9* on the same date. Both listing have 'delegated leadership' beside them. At that time, *Totenkopf* had just been sent back to France and were in the process of becoming a *Panzergrenadier Division*. If you also recall from Volume 1, when they arrived in France, they had suffered high casualties. What could have taken place is, someone like Bochmann overseeing two different *Battalions* due to his experience, but also due to the fact that suitable commanders might not have been identified at that early stage. Another document on the same file lists him as commanding the *II Battalion, SS-Regiment 9* (also known as *Regiment 'Thule')*. We will therefore assume that this is whom he commanded at that time.

With the rest of *Totenkopf,* they were sent back to Russia in early 1943 around the Kharkov area. He conducted actions in early March that would result in his recommendation for the Oakleaves to the Knight's Cross. This recommendation was written by his *Divisional Commander,* Max Simon, on the 27th of March 1943 and contained the following information:

'On the 9.3.1943, *Battalion Bochmann* occupied the security line in Schelstovo, as soon as aerial reconnaissance reported disengagement operations of the enemy, *SS-Sturmbannführer* Bochmann dispatched a battle-strong reconnaissance patrol, after he approached the enemy without being noticed, some 13 km from his own lines, he was able to inflict high bloody casualties and claim four driveable trucks, one anti-tank gun (7.62cm) as booty and was able to destroy various cannons, vehicles and sleds. He returned to his point of departure having suffered no casualties.

The task of his *Battalion* on 10.3.43, was to take the village of Krassnokutsk as quickly as possible. This task was accomplished by *SS-Sturmbannführer* Bochmann by utilising an especially clever action of his *Battalion*. He led the lead *Zug* himself and was able to get a very clear picture of the enemy occupation of the village. Since evening had fallen, he decided to avoid a night street fight and attacked the village from three sides. The attack, which he personally led, was a great success. Many enemy dead, numerous cannons, anti-tank guns and much equipment was abandonded by the opponent.

The *Battalion Bochmann* had the task, on 17.3.43 to take the forested area located 3 km southeast of Ssorokovka and with that the villages of Saroshnoje and Tetlega, in conjunction with the *I. SS-Totenkopf-Kradschutzen Regiment "Thule"*. During these attacks *SS-Sturmbannführer* Bochmann displayed excellent bravery.

After the infantry rolled over the first field positions, he roared into the positions on an armoured car and confused the enemy so much that they fled their positions. To take full advantage of this situation, he advanced immediately and with that, gave his *Battalion* the opportunity to quickly approach the village. In the village of Tetlega, which the enemy was bitterly defending, he pushed forward with his *5. Kompanie* and immediately recognized the opportunity to run over the enemy positions in the village and in the shortest time was able to take the northern section of the village. He was also able to establish contact with the *Kampfgruppe* approaching from the south.'

This recommendation was approved on the 17th of May 1943 and gave *Totenkopf* their second Oakleaves holder to date. This award would not end Bochmann's association with the various grades of the Knight's Cross, further details of his actions and subsequent awards will follow in future volumes.

Willi Esslinger

Date of birth: 02.06.1916

SS Number: Unknown

Born in Markertshofen, very little detail of this soldier exists. It is known that he volunteered for the *SS* prior to the outbreak of the war and fought in Poland, holding the rank of *SS-Unterscharführer,* commanding an anti-tank gun crew.

He went west in 1940 and his gun was credited with six 'kills' during that campaign. He was awarded the Second Class Iron Cross on the 27th of May. He joined the newly created *SS-Wiking Division* after that campaign and he moved east with them in 1941. The Frist Class Iron Cross came in the early opening stages, on the 13th of July.

It was whilst fighting in Russia in the first half of 1943 that he was credited with knocking out a further 19 enemy tanks. He was serving in the *3. Kompanie, Panzerjaeger Abteilung 5* at that time and holding the rank of *SS-Hauptscharführer.* He was awarded the Knight's Cross to the Iron Cross on the 19th of June by the *Army Commander.* He was given his high award, not due to the number of destroyed enemy tanks, but more in recognition of his unwavering courage in the face of the enemy.

Details of the action are very limited, but the following is known; he was on the way to refuel with his heavy gun when word arrived that an enemy tank attack was underway, supported by strong infantry elements. Esslinger immediately took his gun towards the enemy and deployed into a firing position. This was in order to delay the enemy attack, whilst he awaited the arrival of his own stronger forces.

SS-Hauptscharführer Willi Esslinger shown wearing his Knight's Cross

He immediately destroyed 3 T-34 tanks, before having to pull back. The enemy called in its' own heavy weapons and under the cover of these, they began their infantry attack. Esslinger changed his firing position several times and carefully selected which enemy target he was going to attack, all the while not letting the enemy infantry attack put him off. By perservering in the face of the enemy, he brought this enemy threat to a halt through his well directed fire.

No other details of the soldier exist after this high recognition. He was killed in Guzowatka, on the eastern front, on the 25th of August 1944 whilst still serving with the *3. Kompanie*. Besides the Knight's Cross to the Iron Cross, he was also awarded the General Assault Badge.

Overview

This almost completed the list of *Waffen-SS* soldiers who were recognized for their actions during the battle of Kharkov alone between February and March 1943. Two more would follow in early July, but at least five others who were later awarded the Knight's Cross, received this award in part for their actions during the Kharkov battle.

As an overview, here was the situation between January and the end of June 1943:

Leibstandarte Adolf Hitler – 1 set of Swords, 2 sets of Oakleaves and 12 Knight's Crosses
Das Reich – 9 Knight's Crosses, 1 set of Oakleaves
Totenkopf – 5 Knight's Crosses, 1 set of Oakleaves
Polizei – 1 Knight's Cross
Wiking – 4 Knight's Crosses, 1 set of Oakleaves
SS-Legion Niederlande – 1 Knight's Cross
SS-Kavallerie Division – 2 Knight's Crosses
SS-Kampfgruppe Schuldt - 1 set of Oakleaves

This was a total of forty-one separate awards for bravery to the men of the *Waffen-SS* and 1943 was only half way through! This was more than the amount awarded during the whole of 1942 for *Waffen-SS* soldiers. We have not finished this volume just yet and there will be further awards before we bring it to a close. So, for now, let us move to the next major battle that grabbed everyone's attention in 1943.

This battle would of course add further Knight's Cross related awards for the men of the *Waffen-SS*, so let's see why.

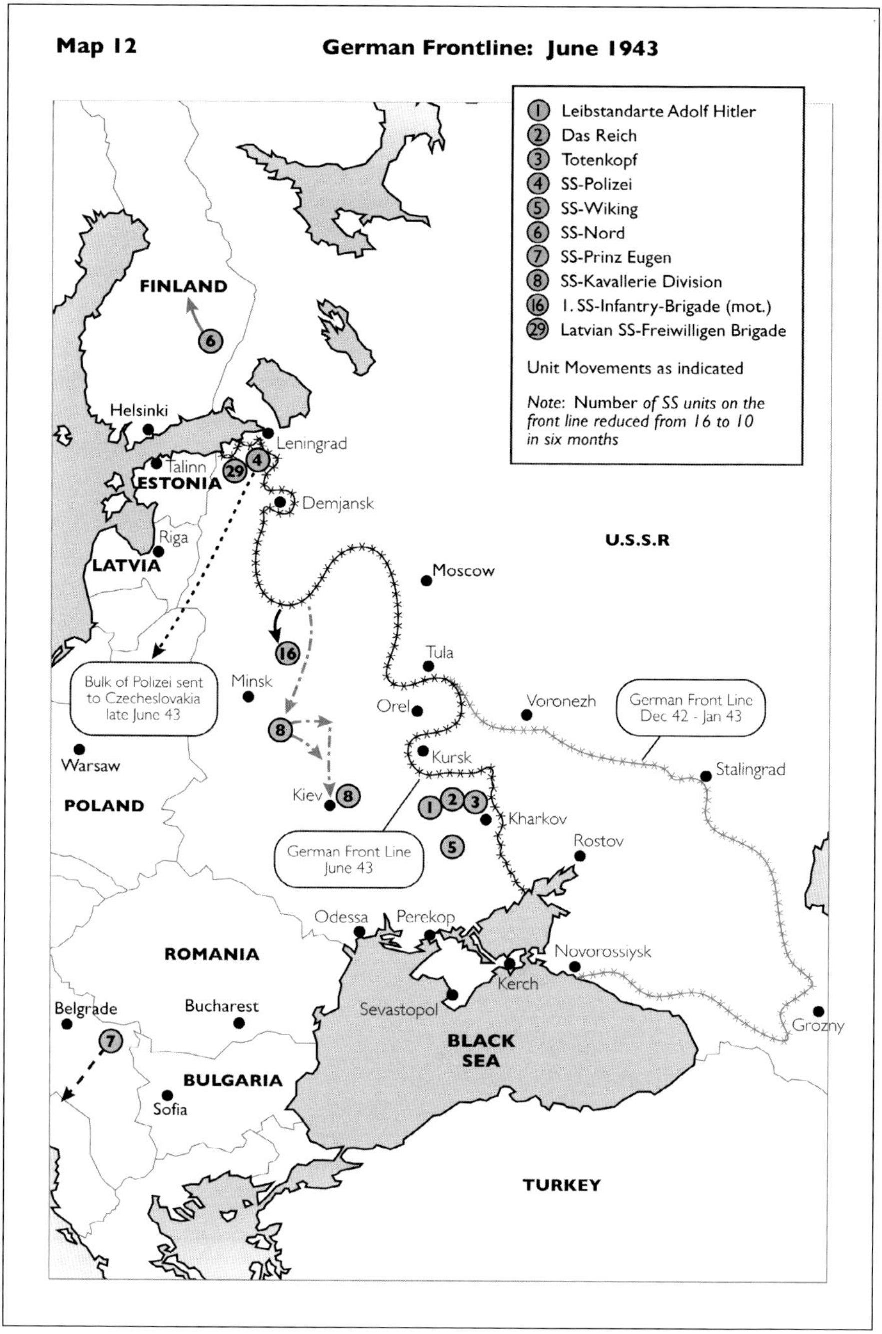
Map 12
German Frontline: June 1943
1 Leibstandarte Adolf Hitler
2 Das Reich
3 Totenkopf
4 SS-Polizei
5 SS-Wiking
6 SS-Nord
7 SS-Prinz Eugen
8 SS-Kavallerie Division
16 I. SS-Infantry-Brigade (mot.)
29 Latvian SS-Freiwilligen Brigade
Unit Movements as indicated
Note: Number of SS units on the front line reduced from 16 to 10 in six months
FINLAND
Helsinki
Leningrad
Talinn
ESTONIA
Demjansk
Riga
LATVIA
U.S.S.R
Moscow
Tula
Bulk of Polizei sent to Czecheslovakia late June 43
Minsk
Orel
Voronezh
German Front Line Dec 42 - Jan 43
Warsaw
Kursk
Stalingrad
POLAND
Kiev
Kharkov
Rostov
German Front Line June 43
Odessa
Perekop
ROMANIA
Novorossiysk
Kerch
Belgrade
Bucharest
Sevastopol
Grozny
BLACK SEA
BULGARIA
Sofia
TURKEY

CHAPTER FIVE

THE KURSK OFFENSIVE

The re-capture of Kharkov back in mid-March was part of the overall German moves to halt the Russian onslaught that was started with the surrender of Stalingrad in the opening weeks of the year.

The focus of the Russian advances was in the south, mainly due to the huge gap opened by the loss of the 6th Army. The Russians also tried to advance in the central and northern regions, but the various German units positioned there did manage to hold their ground on the whole.

This overall situation left a large 'bulge' in the Russian front line. The bottom sector was close to Bjelgorod and the top sector was around the Orel area, in the middle was Kursk and this was the objective for both attacking forces. The furthest extent of this bulge was as far west as Rylsk (Ryl'sk). The German plan, given the code-name of Operation Citadelle, was to cut-off this bulge and destroy the enemy forces within it. The original start date was for early May, but was then postponed again and again until the final start date of 5th July 1943. One of the main reasons for this was Hitler's insistence that the new Panther tanks and Ferdinand assault guns were ready to help in the assault.

Before going into the German preparations for this upcoming assault, we will take the unusual step, within the existing context of this project, of going into more detail than before on the enemy preparations and situation for this forthcoming battle. So, why do this? The reason is due to the fact that, up to this point, the Germans had pretty much had the upper hand. Right from the outset in September 1939, they had pushed back all before them. Although the Russians had prevented the Germans from taking Leningrad and Moscow, they had been unable to seize the initiave. Stalingrad was the start of that process, but as we have seen, the *I SS-Panzer Korps* had been principally responsible for checking these attempts and they well and truly took back the initiative.

So, what had the Russians been up to since their recent defeat in and around Kharkov and the realization that the Germans were not finished yet in respect of their fighting ability? Anyone who looked at the maps at that time could see the overall situation and what the obvious answer would be for an army that wanted to maintain the initiative. The need to 'cut-off' the bulge was obvious, so the Russians set about preparing for this. They spent the intervening months since Kharkov preparing a series of defensive 'belts', designed to blunt the power of any German advance. The belts totaled five separate lines of defense and had multiple, individual gun positions within them, backed up with thousands and thousands of mines in front of them. Within all of this lay the strength of the Russian forces, together with the strong build up of reserves in the rear lines. Approx 1.3 million men, over 3,500 tanks and almost 3,000 aircraft were crammed into this bulge, or positioned behind it. The final 'weapon' that the Russians possessed was the information flowing to them all the way from Bletchley Park in central England. This was where the German enigma code had been broken. The British were able to tell their Russian friends the exact date (each time it was moved back) and time of the upcoming attack. There are accounts on file that show Russian defectors coming over to the Germans in the few days prior to the attack, who were able to tell the exact German troop positions and units in position around the Kursk bulge area.

Now let us look at what the Germans had gathered together in order to destroy their enemy. They amassed around 900,000 men, 3,000 tanks and just over 2,000 aircraft. Around ten percent of the German tank force consisted of the new Panthers and Ferdinands. They did not have the flow of intelligence information that the Russians did regarding the extent of what awaited them, but they did build up a good picture of what was in the immediate area facing them and also used aerial reconnaissance to get an idea of the enemy defences. They too, did not remain idle in the months following Kharkov. They conducted multiple large exercises that were designed to ready them for the upcoming battle, re-equipped their forces and retrained their men. The Germans had proved to the Russians that the war was far from finished and they were extremely confident of success (as were the Russians!). With this huge build up of men and machines, the only thing certain was that there was about to be a mighty and costly clash. So let's see what unfolded for the men of the *Waffen-SS* positioned in this region at that time.

The *SS-Panzer Korps* were still in position in the south around the greater Kharkov area. They were renamed during June to the *II SS-Panzer Korps*; the *I SS-Panzer Korps* was held for use by the *LAH* and *Hitler Youth Divisions,* but would not see action as a *Korps* until one year later. They became part of the *Fourth Panzer Army,* under Hermann Hoth and were positioned in along the southern edge of the bulge, therefore in a prime position to lead the advance towards the goal of Kursk. There has been much written on the climactic battle since the end of the war and many accounts will tell you of the Tiger-tank led *Waffen-SS* advances and the large numbers of these types of tanks that they had. The reality is that there was a total of 34 *Waffen-SS* Tigers within the various heavy tank *Kompanies* that they had at that time. These were divided into eleven each for the *LAH* and *Totenkopf,* with *Das Reich* having twelve. This equates to three-quarters of the normal strength of the later-war heavy tank *Battalions* – hardly a force of hundreds of *SS* Tigers, as some have claimed! The *Waffen-SS* were not given any of the new Panther tanks at this stage, so had to rely on the trusty Panzer IV, the less capable Panzer III and the obsolete Panzer II, as well as numerous Stugs. They would enter this battle with just under 500 armoured fighting vehicles.

SS-Panzer Korps/II. SS-Panzer Korps

As covered previously, the *SS-Panzer Korps* was formed in mid-1942 in France, under the command of Paul Hausser. This *Korps* was used for the first time in the successful Kharkov campaign. With this campaign over, the plans were put in place to raise additional *SS-Korps* that would contain mainly *Waffen-SS Divisions* and build on the recently proven abilities of this fighting force.

The long-term view was to have the *LAH* in the *I SS-Panzer Korps* under the command of Sepp Dietrich, with the *Das Reich* and *Totenkopf Divisions* being in the *II SS-Panzer Korps*. The ability to use the *LAH* leading their own *Korps,* under Dietrich, was not possible in mid-1943, so they remained under Hausser's overall command and became part of the renamed *II SS-Panzer Korps* for the time being. The *II SS-Panzer Korps* therefore retained the three principle *Waffen-SS Divisions*, the *LAH, Das Reich* and *Totenkopf.*

Before we proceed with Citadelle, it is worth pointing out that the first Knight's Cross to be awarded to a *Waffen-SS* soldier in July 1943, was to Artur Phleps. This was on the 4th of July, the same time as the men of the *II SS-Panzer Korps* were moving into their jumping-off points, and will be covered in detail later in this chapter.

So let us now get down to coverage of the individual *Waffen-SS Divisions* who would take part in Operation Citadelle.

LAH

We will start with this unit, as the first 'Citadelle' related *Waffen-SS* Knight's Cross was awarded to a soldier from this *Division.*

Between the 1st and 4th of July 1943, the men of the *LAH* moved from the Kharkov area, up to the northeast, closer to the front line and prepared for their next advance. It was also on the 4th of July that Theodore 'Teddi' Wisch took over control of the *Division* from Sepp Dietrich.

In the closing hours of that day, men of the *LAH* made their initial moves forward to take the important high ground, which included moving towards Jachontoff. This objective was taken in the early hours of the 5th of July and during the remainder of this day the penetration of the Russian lines was deepened. Bykowka was reached by the evening hours and this objective became the extent of the *LAH's* advance on day one.

In relation to this project there were Knight's Cross related actions even on this first day of the operation. Georg Karck conducted actions around Hill 228.6, near Jachontoff in the night of 4th/5th July that resulted in him being awarded the Knight's Cross. Albert Frey was also involved in activities around Jachontoff on the 5th that formed part of his later Oakleaves recommendation. Both of these awards will be detailed in Volume 3. The fighting at this objective would also yield an additional Knight's Cross holder for *Das Reich* and this will be covered in the following pages.

Hermann Dahlke, who had been awarded the Knight's Cross for his actions around Bereka, south of Kharkov during the last campaign, was mortally wounded during the advances on this day. He was not killed instantly, but died later the same day due to the severity of his wounds. The price exacted on the Knight's Cross holders of the *Waffen-SS* was increasing!

The attacks continued on the 6th with them advancing through Jakowlewo and on through Lutschki N, further northeast. The advance extended further to Teterewino, with these positions being consolidated on into the 7th of July, even managing to take an area to the west of Pokrowka. The enemy resistance was growing and increasing numbers of enemy tanks were being thrown into the fight. Rudolf von Ribbentrop was involved in the fighting around Teterewino on the 7th, which formed part of his Knight's Cross recommendation, to be covered in this volume. The *Panzer Regiment Commander,* Georg Schonberger, would be awarded his posthumous Knight's Cross for his activities on this day, to be detailed in the next volume. As with above, elements of *Das Reich* were fighting around Teterewino too, and one of their soldiers would also receive a Knight's Cross for his successful actions there – to be detailed below.

Due to the developing situation and strong enemy tank forces, the thrust was switched from northeast to northwest, through Bol Majatschki, with elements remaining northeast. It was in this eastern sector that Franz Staudegger fought a strong enemy tank force in Teterewino. This action formed the basis of his Knight's Cross award and will be covered shortly. This would be the first of many Kursk-related Knight's Crosses to be awarded. The *LAH* elements fighting in the western sector, fought alongside *Totenkopf* and *Das Reich*.

On the 9th, Rylskij and Ssuch Ssolotino were reached by the *1. Regiment,* where a link was made with *Heer* forces. The attack to the north and northeast could continue in earnest.

The 10th was used for the men to catch their breath and only limited advances were made on this day, the next objective was Prochorowka. Karl Rettlinger and Emil Weisemann were involved in fighting on this day that resulted in them both receiving the Knight's Cross, both of which will be detailed in the next volume. The move on Prochorowka began on the 11th with the *LAH* moving in the centre, *Das Reich* on the right and *Totenkopf* on the left. Limited advances were made through the hilly terrain, but the objectives of Storoshewoje and Wassiljewka were reached. Prochorowka remained out of reach on that day. Rudolf von Ribbentrop added further actions to his Knight's Cross recommendation on this day. The push forwards continued in the early hours of the 12th of July, but even these moves ran into the enemy who were thrusting westwards.

One fight started at 8:00 a.m. near Sw. Stalinsk that involved Kurt Sametreiter and his Panzerjaeger Zug. They engaged and successfully battled with dozens of enemy tanks, this fight resulted in Sametreiter's subsequent award of the Knight's Cross. This will be the final such award to be covered in this volume.

Even before this fight was concluded, further *LAH* elements were beginning their own struggle against additional Russian tanks, slightly north of Sw. Oktjarbrskij. This particular fight involved *Kompanie Commander,* Rudolf von Ribbentrop and also *Battalion Commander,* Martin Gross. They fought at close range against a numerically stronger enemy force and after three hours, succeeded in blunting this enemy thrust. This formed the last part of Ribbentrop's Knight's Cross recommendation and was also the basis for Gross' recommendation – both to be detailed in this volume.

Very close to this area is Hill 252.2, where Werner Wolff became involved in actions that resulted in him also receiving the Knight's Cross, but this will be covered in the next volume.

These *LAH* battles southwest of Prochorowka, on the 12th of July 1943, were the extent of the advances made by this *Division* during this critical offensive. What was not apparent to them was that they were engaging elements of the

Russian reserves that had been moved to this sector. Although the fighting on this day is often associated with Prochorowka, the *LAH* did not actually reach that key objective during this battle. Whilst the *LAH* were battling in front of this objective, *Das Reich* were fighting on the right flank, with *Totenkopf* making advances on the left flank.

The 13th of July seen the *LAH* on a defensive posture as they held this line and defended themselves against various enemy thrusts; an enemy who were trying to find a weak spot. The emphasis for potential further advances rested with *Das Reich* on the right and *Totenkopf* on the left. It was also on this day that Adolf Hitler made his decision to suspend the continuation of Operation Citadelle.

Over the next three days the *LAH* held this area, before then beginning their move back southwards. They had been ordered southwards to the Bjelgorod area for reassignment further south. This was along with their *II SS-Panzer Korps Kameraden* from *Das Reich* and *Totenkopf*. Their moves back through Bjelgorod, then onwards to the southeast, took place over the following week. By the 25th of July the *LAH* were in Artemowka, approx 20 miles northeast of Gorlowka (Horlivka). They were destined to move further to the southeast, but developments in Italy would determine their actual next steps. This will be covered in the next volume, but as July came to a close, they handed over their tanks and prepared to be transported out of Russia for the second time. This short, but intensive campaign cost them around 2,500 dead and wounded.

Das Reich

Like their *LAH Kameraden, Das Reich* moved further north to their start positions for the next attack, during the first few days of July.

The first targets for *Das Reich* was Beresoff and Jachontoff, positioned on the right flank of the *II SS-Panzer Korps* route of advance. The moves towards the target started in the early hours of the 5th of July. They quickly became bogged down due to strong enemy defensive fire and counter-attacks, not helped by the sodden wet ground.

The various attempts to break into Beresoff lasted for over 10 hours, until the objective was taken by 1p.m. This was only after heavy aerial and artillery support. This objective was attacked on all sides during these hours. *SS-Regiment Deutschland* were the lead group here and they had to make their attacks without tank support.

During this battle, Gunther Wisliceny led the way and conducted actions around Jachontoff and Beresoff that resulted in his award of the Knight's Cross. Alois Weber was also involved in the fight for Beresoff and he too became a holder of this award. Both of these will be detailed in this volume. Remember that

Georg Karck and Albert Frey from the *LAH* conducted Knight's Cross actions around this objective on this day also – a tough objective indeed!

Elements of *Totenkopf* were fighting close by and Ernst Haussler, from this unit, received the Knight's Cross for his actions on this day. Two other men, Hans Albin von Reitzenstein and Willy Simke, were involved in actions on the 5th of July that would form part of their later Knight's Cross awards – both of these men were serving in *Das Reich*. All 3 awards will be detailed in the next volume.

The objective for the 6th of July was Lutschki, taken by the afternoon with *SS-Regiment Der Führer* in the lead. The advance was extended north of this town later the same day.

The following day *Das Reich* pushed further eastwards and northwards, taking Petrowski, with fighting around Teterewino and Jasnaja Poljana also taking place. The *LAH* were also attacking Teterewino on the same day from the western flank.

One *Das Reich* soldier conducted actions in this area that would add him to the list of *Waffen-SS* Knight's Cross holders. His name was Joachim Kruger and his award would not follow until late June 1944. By this time, he had already been killed in battle. This successful action will be detailed in later volumes. Sylvester Stadler's actions on this day formed part of his Oakleaves recommendation and will be detailed in Volume 3.

During the 8th of July, *Das Reich* fought off enemy armour-led formations at Kalinin and Lutschki. These were the same enemy formations that von Ribbentrop and Staudegger from the *LAH*, were engaging around Teterewino on this day. The list of Knight's Cross related actions grew rapidly during this day. Helmut Schreiber was added to the list for what he done during the 8th and 9th and this will be detailed in this volume. Two more joined the list, Walter Kniep for his fighting in Lutschki and Johann Thaler for fighting near Teterewino, these two will be detailed in the next volume. Limited advance was achieved by *Das Reich* on the 9th, but their focus was on holding the right flank against further enemy intrusion attempts.

This *Division* continued to provide flanking cover for the main push towards Prochorowka during the 10th. The *LAH* would lead this push, with *Das Reich* moving on their flank and rear. As has been detailed, on the 11th of July, the *LAH* advance hit strong defenses around Hill 252.2 (Werner Wolff's Knight's Cross action and also Kurt Sametreiter's Knight's Cross action at Sw. Stalinsk). This position at Sw. Stalinsk was adjacent to the positions of *Das Reich* on the 11th.

Although the activities of the *Das Reich* and *LAH Divisions* would seem limited at this time, this was due to the emphasis shifting to *Totenkopf* on the left flank and will be detailed next. The enemy were also at a critical point and their reserves were being raced towards Prochorowka in a desparate attempt to halt further German advances.

The enemy armoured reserves hit *Das Reich* throughout the 12th of July, but all attempts to break through were held. This even included using *Das Reich's* captured T-34s against Russian crewed T-34s. The objective of Storoshewoje fell to the control of *Das Reich.* Over the next two days they held their line, then prepared to push further north-eastwards. Next on the list was the town of Belenichino, which fell on the 14th of July and Simon Grascher's part in this gave him the Knight's Cross one month later – to be detailed in the next volume. Iwanowka was taken the same evening. Limited movement was achieved on the 15th due to worsening weather conditions.

We have already highlighted the change in task for the *II SS-Panzer Korps* from the 13th of July, when Hitler ordered 'Citadelle' to be stopped. By the 16th of July, *Das Reich* were busy defending themselves against aerial attacks and then over the following two days, they prepared themselves for their imminent withdrawal back towards Bjelgorod.

As they started their moves south, they counted the cost, with approx. 2,500 dead and wounded. Between the 19th and 23rd of July, *Das Reich* were moved southeast, via Kharkov, to an area near Isjum for initial employment there. This was then changed and they traveled further to the southeast via Konstantinowka (Kostjantynivka) and Gorlowka (Horlivka) towards the Mius River area. This new area was reached around the 27th of July 1943 and this was the same time that the *LAH* were being ordered to Italy. *Das Reich* were in Charzyssk at this stage and this is where we will leave the coverage of this unit, as they readied themselves for their next offensive in the south.

Before leaving them, it is worth highlighting the fact that *Das Reich Divisional Commander,* Walter Kruger's later Oakleaves award was made in part for the performance of his unit's actions during the Kursk battles. This will be detailed in the next volume of this project.

Now for details of the remaining *Waffen-SS Division* fighting within the *II SS-Panzer Korps* during July 1943.

Totenkopf

Totenkopf's moves mirrored that of its' sister *Waffen-SS Divisions, LAH & Das Reich,* moving up from the south into position close to the front line, in the opening days of July.

We have touched on the fact that they initially moved alongside *Das Reich* in the opening hours of the 5th of July towards Beresoff. As previously highlighted,

Map 13 **Kursk Offensive: Knight's Crosses awarded to end July 1943**

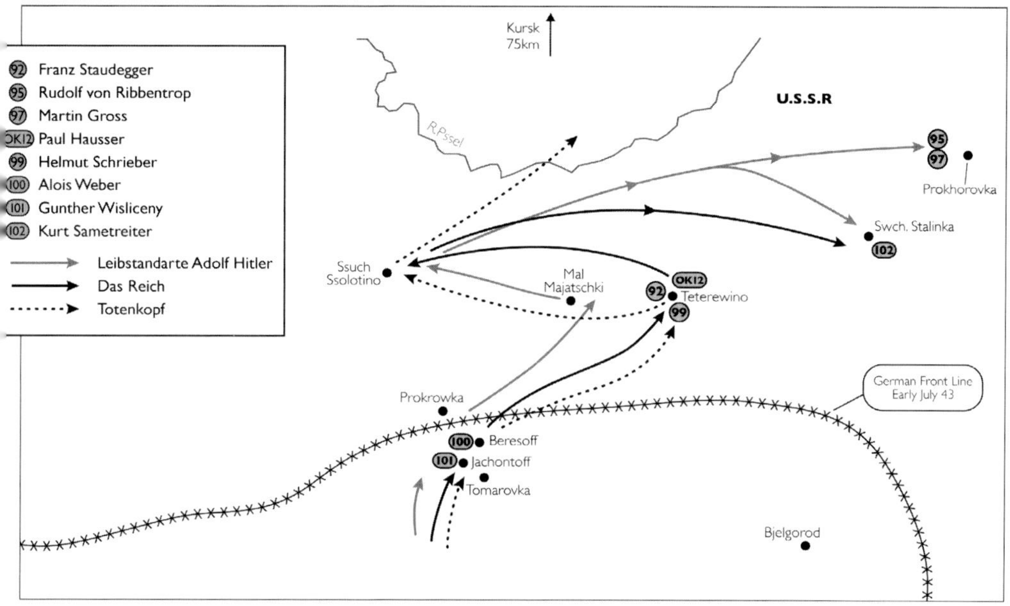

the *II Battalion, Regiment 5 Commander,* Ernst Haussler, led *Totenkopf's* attack around this area and he was later awarded the Knight's Cross, which will be detailed in Volume 3. They fought for control of the hills and forests in this area.

They continued their push on the eastern flank over this first day and the following two days. Due to the developing enemy threat, *Totenkopf* were relieved and moved to the northeast during the 8th and 9th of July. They initially moved through the town of Lutschki and Teterewino, where there were further clashes with the enemy. Elements fought further westwards at Ssuch Ssolotino. They were then given the order to cross the bend in the Psel River, which was west of Prochorowka.

This move was started on the morning of the 10th of July 1943. By the late afternoon they had succeeded in making a crossing and establishing a bridgehead. At the same time, further south, the *LAH* and *Das Reich Divisions* were making limited advances. This *Totenkopf* bridgehead was placed under heavy enemy attacks, as they tried to eradicate this dangerous threat.

This bridgehead and the area surrounding the *Totenkopf* positions to the south of the river were expanded on the 11th, but only under very difficult weather conditions and against increasingly numerical enemy attacks. The enemy was under extreme threat at this time and they were rushing strong reserves into this area to stop further German advances. The focus of these halting moves came on the 12th and has been covered in the preceeding pages, as the *LAH* and *Das Reich Divisions* held their line against this Soviet armoured onslaught. This enemy armoured force also hit *Totenkopf* further northwest, as this was regarded as the most dangerous threat by the Russians.

Ersnt Dehmel, from *Totenkopf's* Stug *Battalion*, fought within the Psel positions on the 11th that resulted in his Knight's Cross award over one month later – to be detailed in Volume 3. Another *Totenkopf Division Kameraden,* Kurt Launer, conducted successful actions also within this bridgehead, on the 12th of July that resulted in him receiving the Knight's Cross. Launer was the *II Battalion, SS-Regiment 6 Commander* and he received his award on the same day as Dehmel and Haussler, all to be detailed in the next volume.

Throughout the 12th, *Totenkopf* dealt with repeated and strong enemy armour-led attacks. These were on both sides of the northern bridgehead and also along the right flank of their positions south of the river. This situation for *Totenkopf* continued over the next five to six days, until they were ordered to pull back. This was due to Hitler's earlier decision to suspend the overall continuation of this offensive. It was only after they withdrew that the enemy was able to take back control of this vital river bend. *Totenkopf* had once again proved their ability to withstand intense enemy attacks without faltering, just as they had done in Demjansk the previous year.

One remaining *Totenkopf* soldier, Erwin Meierdress, was later awarded the Oakleaves to his existing Knight's Cross in part for his actions during the Kursk Offensive between the 7th and 12th of July 1943. This will also be detailed in the next volume.

Totenkopf joined *Das Reich* and *LAH* in the move southeast, although not immediately, so following behind *Das Reich*. They joined their *Das Reich* neighbours in the closing days of July and prepared for their next fight.

They left the Kursk region with the knowledge that they had given their all and held the line. This was at a cost of over 2,000 casualties during these eventful two weeks. We will end coverage of them at this stage and re-join them in their Mius positions in Volume 3.

Now, what had *Wiking* been up to during July 1943?

Map 14 **Isjum Area: Late July 1943**

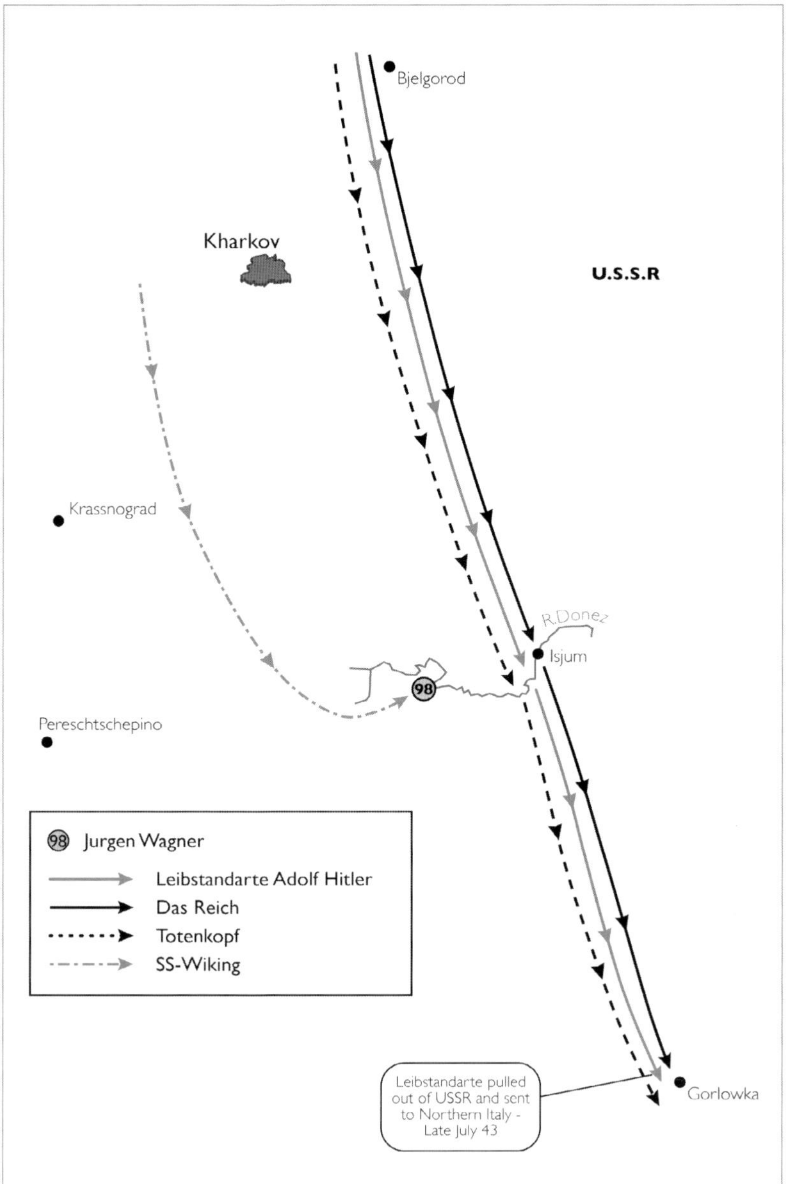

Wiking

We last covered *Wiking* in late June, as they were preparing for the next offensive.

On the 4th of July, *Wiking* were moved from Losowaja, further north to the Slawiansk area and placed as reserve. They were then moved further north again the following day. Would the training during the recent exercise now be put to good use?

As the Kursk attack unfolded between the 5th of July and its' climax one week later, *Wiking* remained in their reserve positions west of Kharkov. They were finally requested to assist on the 13th of July, but before they moved out to get involved in this struggle, they had to move back south to counter a strong Russian push closer to previously held positions. This was the same enemy push that the *II SS-Panzer Korps* were initially sent south to halt.

Wiking led the moves to this area, as their *Waffen-SS Kameraden* still had to disengage from their existing fight. Would we soon be seeing these four *Waffen-SS Divisions* fight alongside each other in one area? *Wiking's* lead elements reached their objective on the evening of the 17th of July and went into the attack the following day. First on their target list was Ssrednij, followed by Ssawodskoj and Andrejewka. Over the next four days, *Wiking* fought in and around these areas against a well-prepared and strong enemy force. They did not succeed in rolling up this enemy incursion, but it did manage to halt further enemy advances in this area at that time. A stalemate developed in this immediate area for the remaining days of July 1943.

In the fighting that took place between the 18th and 21st of July, a number of *Wiking* soldiers were involved in actions that resulted in their subsequent award of the Knight's Cross, or its' higher grades. The first of these was Jurgen Wagner, whose actions will be covered in this volume. The remaining soldiers, Georg Eberhardt, Walter Schmidt, Albert Muller, Hans Juchem, Gunther Sitter and August Dieckmann will all be covered in Volume 3, as their awards came after the end of July 1943.

We will now leave the coverage of *Wiking* at this time and before detailing the Knight's Crosses awarded during July 1943, let us cover the remaining *Waffen-SS* units on the front line and elsewhere in that month.

SS-Kavallerie Division

We left this unit in late June, as they were being moved to the southern sector of the Russian Front. They were engaged in operations between Ovruch and Belekurichi throughout July against a substantial force of Partisans. There were notable successes against this enemy force in late July 1943.

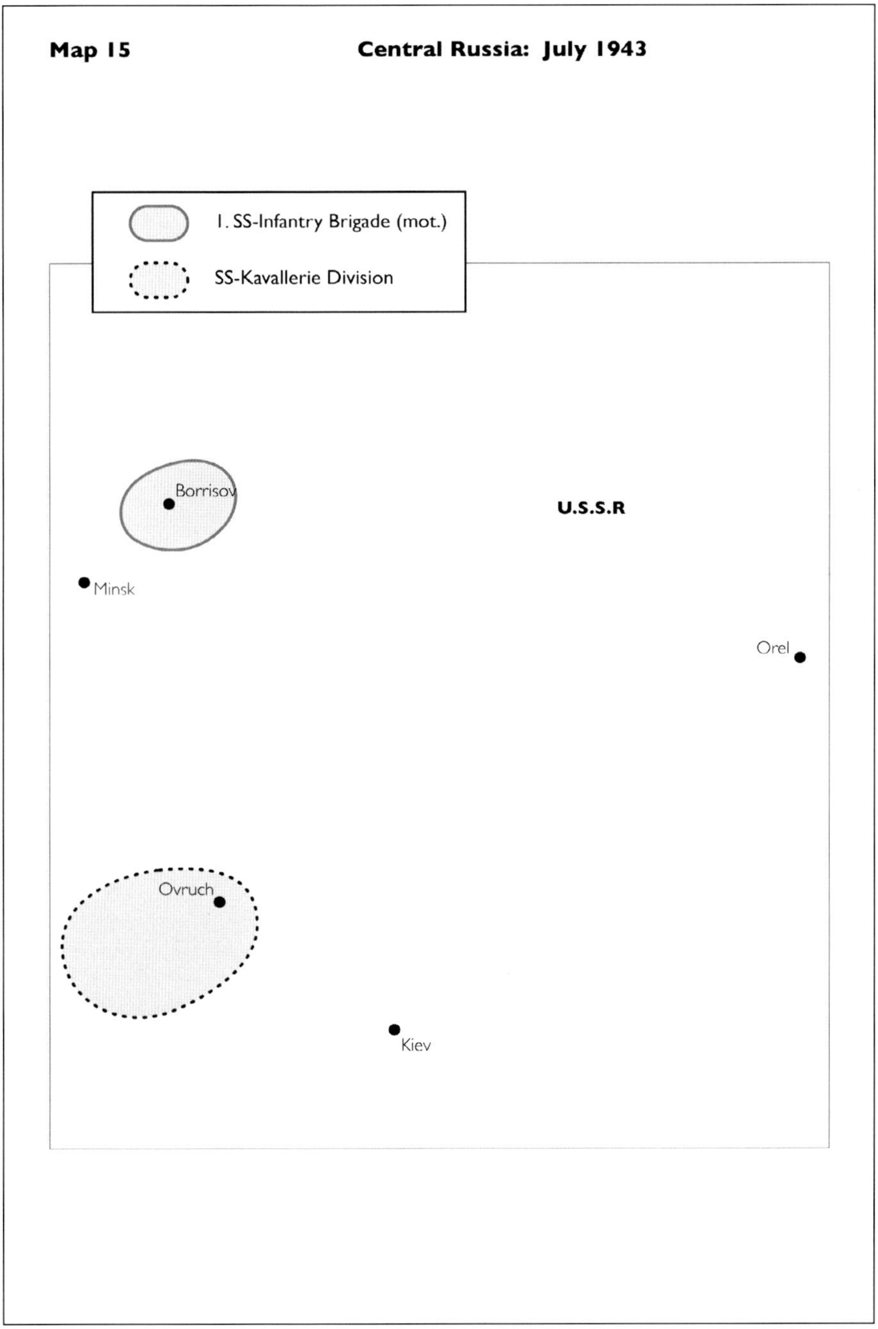
Map 15
Central Russia: July 1943
1. SS-Infantry Brigade (mot.)
SS-Kavallerie Division
Borrisov
U.S.S.R
Minsk
Orel
Ovruch
Kiev

1. SS-Infantry Brigade (mot.)
They became involved in an anti-Partisan sweep near Borrisov, east of Minsk, in early July 1943, known as Operation Hermann.

Nord
There were no significant changes for this *Division* as they remained in their 'static front' positions in July 1943.

Latvian SS-Freiwilligen Brigade
Located near the front line around Leningrad, they continued with the dual task of defending their positions and also training their new recruits. There were only minor engagements for this unit during July, which helped in their overall task of training and expansion.

Prinz Eugen
Now under the command of von Oberkamp, this unit conducted limited activities during July 1943, following their intensive and costly battles against the Partisans that lasted up to the June. There were smaller attacks against the enemy in the northeast of their headquarters position, which was back in Sarajevo.

Within the context of this project, July was very eventful for *Prinz Eugen*. On the 4th of July, Artur Phleps was approved for the Knight's Cross to the Iron Cross for his leadership of this *Division* in the first half of 1943. *Battalion Commander,* Bernard Dietsche was also approved for the Knight's Cross on the 17th of July for his successful leadership around the Krusevic area in late May; both of these awards will be detailed in this volume.

Polizei
As covered in preceding chapters, the bulk of this unit had been removed from the front-line as they underwent re-formation into a *Panzergrenadier Division*. They were considered combat-ready once again and in mid-July they were moved to the Balkans region and prepared for their next tasks. These will be covered in Volume 3.

What about the non-frontline units?

III. (Germanic) SS-Panzer Korps
This additional *SS-Korps* was ordered to be formed, earlier, in April 1943 and was placed under the command of Felix Steiner. They were established in Grafenwohr, Germany, and it is of interest to note that the initial units subordinated to it included *Wiking,* although this was quickly changed.

The units that did come under their control was the newly forming *SS-Panzergrenadier Freiwilligen Division Nordland* and also the *SS-Freiwilligen Brigade Nederland.* As both of these units were undergoing training or formation, this *Korps* would not be active for the time being.

V. SS-Freiwilligen Gebirgs Korps

This specialist mountain-based *Korps* was also ordered to be formed in April 1943 and was placed under the command of Artur Phleps, who at that time was still engaged in fighting in Yugoslavia. Once *Prinz Eugen* finished its' fighting in May/June 1943, Phleps was able to hand over command of his old *Division* and start to place his efforts on the raising of this new *Korps.* His old *Division, Prinz Eugen,* was one of the units designated to be part of this *Gebirgs Korps.* Their formation began in Milowitz, near Prague.

I. SS-Panzer Korps

This new *Korps* was ordered to be formed in late June/early July 1943, as the *II SS-Panzer Korps* finished their preparations for 'Citadelle'. The headquarters was established in Beverloo, Belgium under the command of Sepp Dietrich. There was limited activity for this new formation in July 1943. One of the units designated to serve within this *Korps* was the *LAH,* who were busy fighting in southern Russia at that time.

IV. SS-Panzer Korps

This particular formation is difficult to track, due in part to conflicting information regarding it. This includes the date of formation, which ranges from June through to August 1943; the fact that June is mentioned, is why we have included it in this volume.

The first commander is listed as Alfred Wunnenberg, the former *Polizei Commander.* Their formation location is listed as Potiers in France and they are listed as being responsible for overseeing the raising of the new *SS-Divisions* located in France at that time. This would have meant that *Hohenstaufen* and *Frundsberg* would have come under its' command. However, neither of these units list being part of this formation in their own histories, which only adds to the overall confusion! We will aim to continue the coverage of this unit in the next volume.

The various *Korps* detailed above have been listed in formation date order (apart from the *II. SS-Panzer Korps),* rather than numerical order. This completes the list of *SS-Korps* in existence at the end of July 1943, so now onto the remaining *Divisions.*

Hohenstaufen

As covered in the previous chapter, in early June they moved to Amiens in order to facilitate their training further; they needed a larger training area. Elements of the *Flak Abteilung* were involved in fighting against *Allied* planes and they suffered their first losses, whilst still training! They remained in this area during July 1943.

Frundsberg

In July they focused on their continued training and formation in the Alsace area. They did not have any of the 'excitement' that their *Hohenstaufen Kameraden* had!

SS-Panzergrenadier Freiwilligen Division Nordland
& SS-Freiwilligen Brigade Nederland

Various political arguments ensued regarding this unit, during the summer months of 1943, whilst the principle units of the *Waffen-SS (LAH, Das Reich, Totenkopf, Wiking, etc.)* were fighting their titanic struggles in Russia.

SS-Legion-Niederlande did not remain with this unit, but was extracted and increased in strength to its' own *Brigade*. This *Brigade* was sent to Thuringia for further training and will be covered in more detail in the next volume.

Various name changes took place for this new *Division* that included *'Warager', Germanic Volunteer Division & Freiwilligen Division Nordland. SS-Brigadeführer* Fritz von Scholz, who was awarded the Knight's Cross in early 1942, was placed at the head of this new *Division*.

Hitler Youth

It was during July that the first volunteers arrived at Beverloo, with the *Panzer Regiment* being formed at Mailly le Camp. Unlike some of the other units raised in 1943, the training of the *Hitler Youth Division* lasted a full year, into the opening days of June 1944. There were difficulties in getting enough personnel, *NCO*s and officers. Vehicles and equipment also took time and delayed training. Emphasis was placed on getting the boys physically fit, then they focused on weapons training.

Latvian SS-Freiwilligen Legion/Division

This recently created *Division* continued with its' basic training at the various locations within Latvia during July 1943.

Croat SS-Freiwilligen Division

At the start of July 1943 they were renamed the *Croatian SS-Freiwilligen-Gebirgs Division*. In mid-July they came from the Wildflecken and Goslar camps. Initial training and formation was still in its' early stages.

SS-Freiwilligen Division Galizien

This *Division* was formed on the 30th of July 1943 and based in Heidelager, Debica, Poland – although recruits had been arriving since mid-July. The first *Commander* was *SS-Brigadeführer* Walter Schimana. This unit will be covered in more detail in the next volume.

Estonian SS-Freiwilligen Brigade

This formation continued with their training at Heidelager throughout July, meaning that two of the *Waffen-SS'* units were being trained in the same locations at the same time.

SS-Karstwehr Battalion

This unit was placed on alert in early July 1943, as the political situation in Italy rapidly worsened. When Mussolini resigned in the closing days of that month, *Karstwehr* readied themselves for their first actions. We will cover the details of those actions in the next volume.

Sturmbrigade Reichsführer-SS

You may recall that this formation was sent to Italy towards the end of June 1943 to help in the worsening situation. They did not remain in Italy for long, as in July, they were transported by ship and plane from Livorno in Italy to the island of Corsica, off the west coast. They continued in their preparations for their involvement in actions.

SS-Sturmbrigade Langemarck

They continued their training in the Heidelager area, near Debica during July 1943.

SS-Sturmbrigade Wallonien

Positioned in the Wildflecken training area, south of Fulda, they too continued their focus on training under *SS-Sturmbannführer* Lucien Lippert's watchful eye.

SS-Sonderverband z.b.V. Friedenthal

This unit was the foundation of what became the *SS-Jagdverbande,* but they started life under the title *Sonderlehrgang z.b.V. Oranienburg* in mid-April 1943. They were very small at the outset, but expanded to three *Kompanies*. It was placed under the command of *SS-Hauptsturmführer* Otto Skorzeny and by June 1943 they had changed their name to *SS-Sonderverband z.b.V. Friedenthal.*

This unit was 'officially' formed on the 5th of August 1943, although just over one week before, Skorzeny had received a direct order from Hitler that would catapault him and his new unit into the world's glare and infamy. That order from Hitler was to rescue his old ally Benito Mussolini from his imprisonment in Italy. This unit and its' first operation will be covered in detail in the next volume.

Kursk Summary

Following on from the success at Kharkov, we have once again seen the focus of the fighting on the Russian Front remained in the southern sector. The delays that took place regarding the start date only allowed the Russians to build extensive and effective fortifications, designed to halt any German advance attempts.

We have also covered how these defenses did indeed make life very difficult for the soldiers of the *Waffen-SS* as they aimed to punch forward. The actions in overcoming these extensive obstacles resulted in further recognition and awards of the Knight's Cross for some of these men.

A lot of myth and inaccuracy exists regarding this offensive, but it only requires the reader to dig below the surface of these inaccuracies to see what the facts are. Everything from grossly exaggerated accounts of the number of tanks involved in the 'Prochorowka' battle on the 12th of July (although actually fought in the area to the west of Prochorowka), to 'hundreds' of *Waffen-SS* Tigers being destroyed – despite the fact that they had no more than 35 available at the start of July, through to accounts of these *Waffen-SS* soldiers being completely exhausted and incapable of fighting after Prochorowka. The reality of this last inaccuracy is that they had managed to make their most significant gains (*Totenkopf* on Pssel River bend) at the height of this battle. If they were incapable of fighting at this stage, why were the Russians so concerned at this *Totenkopf* advance and why did they throw so much resource into trying to stop it? Also, if they were incapable of fighting, why were two of the *Waffen-SS Divisions* engaged in new actions in the southern area of Russia before the end of the month, whilst the *LAH* were being rushed to Italy to help there?

The reality is that decisions at the highest levels dictated what unfolded for the soldiers of the *Waffen-SS,* not their fighting abilities. We will go into this in more detail at the end of this volume.

The Kursk Offensive became the last major attack launched on the Russian Front, although other, smaller offensive actions would take place against this 'eastern enemy' before the war's end, as they advanced towards Berlin.

A total of 8 Knight's Crosses, plus 1 set of Oakleaves were awarded by the end of July for actions during the recent Kursk Offensive. All of these will be detailed in the following pages, but add to this, the 21 other Knight's Crosses or higher grades that would be awarded solely, or partly, for actions during the Kursk offensive. These will be detailed in the next volume of this project.

One remaining consideration should be made when thinking of 'Kursk'. We have detailed how *Wiking* were held in reserve, west of Kharkov. What difference would have been made to the outcome of this battle, if they had of been added to the fight around the 10th or 11th of July, when the *LAH* and *Das Reich Divisions* were becoming bogged down? They had proved their worth up to this point and their fighting capability. They had been training hard for this forthcoming action in the months preceding the attack, but were left idle as the initiative passed from the Germans to the Russians.

Their involvement and difference to the final outcome is something that will have to remain as speculation, but this unknown outcome is still a topic of discussion amongst surviving *Wiking Kameraden* today!

Now that we have covered all of the activities of the various units up to the end of July 1943, let us detail the individuals that were awarded the Knight's Cross or higher grades up to the same point in time.

Artur Phleps
Date of birth: 29.11.1881
SS Number: 402 214
He was born in Birtholm, Siebenburgen – this was part of the former Austro-Hungarian Empire, but was ceded to Romania after World War I – and started his military career at the age of 14. He finished his initial training with the rank of officer cadet four years later; he then moved to start his long career as a mountain soldier.

He became a *Second Lieutenant* in late 1901 and then *First Lieutenant*, six years later. In that time he changed *Battalions*. He attended a further training course and in the first half of 1908 he joined the *General Staff Corps*. He became a *Captain* in late 1911, having served in various positions during this interim time. He moved to a posting in the Balkans prior to World War I.

The highly experienced and multi-decorated Artur Phleps photographed after he added the Knight's Cross to his long list of existing awards from both World Wars and inbetween!

During World War I he moved to the rank of *Major* in 1916, then to *Lieutenant-Colonel* a few weeks prior to the end of the war. He had held a variety of postings during the war that included *Quartermaster.* By the end of this war he had been awarded the Second Class Iron Cross and the Black Wound Badge, as well as twelve other awards.

In the inter-war years he initially served in the National Guard within his home area, but in early 1919 he took on Romanian nationality and joined their army. He stayed with the Romanian Army until mid-August 1940. In that time he rose to the rank of *Lieutenant-General* and had been the *Commanding General* of the Romanian Mountain Troops during this time. He had been very busy during that time and had commanded *Regiments, Brigades* and *Divisions* and also held *Korps* level commands. By the time he resigned from the Romanian Army, he was regarded as one of *the* best mountain warfare experts.

His services were in demand and he was persuaded to join the *SS* at the end of June 1941, given the initial rank of *SS-Oberführer.* He was sent to *Wiking* and a few days later assumed command of *SS-Regiment Westland.* In July 1941 he was awarded the Clasp to the Second Class Iron Cross and also the First Class Iron Cross, as well as the Infantry Assault medal. He stayed with them until late January 1942 and in that time fought in their difficult battles in southern Russia in the second half of 1941. In late 1941 he had been promoted to *SS-Brigadeführer und Generalmajor der Waffen-SS.*

He was tasked with raising a new *SS Mountain Division* by Himmler himself and this process began in February. You will know from Volume 1 that this new unit came to life at the start of March 1942. Seven weeks later he was promoted to *SS-Gruppenführer und Generalleutnant der Waffen-SS.* He raised this new *Division* throughout the rest of 1942 and led them in their first battles in the Balkans at the end of this year and into early 1943, as has been covered in the preceding chapters of this volume. During September 1942, he was awarded the Russian front Medal for his services with *Wiking.*

His experience at higher-level commands was needed and in June he was ordered to raise the *V. SS-Gebirgs Korps.* Before the end of that month he had been promoted to the rank of *SS-Obergruppenführer und General der Waffen-SS.* On the first day of July 1943 Heinrich Himmler penned a recommendation for the award of the Knight's Cross for Phleps for his recent successes in the former Yugoslavia. The recommendation read as follows:

'*SS-Obergruppenführer und General der Waffen-SS* Artur Phleps, as *Commander* of the *SS-Freiwilligen Division "Prinz Eugen",* has carried out in the period from 20. January through to the 9. March 1943, Operations "White" I and II.

In these actions he has proved his worth through this far-sighted, energetic and flexible troop leadership. During the decisive attack from the area of Bos. Petrovac in the general direction of Bos. Grahavo in the period from 23. to 28.2.43 it must be credited only to the personality of the *Divisional Commander* that the *Division* could reach the Petrovac-Drvar road. This was accomplished in spite of the snow more than one meter deep in the mountainous area, that they had to cross, and the countless tree and road blocks.

Through a wide deployment of all forces the opponent, in a strength of four brigades, was surprised. His will to fight was definitely broken, so that in the subsequent course of the operation he was unable to offer any more serious resistance.

Only through the personal action of *SS-Obergruppenführer* Phleps, the *Division* managed to reach Livno and later the bauxite mines west of Mostar. The losses of the enemy amounted to 1,930 counted and 1,673 more estimated enemy troops dead, 2,378 wounded. In addition a large booty of heavy and light machine guns and a large number of horses and vehicles were taken.

In the ensuing development of the mopping-up in this zone, on 15.5.43 the *SS-Freiwilligen Division "Prinz Eugen"* pushed from the area of Mostar and Capljina further to the southeast. That made it impossible for the Tschetnik units to accomplish an orderly retreat out of the area. Within the shortest time the *Division* was able to reassume the advance in a southeastward direction over the completely desert-like and strongly mountainous land in the areas of Niksic and Gornje-Polje. With his initiative, the *Divisional Commander* made it possible to overcome this arid terrain. The *Division* won a favourable starting position for the encirclement of the opponent withdrawing from the Turmidor mountain area.

The advance towards Savnik against tough resistance by the enemy was worked out in three days. The *Division* succeeded in capturing, through sudden attacks, the three crossings over the 400-meter deep ravine near Savnik. With that, the way for a later advance in the direction of Zablaj was opened.

In cooperation with the *Army 1. Gebirgs Division,* which advanced to the east of the *SS Division,* they prevented the escape of the enemy in a southeastern direction. During this time, to the north of the *Division's* flank, the Partisans had assembled strong forces in the area of Piva, Drina and the Sutjeska arch. They wished to force a breakthrough in the southern and northern directions.

In the night of 30. to 31. May the *Division* reached the order to relieve all available elements from the area of Savnik. They were hastily thrown in the left flank to hinder the enemy breakthrough from the area of Mratinje in a southerly direction. Thanks to the personal energy of *SS-Obergruppenführer* Phleps, within two days and two nights the hurriedly assembled vehicles, three *Battalions,* two heavy motorized *Batteries,* two Flak *Platoons* and two tank *Kompanies* could be thrown into the area of Avtovac, 180 kilometres further away.

Through the ruthless advance over the 2,000-meter high Maglic mountain and wide frontal pressure in the area north of the Cemerno-Sattels the *Division* succeeded. In cooperation with the right flank of the *118. Infanterie Division,* they closed the pocket in the north.

The physical and fighting performance of the *SS-Freiwilligen Division "Prinz Eugen"* in this wild, rough and remote mountainous area, in the middle of snowstorms, rain and fog, must be considered excellent. The actions crown all to date services of this kind by the *SS-Gebirgs-Division "Prinz Eugen".*

The quick carrying out of the operations starting out from the Narenta until Piva. Next came the tactically difficult task involving a big movement switch of the focal point of the *Division* from the right to the left flank. The operation closed the pocket in Maglic area and denied the harassed enemy any rest. It broke down his will to resist in such a way that he collapsed.

SS-Obergruppenführer Phleps has in these operations especially distinguished himself through his personal bravery and superior troop leadership. The successes of his *Division* must be credited, in the first place, to the fighting procedures developed by him and to the extreme toughness employed in the training of his *Division.*

I ask that the *Commander* of the *SS-Freiwilligen Division "Prinz Eugen", SS-Obergruppenführer und General der Waffen-SS* Artur Phleps, in consideration of his outstanding performance, be awarded the Knight's Cross of the Iron Cross.

The *Reichsführer-SS*
Heinrich Himmler'

It must have been an honour indeed to have been personally recommended by the *Reichsführer-SS* for such a high award. Although he was not held in high regard by the men within the *Waffen-SS,* he was afterall, the head of that organization. The author has not come across any other recommendations written by Himmler up to this point. This recommendation was approved very quickly and only three days later, on the 4th of July 1943, Artur Phleps became the first Knight's Cross holder of *Prinz Eugen,* although he had moved on from command of that unit by then. This recognition would not end his association with this medal or its' grades, but details of that will follow in future volumes.

Franz Staudegger
Date of birth: 12.02.1923
SS Number: Unknown
Born in Bleiburg, Austria, he served in the *Hitler Youth* in the 1930s, before joining the *LAH* in July 1940. By March 1942 he was holding the rank of *SS-Sturmmann*. He was a Panzer III *Commander* during the Kharkov fighting (serving in the same *Light Platoon* as Michael Wittmann) and was awarded the Second Class Iron Cross on the 20th of March 1943; this was quickly followed by the Tank Assault Badge in Silver at the start of April. He then moved to the *LAH's, 13. (Schwere) Kompanie,* within their *Panzer Regiment*. This *Kompanie* was equipped with the Tiger tank and it was as a *Commander* of one of these Tiger tanks (tank number 1325) that Staudegger entered the Kursk offensive. On the second day of the Kursk offensive he was awarded the Iron Cross First Class. Two days after this, on the 8th of July, he conducted actions in his Tiger that resulted in his rapid recommedation for the Knight's Cross.

This recommendation was written by his *Regimental Commander,* Schonberger, on the 9th of July and went as follows:

'On 8.7.1943 the *SS-Panz. Reg. 1/LSSAH* launched an attack west from Teterevino. The *Regiment* had been relieved by elements of the *"Deutschland" Rgt.* on the morning of the same day. Several hours after the *Regiment's* departure an armoured formation of 50-60 T-34s was sighted attacking from the northeast.

As *Commander* of an unserviceable tank, *SS-Unterscharführer* Staudegger was unable to take part in the attack and therefore remained in Teterevino. After he learned of the tank attack he employed all available means to make his Pz. Kfw VI driveable. He set out alone against the attacking enemy tanks and destroyed 17 T-34s in a two-hour tank battle.

The enemy armoured formation subsequently broke off and withdrew into a gully. Without waiting for orders, *SS-Uscha.* Staudegger now decided to attack the enemy unit, which had meanwhile regrouped. Driving far beyond his own lines and without support, he knocked out 5 more T-34s. The rest fled.

SS-Uscha. Staudegger carried out this exceptional act on his own initiative, giving his all and without loss. In so doing he prevented an otherwise unavoidable penetration by tanks into our covering positions, decisively weakened the enemy tank formation and thus frustrated the enemy's tactical objective, the opening of the main road for his units in the southwest, which were virtually cut-off from their supplies.

Staudegger was decorated with the EKII for bravery during the winter fighting in the battle of Kharkov while serving as the driver of a Pz. Kfw. III.

An official portrait photograph of Franz Staudegger showing his neatly positioned Knight's Cross to the Iron Cross.

He received the EKI for especially courageous conduct with his tank during the breaching of the enemy defensive position northeast of Tomarovka.

He is worthy of receiving the highest decoration, the Knight's Cross of the Iron Cross.'

This recommendation was countersigned by *SS-Oberführer* Teddi Wisch. It did not take long for approval and on the 10th of July 1943, Franz Staudegger became a Knight's Cross holder. This award made Staudegger the very first Tiger tank connected Knight's Cross holder of the *Waffen-SS*. He would be by no means the last!

Before leaving the coverage of Staudegger it is worth detailing this action further. As highlighted, he knew the extreme danger posed by this large enemy tank breakthrough. He set upon it with vigour and it has to be remembered that he was the only Tiger tank in this melee of enemy T-34s. Every one of them focused on Staudegger's huge tank that sat alone in this nest of enemy armour. Destroying three initially, followed by a further two, then proceeded by another five. All the time under attack himself. A further seven fell victim to his powerful main gun, with all of the crew working feverishly.

Most people would have moved to the relative safety of their own lines at this stage, but Staudegger wanted to finish the threat, instead of letting this become one of his *Kameraden's* worry. He followed after the retreating enemy tanks and came across them a short time later. He set about what was left and used his remaining armour piercing rounds to destroy five more tanks. Switching to high-explosive rounds he continued to fire into the mass of enemy armour. He is recorded as hitting at least four more in this manner.

The reason for providing this addition detail of his fight is to highlight what it meant to take control of one of these huge machines and turn it into the effective weapon that it could be – actions like this helped to forge the reputation of the Tiger tank and made it the fear of many an *Allied* Army!

This feat was so significant that Adolf Hitler himself wanted to hear all about it. Franz Staudegger was sent to Führer HQ to give Hitler a personal account of what had taken place. He followed this by a spell of leave.

There is no detail of what took place for Staudegger inbetween this action in July 1943 and the start of June 1944. He shows up again as *Commander* of Tiger I, number 123, within the *II Platoon, 1. Kompanie, 101st SS-Panzer Battalion*. He was holding the rank of *SS-Standartenjunker*. He retained this tank number, position and rank as the Ardennes offensive began in mid-December 1944, this time being in a Tiger II. He is then listed in late March 1945 as being in the *2. Kompanie,* tank number unknown. His last action was in his Tiger II in April, when he was forced to abandon it in eastern Austria, making his way back to his own lines on foot. His final rank is listed as *SS-Oberscharführer*. He survived the war and died on the 16th of March 1991 in Frankfurt am Main.

Karl Kloskowski
Date of birth: 09.02.1917
SS Number: 310 800
Born in Lankow, his first taste of service was with the *R.A.D.* from the start of October 1935 to the end of September 1936. This was followed in mid-December with a move to the *SS*. He served with *SS-Regiment Germania* and was involved in the Sudetenland and Austrian campaigns, earning the medals for these.

It can be presumed that he fought in the west and the Balkans in 1940 and early 1941. There is no information to verify these assumptions on the part of the author. What is without question is that he went into Russia with *SS-Division Reich* in mid-1941 and had served in the *Kradschutzen* up to this point.

He quickly earned the Infantry Assault Badge on the 3rd of July, followed by the Second Class Iron Cross on the 19th of July. On the 2nd of October he was awarded the First Class Iron Cross and by this stage he was holding the rank of *SS-Oberscharführer*. The Black Wound Badge followed on the 16th of November; 1941 was indeed a busy time for him! Whilst in France in August 1942 he was also awarded the Russian Front Medal. In early September he attended a training course that lasted until late November. He held the rank of *SS-Hauptscharführer* by the end of the year, but in late April 1943 – after the Kharkov fighting had concluded – he was promoted to *SS-Untersturmführer*.

It was during the fighting, whilst serving with the *Panzer Abteilung* of *Das Reich* in Kharkov, that Kloskowski conducted actions that resulted in him being awarded the Knight's Cross. The recommendation for this award was written on the 6th of July 1943, as the Kursk offensive was in full swing! The author was his *Abteilung Commander*, Christian Tychsen and he wrote the following:

'Kloskowski was already recommended for the Knight's Cross to the Iron Cross in November 1941 because he prepared the way with his *Spahtrupp* into Moshaisk. He made his own decision to attack a stronger enemy and using adept leadership, took the area. Through this action the *Division* succeeded in reaching this goal.

That recommendation for the Knight's Cross was rejected by the *Division* because he had recently been awarded the Iron Cross First Class.

Karl Klowskowski photographed whilst on the front line, after he was awarded the Knight's Cross, just visible in the opening of his reversible parka.

In new actions, Kloskowski maintained himself as a *Zugführer* once again and proved extraordinary bravery and selfless battle craft, he undertook and distinguished himself in several areas and his *Kompanie* destroyed 9 heavy and medium PaK, 12-15 anti-tank rifles, 8 heavy mortars and 1 gun with security.

Kloskowski distinguished himself outstandingly in the action against Pawlograd. Within 10 minutes of starting and with his *Abteilung* as the lead *Zug* of the advance along the single narrow passable road, they fought up to the outskirts with 4 anti-tank guns, 1 armoured car and 8 trucks. In the west part of the city of Pawlograd, Kloskowski ran into a Pakfront and enemy infantry on the large bridge over the Woltschja. They took up position, especially at the bridge supports. Kloskowski gave the order to hold against the strong enemy resistance and get the *Abteilung* as close to the enemy as possible. From this decision, he advanced over the bridge and destroyed the 3 enemy Pak and the Russians who were working on the bridge. They hunted the 3 T-34s in their positions and later, using concentrated fire upon one of them, destroyed it. With this, in the lead of his *Abteilung* he pushed on into the area and at the same time destroyed 3 T-34s, 4 PaK, 1 recovery vehicle and 12 light vehicles that were full of Russians.

Through the fast occupation of the bridge and through his resolute attack through the 8km long village in the lead, his *Kompanie* was involved decisively in the successful outcome. Only through his fast and selfless and calm decision was the *Division* able to take the place and divide a large Russian Brigade and to destroy a large part of it with slight losses to their own.

Kloskowski is also due this honor because of his lasting exemplary devotion to duty.

He has a vigorous outstanding character exemplary in all crises and saved his *NCO*s.'

The recommendation was also warmly approved by Kurt Brasack, who was the acting *Divisional Commander* at that time. It was also countersigned by Paul Hausser, the *SS-Panzer Korps Commander.*

This recommendation was approved on the 11th of July 1943 but would not end Kloskowski's association with this medal, or his multiple demonstrations of his bravery. Details of those will follow in later volumes.

Waldemar Riefkogel
Date of birth: 07.01.1913
SS Number: 229 338
Born in Celle, he began his service with the Police in late 1934. Two years later he moved to the *Schutzpolizei* after attending an *NCO*'s training course. During the campaign in Poland he remained with the *Schutzpolizei*. He moved to the *Polizei Division* in May 1940 and fought with them during the campaign in the west. He was promoted to *SS-Untersturmführer* and by August 1941 was serving with the *10. Kompanie, Polizei-Regiment 2*. His next campaign was the invasion of Russia in the summer of 1941. He quickly earned the Second Class Iron Cross, on the 5th of August. In mid-January 1942 he was awarded the First Class Iron Cross and by that stage was holding the rank of *SS-Obersturmfhurer.*

He next moved to France where he joined *Totenkopf* in late 1942, serving in their *Panzer Abteilung,* but once again returned to Russia in the early part of 1943 with the *3. Kompanie*. It was during the latter stages of the Kharkov battles that he conducted actions that resulted in him being awarded the Knight's Cross. The recommendation was written on the 6th of July 1943, just as the Kursk campaign was getting under way, by his then *Divisional Commander* Max Simon and covered the following:

'In the fighting to take Tschugujew *SS-Obersturmführer* Riefkogel was with his *Panzer Kompanie* during the night of 16. and 17.3.1943, as part of the *I. /SS.-Pz.Gren.Rgt. "Totenkopf"*. The Russians attacked strongly during the night with tank support upon Tschugujew in order to take possession of this important city, the enemy suuceeded in breaking in.

SS-Obersturmführer Riefkogel, whose *Kompanie* consisted of only 2 useable tanks, moved against this break-in without infantry support, shot up 2 enemy tanks and forced the accompanying enemy infantry out through his lightning-quick successful action. An immediate enemy counter-attack also failed due to the courageous defense of the hero *SS-Obersturmführer* Riefkogel.

Some hours later came a new strong enemy tank attack, followed behind by truck-borne infantry. *SS-Obersturmführer* Riefkogel, who at that time was occupied with the salvaging of an unusual tank, took the immediate decision to use his two useable tanks against the counter-attack. After he had shot down a further 4 T-34s, he noted that the enemy infantry were preparing to attack the positions of the *3. Kompanie*. *SS-Obersturmführer* Riefkogel gave the order to boot out the enemy infantry and boldly led his few men against this enemy counter attack, destroying a large part of the attacking Russians.

Waldemar Riefkogel photographed in 1944, after his promotion to SS-Hauptsturmführer, showing the Knight's Cross he was awarded in 1943.

Through this immediate brave interference *SS-Obersturmführer* Riefkogel broke up the Bolsheviks completely. During this fighting *SS-Obersturmführer* Riefkogel did not leave his men, despite being wounded through mortar shrapnel. His interference prevented an enemy break-in to the important city of Tschugujew.

I please ask that *SS-Obersturmführer* Riefkogel, in recognition of his heroic courage and its' connected result, be awarded the Knight's Cross to the Iron Cross.'

This was approved on 11th of July 1943. By this stage he was commanding the *1. Kompanie* within *Totenkopf's Panzer Regiment.* There is virtually no information on this officer after this date, but it is known that he was commanding the *3. Kompanie* and holding the rank of *SS-Hauptsturmführer* one year later. It was also during this month, on the 30th of July 1944, whilst *Totenkopf* where in Poland, that he was killed in action.

Rudolf von Ribbentrop
Date of birth: 11.05.1921
SS Number: 400 121
Born in Wiesbaden and the son of the German Foreign Minister, Joachim von Ribbentrop, his military experiences started at a young age when he joined the *Hitler Youth* in late April 1933 and stayed with them for two years. At the age of fifteen, in 1936, he spent a year in London for studies. He then returned to Germany to finish his schooling, which lasted until 1938. In the early part of 1939 he spent a stint with the *R.A.D.*

On the same day that the Germans crossed the Polish border, the first day of September 1939, he volunteered for the *SS.* He was placed with *Deutschland's Replacement Battalion,* thereby missing out in the action in Poland. He did move to join the main *Regiment* in October and was placed with the *11. Kompanie.* In early May 1940 he was holding the rank of *SS-Sturmmann* and was selected for officer's school. This was the day prior to the start of the campaign in the west. Ribbentrop had the impression that he would be able to go with his unit westwards, but was soon very disappointed to learn that he would still be going to officer's school, thereby missing out on another campaign. Determined to ensure this would not happen he began a series of frantic phone calls and conversations between his *Commanding Officer* and his Father. The end result of a very busy 24-hours was that he did indeed find himself at the front with his unit.

Rudolf von Ribbentrop shown here after his Knight's Cross presentation.

He fought into the Beveland Canal area and received his first wound. He continued westwards after this and fought at Merville – where he learned that he had to go to officer's school at the end of May. Prior to arriving at this school he had been promoted to *SS-Unterscharführer,* been awarded the Black Wound Badge – on the 18th of May – and the Second Class Iron Cross – on the 19th of June and the Infantry Assault Badge at the start of October 1940. He remained at Braunschweig until the early part of 1941.

He left Braunschweig in February and followed this on the 20th of April by promotion to *SS-Untersturmführer.* He then went northwards with *SS-Kampfgruppe Nord's Aufklarungs Abteilung* into Finland. In early September he received his second wound, one that removed him from service until February 1942. He did however, earn the Finnish Freedom Cross, Fourth Class. Following his convalescence, he moved to the newly created *Panzer Abteilung,* within the *LAH.* He spent time in various positions in this *Abteilung* before finally being moved to the *6. Kompanie.* It was with this unit that he moved into Russia in early 1943. He fought in and around Kharkov from early February and some of these actions formed part of his recommendation. After Kharkov and Bjelgorod he fought in the Kursk offensive. It was during this fighting that he conducted additional actions that resulted in him being recommended for a high award. Back on the 1st of March 1943 he had been awarded the First Class Iron Cross, then promoted to *SS-Obersturmführer* on the 20th of April, followed by the award of the Silver Wound Badge on the first day of May.

This award submission was written by his *Regimental Commander, SS-Obersturmbannführer* Schonberger on the 13th of July and was actually aimed at awarding him the German Cross in Gold. This document contained the following overview:

'*SS-Ostuf.* v. Ribbentrop was himself a *Zugführer* in the winter fighting this year and later as *Führer* of a *Pz. Kp.*, as in the present break-in fighting he has especially distinguished himself through outstanding courage, coldblooded bravery and circumspect leadership.

After successful close combat in the area Nowaja Wodolaga, he was awarded the Iron Cross First Class on the 1.3.43 for proven and outstanding courage.

In the hard fighting north of Kharkov, he penetrated, on the 12.3.43, the established defenses in street fighting and the connection was made with the other *Grenadiers* around Red Square, which provided further bases for the advance into the city.

After the occupation of the city of Kharkov, the resulting push on Bjelgorod placed him in the lead *Kompanie.* He penetrated into the city on 18.3.43 at the head of his *Kompanie* under his personal bold actions. He has to take an outstanding share of the success of the action in Bjelgorod.

On the 7.7.43, stood the *II./SS Pz. Rgt. 1/ LAH* after a successful attack in Teterewino, where they were attacked numerous times themselves in the flanks by stronger Russian tanks. From a favourable attack position marched a Russian panzer group of 40 T-34s driving in front of the *Kompanie* of *SS-Ostuf.* v. Ribbentrop. He immediately overseen the situation, attacked the enemy with his smaller force and without loss to himself, shot up 6 enemy tanks. This courage and boldness resulted in the failure of the enemy attack, also forcing them to retreat.

On the 8.7.43 the *Abt.* attacked Rylski. *SS-Ostuf.* v. Ribbentrop again took part in the comprehensive attack, within the framework of the *Abt.* The village area was occupied by 80 enemy tanks. He himself shot up numerous tanks and forced the remainder to flee. A large amount of these remained stuck in the swamp. Of the 30 shot up tanks from the *Abt.* by far the largest part fell to the *Kp.* of *SS-Ostuf.* v. Ribbentrop.

On the 11.7.43, the Russians penetrated in Prochorowka with about 150 tanks of the type T-34 in the early morning, threatening the security of the positions of the *Grenadiers*. The combat-ready *Kp.* of *SS-Ostuf.* v. Ribbentrop threw itself toward this enemy and became engaged in battle with a much stronger enemy. The *Abt.* fought through a hard 3-hour tank battle and the most important share of the success was down to the decisiveness and fearlessness of *SS-Ostuf.* v. Ribbentrop. He destroyed, in this fight, 14 enemy tanks.

For repeated displays of bravery and outstanding courage by *SS-Ostuf.* v. Ribbentrop, I ask for the award of the German Cross in Gold as he is worthy of this high award.'

As highlighted above, this recommendation was for the German Cross in Gold, but at a higher level it looks as though this recommendation was felt worthy of even higher praise. The result was the award of the Knight's Cross to the Iron Cross for Rudolf von Ribbentrop on the 15th of July 1943.

Soon after this, at the start of August, he was moved to the newly forming *Hitler Youth Division*. He assumed command of the *3. Kompanie,* within the *12th SS-Panzer Regiment,* which was equipped with Panthers. He stayed with this unit throughout the remainder of 1943 and on into 1944, right up to the D-Day invasion. He received his fourth wound two days prior to the landings and in well-used photographs you will see him riding in a motorcycle combo, still recovering from these wounds. He fought against the Allies and for actions conducted in this difficult fighting he was awarded the German Cross in Gold on the 25th of August

1944. He had spent all of August in hospital, but was able to return to his unit in September, in his new posting of *Regimental Adjutant*.

His next battle was the Ardennes, where he was wounded for the fifth time – receiving the Gold Wound Badge. He next fought in the battles in Hungary from early April – his unit being sent to Germany inbetween for a re-fit. He commanded a *Kampfgruppe* made up from units within the *I Battalion* of the *Panzer Regiment*. He fought with them into Austria and finally surrendered in May along with the rest of his *Kameraden*. Back in February he had been promoted to *SS-Hauptsturmführer*.

Rudolf von Ribbentrop survived the war and was still alive at the time of writing this volume.

Bernhard Dietsche

Date of birth: 03.02.1912

SS Number: 13 578

Born in Singen, Dietsche was an early member of the *SS*, joining in April 1931. He initially served with the *13./SS-Standarte*. On the 20th of April 1934 he attended an *NCO's* course at Bad Tolz, at that time holding the rank of *SS-Unterscharführer*. On the first day of 1935 he was promoted to *SS-Scharführer*, followed two months later by a move to *SS-Oberscharführer*. His training and skills development did not end there and in mid-January 1936 he attended a *Führeranwarter's* training course also at Bad Tolz. Six months later he had obtained the rank of *SS-Standartenjunker*. At the start of February 1937 he started a short *Zugführer's* training course at Dachau. Two weeks after this he was moved to *SS-Standartenoberjunker*. This was followed on the 20th of April 1937 by a promotion to *SS-Untersturmführer*. At the start of May he moved to serve with the *12.Kompanie, III Battalion* within *SS-Regiment Germania*. On the 11th of November 1938 he was promoted to *SS-Obersturmführer*, still serving with *Germania*.

This was the unit that he entered the Second World War with and his first action was in Poland. He earned the Second Class Iron Cross in October the same year. He is not listed as serving in the west, although his file does not mention what he done during this time. In mid-September 1940 he moved to the newly created *SS-Regiment Westland* and was placed with their *13. Kompanie*. At the end of January 1941 he was promoted to *SS-Hauptsturmführer* and stayed with the *13. Kompanie* until late June 1942. He did go into Russia in mid-1941 and quickly earned the First Class Iron Cross, on the 27th of June 1941. He also received two wounds prior to the end of 1941, the first at the start of August and the second

SS-Sturmbannführer Bernhard Dietsche photographed wearing his Knight's Cross and other awards.

at the start of December; he earned the Black Wound Badge because of these. He was also awarded the Infantry Assault Badge, although the award date is not listed. He then left *Westland* on the 25th of June 1942, just prior to *Wiking's* new summer offensive southwards.

He next served with *Prinz Eugen,* under the leadership of his old *Westland Regimental Commander* Artur Phleps, and was in the Balkans from the start of August 1942. He received a further promotion to *SS-Sturmbannführer,* this taking place at the end of January 1943. He was commanding the *II Battalion* within the *2. SS-Gebirgsjaeger Regiment* at that stage. He took part in the initial actions of *Prinz Eugen* that started at the end of 1942, but carried on into 1943. This was Operation White and after a period of rest and re-fit, they began Operation Black. This started in mid-May 1943, and it was actions during this operation that Dietsche was recommended for the Knight's Cross to the Iron Cross.

This recommendation was written by Artur Phleps on the 16th of June and contained the following information:

'As leader of the motorized *Abteilung* from the *II Battalion/SS-Geb.Jg. Rgt. 2,* 1 Flak *Zug* and a *Panzer-Kp. SS-Sturmbannführer* Dietsche advanced towards Niksic along the main road from Plevlja, in order to quickly take possession of Bukovica, by crossing into Savnik. These crossings (3 road bridges) over the 400m deep valley were under the control of the enemy, but because the *Division* made attacks upon Zabljak, they later made this possible.

There were roadblocks, which hindered and slowed their attack, but the lead *Abt.* made it into southern Savnik and the attack group Schmidhuber advanced into the north, with Peterson developing the attack with his *8. Kompanie* and all other *Kompanies* becoming involved in the fight.

On the 29.5.43, *SS-Sturmbannführer* Dietsche advanced with the *8. Kompanie* and the 1 *Kradschutzen-Gruppe,* with support from heavy mortars and anti-tank *Zug* of the *Battalion,* as well as the fire from the 10cm cannon. They pushed northwards and eastwards dividing Krusevic and out of this area towards Mokrovor. They also took possession of the winding roads south and southwest of Savnik. Eastwards from here was *Kampfgruppe* Bachmann (*III./SS-Geb.Jg.Rgt.1)* on Hill 1257. They succeeded thanks to the very skillful use of the supporting fire from the heavy weapons and artillery, and the *8. Kompanie* and the *Kradschutzen-Gruppe* of the *Geb. Jg. Rgt. 2.* fairly quickly took possession of the high winding roads southwest of Savnik.

The *Panzer-Kp.* and the *Flak-Zug* could not get through the roadblocks north of Krusevic and the *Pioneer-Kompanies* of the *Division* worked on these. I attended this location of the roadblocks along with *SS-Sturmbannführer* Dietsche and referred him to the importance of crossing the Savnik once again. He took the

8. Kompanie and the *Kradschutzen* and moved towards Mokro. I knew this brave and bold officer and knew that he would master the difficulties.

Recognising the importance of this order, Dietsche, without delay, worked through the roadblock and took possession of the hill southwest of Savnik. He took the decision to go further, without waiting for the *Panzer-Kp.,* only with the *Kradschutzen-Gruppe,* and in spite of the enemy machine-gun fire forcing them to take cover. After Savnik they moved down and took possession of the first of two bridges, clinging onto the north of the mountain. They did not locate the second bridge until 30 minutes later (12:45 hours) and the 1. *Zug* of the *8. Kompanie* advanced to Cuklin hill. In heavy machine-gun and mortar fire from all sides, they held this weak base until around 15:00 hours, when finally the remainder of the *8. Kompanie* arrived. In that narrow area they held on against enemy counter-attacks only thanks to his brave leadership. This unfavourable situation on the flank of tightly packed right wing of the *Kompanie* lasted until 16:00 hours, then the *Panzer-Kp.* interfered and brought a reversal of the situation and forced the enemy to retreat.

Thorough preparation, superior leadership and rare boldness gave his undertaking and all preceding actions the stamp of exemplary *SS* leadership.

A short time afterwards, with his *Battalion,* he moved in motorised transport on the right wing of the *Division,* out of the Savnik area and advanced on the left wing of Avtovac. He succeeded again, through circumspect leadership, in throwing this improvised force out and abandoning their positions.

They moved east out of the Avtovac area and threw the broken enemy onto Stabma and Jasen and in cooperating actions pushed them back to the north. They took possession of the important Presjeka-Saddle (2198 m). After forcing the strong enemy to retreat from the Presjeka-Saddle, he took the decision to take control of the Maglic-Heights (2386 m). When he reached this area, he could see the enemy streaming to the west, trying to force a breakthrough over Sutjeska. With Pak and machine-gun fire and through adept direction of the fire of the 10cm long cannon on the Cemerno saddle, he succeeded in causing the enemy heavy losses and dispersed the remainder. He also helped to close the pocket around considerable enemy forces west of Sutjeska, from which their destruction could begin.

On this inhospitable mountain range, in the snow-storms and through the loss of their rations column, stood Dietsche with his *Abteilung* like a rock, mastering the heaviest of situations.

Through this he has proved himself worthy, as the first leader of the *SS-Freiwilligen-Gebirgs-Division "Prinz Eugen",* for the high award of the Knight's Cross to the Iron Cross and I recommend he receives this.'

This recommendation was approved for Bernhard Dietsche on the 17th of July 1943. He had been wounded two weeks earlier and actually received news of this award whilst still in hospital. This also gave *Prinz Eugen* their second Knight's Cross holder.

He stayed with *Prinz Eugen* and by the end of 1943 had received two further wounds, one in early July and the other at the start of December; these earned him the Silver Wound Badge. He moved from this unit at the end of March 1944 and took up a teaching post at Bad Tolz. This posting lasted until mid-July the same year, when he moved to the officer's school at Braunschweig. He followed this by returning to Bad Tolz at the start of October 1944. His file does not list anything different after this move, although some sources state that Dietsche was sent to the newly forming *'Skanderberg' Division* in November. If that was the case, he would in fact have ended up serving alongside his old unit, *Prinz Eugen,* as *Skanderberg's* formation as a *Division* was never completed. If he stayed in Bad Tolz until the end of the war, he would have been incorporated into *Nibelungen.* Bernhard Dietsche's name does not appear on any of the officer lists for either *Skanderberg* or *Nibelungen,* this lack of information only adds to the confusion! Some sources also state that he was awarded the Gold Wound Badge, but this cannot be verified.

Although the facts may be in dispute, what is fact is that he ended this conflict with the rank of *SS-Obersturmbannführer,* being promoted to that rank at the end of January 1945.

He survived the war, was involved in the Nuremberg war-crimes trials, although for what reason is unclear. He died on the 28th of January 1975.

Martin Gross

Date of birth: 15.04.1911

SS Number: 6 684

Born in Frankfurt am Main, he spent just over one year in the *Hitler Youth* from early 1928 until May 1929, when he moved to the *S.A.* This was followed by a voluntary move to the youthful *SS* at the start of February 1931. On the 10th of May 1933 he moved to the recently created *SS-Sonderkommando Berlin (LAH).* He was a *Platoon Commander* in the *3. Kompanie* from October 1934. His file does not mention which officer school he attended, but he was promoted to *SS-Untersturmführer* on the 10th of March 1935. His next promotion came on the 9th of November 1936 with a move to *SS-Obersturmführer.* Prior to the outbreak of the war he took part in the march into the Saarland (1935), Austria (1938), Sudetenland (1938) and Bohemia and Moravia (1939).

An autographed photograph of Martin Gross, his Knight's Cross clearly visible.

He took part in the campaign in Poland in 1939, at that time serving as a *Platoon Commander* in the *LAH's, 1. Kompanie*. He earned the Second Class Iron Cross at the start of October. In December he assumed command of the *1. Kompanie,* then followed this at the end of January 1940 with a promotion to *SS-Hauptsturmführer.* He led this unit during the campaign in the west in the early summer of 1940. He received his first wound on the 27th of May, earning the Black Wound Badge for this. When the campaign had concluded, he was awarded the First Class Iron Cross on the 20th of July 1940. This was followed in October with the award of the Infantry Assault Badge.

His next campaign was in the Balkans, now serving with the *5. (heavy) Kompanie*. He earned the Star of Romania Medal and Royal Bulgarian Bravery Medal, III Class, I Grade quickly followed by the advance into Russia in mid-1941. In the second half of November 1941 he suffered his second wound. He moved to the *Replacement Battalion* of the *LAH* at the start of May 1942. At the start of June he became a *Commander* of the tank-training school at Wunsdorf, training the *Tank Battalion* for the *Totenkopf Division*. He stayed there until late October, when he moved to the *LAH's Panzer Abteilung,* taking command of their *II Battalion*. At the end of January he was promoted to *SS-Sturmbannführer.*

He went with this unit into Kharkov in early 1943. For his bravery and actions around Nowaja Wodolaga, Dergatschi and Bjelgorod during that campaign, he earned the German Cross in Gold on the 28th of March. He remained with the *II Battalion* and conducted actions during July that would result in his recommendation for the Knight's Cross to the Iron Cross. This recommendation was written by his *Regimental Commander, SS-Obersturmbannführer* Georg Schonberger on the 13th of July 1943 and read as follows:

'On the 12.7.43 the *II/SS-Pz.Rgt. 1* and the *2. Pz. Gren. Rgt. LSSAH* were in position around Point 252.2 on the railway line around 2.5 km southestwards of Prochorowka, in the immediate rear area behind the first infantry positions. At 8:15 hours around 150 enemy tanks of the type T-34, broke through the security positions of the infantry and stormed through on a narrow front, firing all of their weapons. *SS-Sturmbannführer* Gross hurridly organized his men and engaged the enemy on three sides. He himself stood in the middle of his men and took part in the fight on all sides. Through his courageous example he led the entire *Battalion,* which destroyed about 90 enemy tanks during a three-hour tank battle. The remainder were set upon by the infantry ammunition and the artillery. They inflicted further losses.

Through the cutting-edge circumspect leadership of the *SS-Sturmbannführer,* the powerful tank attack of the Russians was thwarted.

This unique act justifies the high honour of the award of the Knight's Cross to the Iron Cross for *SS-Sturmbannführer* Martin Gross. He is therefore worthy of this award.'

This was signed by Schonberger and also endorsed by the *Divisional Commander,* Teddi Wisch. The recommendation was approved on the 22nd of July 1943.

He remained with this *Battalion* until mid-February 1944. He then moved to the *Panzer Training and Replacement Battalion.* In August 1944 this *Battalion* became part of a newly created unit, *Panzer Brigade Gross,* led by Martin Gross. This unit began with a strength of 2,500 men and fought in Latvia against the Russians. It contained various elements throughout it's short life that included parts of the *19th Waffen-Grenadier-Division der SS (Lettishces Nr. 2)* and also parts of the *(heavy) SS-Panzer Battallion 103.* In November it was moved to East Prussia, after suffering heavy losses the same month that Gross was promoted to *SS-Obersturmbannführer.* His *Brigade* was broken up towards the end of 1944 and various elements, numbering less than 200 men, were sent to the main *SS Tank Divisions.* Martin Gross himself was sent to the *12th SS-Panzer Division Hitler Youth* in March 1945, whilst they were fighting in Hungary. His last posting was as commander of *Hitler Youth's Panzer Regiment.*

Martin Gross survived the war and died on the 1st of March 1984.

Jurgen Wagner

Date of birth: 09.09.1901

SS Number: 23 692

Born in Strassbourg, he began his military career at a young age when he joined the Cadet Corps aged 14. As part of his training he found himself at the future home of the *LAH,* Berlin-Lichterfelde, two years later. He stayed with the cadets until 1921 when he moved to the *Army,* staying there for five years. He then conducted a non-military career for the next five years.

He joined the *SS* in mid-June 1931 and ten months later gained his first promotion to *SS-Scharführer (SS-Unterscharführer).* He led the *3./IV./21. SS-Standarte* until July 1933 and in that time he had been promoted twice and held the rank of *SS-Sturmführer (SS-Hauptsturmführer).* He was an instructor at the Juterbog training ground for the *Sonderkommando Zossen* and *Sonderkommando Berlin* – who were soon to become the *LAH.* By the start of October 1933 he is listed as serving with the *LAH* and was holding the rank of *SS-Sturmbannführer,* taking command of their *II Battalion.* In early July 1934 he was promoted further to the rank of *SS-Obersturmbannführer.* He remained with the *LAH* for the

A happy looking Jurgen Wagner shown here with the rank of SS-Brigadeführer, wearing the Knight's Cross he was awarded whilst holding the rank of SS-Oberführer.

remainder of their pre-war life, then moved to *Deutschland* in early June 1939 as a *Staff Officer.*

He fought in the west during 1940 and was heading up *Deutschland's, II Battalion* by then. He earned both classes of the Iron Cross during that campaign, 16th of May and 1st of July respectively. He stayed with this unit as they went into the Balkans in 1941 and also into Russia. At the start of July 1941 however, he moved to command the *SS-Infanterie Regiment 11*. Three months later he was promoted to *SS-Standartenführer,* followed six weeks later by a move to the command of *Deutschland.* Wounds received at the front line removed him from active service in late November 1941, receiving the Black Wound Badge before the end of that year.

In mid-1942 he returned to active duty and took command of *Germania,* at that time getting ready for their next push southwards. For his actions with this unit he received the German Cross in Gold and a promotion to *SS-Oberführer* in early November. The actual date for the award of his German Cross in Gold differs. One document on his file lists the 1st of September, Mark Yerger lists the 11th of December and Joss Schneider lists the 14th of December 1942. This was whilst *Wiking* were advancing through the Caucausus and then moving back towards Rostov. The award date may be in doubt, but the facts are that he definitelty held this award by the time 1942 closed.

Caught up in the summer push with *Germania* in July 1943, he conducted actions that resulted in him being recommended for the Knight's Cross. This recommendation was penned by Herbert Gille and it is also of note that this same document lists the 14th of December 1942 as the award date of his German Cross in Gold. The document read as follows:

'During the attack of the Donez west of Isjum carried out by the opponent since the 16.7.43 with strong forces and the support of numerous tanks, the reinforced *Regiment "Germania"* under the leadership of its' *Commander, SS-Oberführer* Wagner, was engaged in the focal point of the battle. On the 17. and 18.7.43 counterattacking the enemy who had broken in, and on 19.7.43 fighting back strong enemy attacks. In the course of the counterattack on 18.7.43 the *Regiment* captured the important villages of Ssawodskoj and Ssrednij, and on 19.7.43 repelled attacks from the 20. Rifle Guard Division and two Tank Brigades.

Thanks to the quick capture of the villages of Ssawodskoj and Ssrednij, an enemy breakthrough attempt that could have endangered the whole front south of Isjum was prevented, and the further dispatch of strong forces over the Donez was avoided. On 19.7.43 the opponent broke through to the north of Andrejewka with two tank Brigades and strong infantry units and pushed in a southeasterly direction towards Andrejewka.

Seeing the danger of this assault due to the depth of the penetration achieved by the enemy battle group, as the prisoner statements later corroborated, *SS-Oberführer* Wagner, under his own decision deployed the *II/SS-Panzergrenadier Regiment "Germania"* for an immediate counterattack. He did this although this *Battalion* had orders to finish off an enemy penetration by Ssawedskoj. During this heavy battle *SS-Oberführer* Wagner was the soul of the fight. Thanks to his personal impulse and his readiness for action he accomplished, always staying in the focal point of the fight, the annihilation of the numerically vastly superior opponent and the destruction of 35 - 40 tanks with proportionally weak forces. With that, the planned breakthrough of the opponent was prevented and the main fighting line was won back and again firmly in our hands.'

This recommendation was approved on the 24th of July 1943, but this award of the Knight's Cross to the Iron Cross would not end Wagner's assocation with this medal. We will cover the details of that in later volumes of this project.

Paul Hausser
Date of birth: 07.10.1880
SS Number: 217 862
Early details of Paul Hausser were last covered in August 1941 when he became the 10th *Waffen-SS* soldier to receive the Knight's Cross. He remained active from that time and led his *Division* southwards from Smolensk towards the area north of Kiev, where they successfully helped to contain the enemy in the massive encirclement that occurred there during September 1941. He then took them back northwards to they could continue their push towards Moscow. As they got closer, the enemy resistance stiffened and the losses to this *Division* mounted. One of the casualties during mid-October 1941 was Paul Hausser himself, receiving a serious eye wound that removed him from front-line service for the time being. Back at the start of October, he had received a promotion to *SS-Obergruppenführer und General der Waffen-SS*.

His next assignment after recovering from these wounds was to form the *SS-Panzer Korps* in May 1942 in France. This new *Korps* incorporated the *LAH, Das Reich* and *Totenkopf Divisions,* as each of these units was withdrawn from Russia throughout the second half of 1942. Just after taking on this new task in May, Hausser was awarded the Silver Wound Badge. He took his *SS-Panzer Korps* back to Russia in the January 1943 to deal with the looming crisis in the southern sector. The actions of this *Korps* and the *Divisions* contained within it have been detailed in the preceding chapters and it was for these successes that

Paul Hausser shown in an enhanced photograph, with superimposed Oakleaves on top of his existing Knight's Cross to the Iron Cross.

Paul Hausser was recommended for the Oakleaves to the Knight's Cross. This recommendation was written by *Generaloberst* Hoth on the 28th of July 1943 and read as follows:

'I am applying for the award of the Oakleaves to the Knight's Cross to the Iron Cross for the *Commanding General* of the *II SS-Panzer-Korps, SS-Obergruppenführer und General der Waffen-SS* Hausser, for his repeated exceptional leadership during the attack operation north of Bjelgorod (Zitadelle).

On the first day of the offensive, July 5, 1943, the attack of the *Leibstandarte* faultered due to overwhelming enemy artillery fire from the hills at Schurawliny and south of Olchowka. The *Commanding General,* being up at the front, recognized the crisis and immediately issued the highest measure of appropriate orders. Almost all the artillery of the *Korps* was used for counter fire and the entire *8th Luftwaffe Korps* was directed on the enemy batteries. Realising that an attack by the *Division 'Das Reich'* would result in the necessary relief, Hausser hurried further towards the front and deployed the tanks of this *Division*. He also ordered an immediate attack by *Totenkopf,* which according to the plan was to have been committed later to the rear of *Das Reich*; the effect was telling. The attack of the *Leibstandarte* through the deeply built enemy defensive line again gained momentum. The stronghold of Schurawliny was taken by assault in a pincer movement and by evening, the second enemy defensive line was almost breached. The mopping up of the enemy on the right flank began.

On the second day of the offensive, the *II SS-Panzer Korps* had broken through the second enemy line when strong enemy armour forces were reported approaching from Prochorowka. The *Commanding General,* having hurried to the front, realized the favourable situation. He decided to turn the bulk of his *Korps* towards Prochorowka to keep the enemy located there, as far away from the battlefield as possible. He did this even though it was clearly visible that the *XXXXVIII Panzer Korps* was still engaged in hard fighting at the second enemy defensive line northwest of Olchowka from where the advance of *II SS-Panzer Korps* had been flanked. Leaving behind security forces at Pokrawa, Hausser personally led the tanks from *Das Reich* and *Leibstandarte* along the Lutschki-Prochorowka road. In heavy armoured combat, it was possible to throw the 2nd Soviet Tank Corps and the 5th Guards Mechanized Corps back to Prochorowka. Heavy losses were inflicted on the enemy and the heights at Teterewino were taken. Through these actions it was possible to turn the tanks again to the east and engage the 3rd Motorised Corps from the rear, which was fighting opposite the *XXXXVIII Panzer Korps*.

On July 7, 1943, a crisis developed with the forces of *Das Reich* left behind to cover the right flank at Teterewino. They were attacked from the east by the newly committed Russian 6th Tank Corps, 2nd Tank Corps and 5th Guards Tank Corps. The enemy broke through in great depth through the infantry of *Das Reich,* which had only itself to depend on. The *Commanding General,* again in the appropriate location, decided to continue with the armoured attack to the west despite the threat of a complete breakthrough. Thanks to the personal presence of Hausser, who aroused the tenacity of the armoured infantry, they succeeded in finishing off the penetrated tanks in close combat and prevented a total breakthrough.

I hardly ever met *SS-Obergruppenführer* Hausser during their operation at his advance headquarters, only up front with his *Divisions* or returning from his troops. Despite his handicap from a previous serious wound, he un-tiringly led all day from the front. His presence, bravery and personal humour in even the most difficult situations, gave his troops buoyancy and enthusiasm while he held command of the *Korps* tightly in his hand. As he had already shown during the offensive fighting at Kharkov,

SS-Obergruppenführer Hausser showed far sightedness in recognizing the operational situation and executed combat operations with bravery and energy. Again and again he has proved himself as an unusually qualified *Commanding General.*

Signed Hoth, *Generaloberst u. Oberbefehlshaber d. 4. Panzerarmee.*'

The recommendation was approved on the 28th of July 1943, the same day it was written, making Hausser the twelfth *Waffen-SS* holder of this award. One other important factor to bear in mind is that the actions detailed above were achieved by a man who was aged 62 at that time and after he had suffered a serious eye wound back in late 1941. You may also note that there is very little reference to the previous success in and around Kharkov, but the focus is placed on the Kursk offensive instead – no doubt a deliberate act on the part of Hoth to possibly help ensure a successful approval?

His connection to this award and its' various grades would continue, but more details of that in later volumes.

Helmut Schrieber
Date of birth: 25.03.1917
SS Number: 361 292
Born in Giessen, Schrieber spent time with the *Hitler Youth* from the start of June 1933 until early April 1938. He followed this by moving to the *R.A.D.* until late October, he then joined the *SS* on the first day of November, being placed with *Deutschland.*

He fought in Poland as a squad leader and the skills he displayed during that campaign resulted in him being sent to Bad Tolz to train as an officer. The dates he attended are not listed, but he received a promotion to *SS-Untersturmführer* on the 1st of August 1940, by which time he had also fought in the campaign in the west. He is listed as taking part in the campaign in the Balkans in early 1941. By mid-October he was back with *Das Reich* and advancing with them into Russia. He earned the Second and First Class Iron Crosses on the 1st of December. He spent time as *Deutschland's I Battalion Adjutant*. He was awarded the Black Wound Badge in mid-February 1942. His next promotion came on the 21st of June, when he moved to *SS-Obersturmführer.* The Infantry Assault Badge came on the 20th of July and the Russian Front Medal at the start of August. In the second half of 1942 he was commanding *Deutschland's, 10. Kompanie*.

He went back to Russia during the Kharkov battles and for his actions and bravery there he received the German Cross in Gold on the 28th of March 1943. On the 21st of June he was promoted to *SS-Hauptsturmführer,* still with the *10. Kompanie*. He conducted actions in the first few days of Operation Zitadelle that would earn him a recommendation for the Knight's Cross to the Iron Cross from his *Regimental Commander, SS-Standartenführer* Heinz Harmel. This recommendation was written on the 11th of July and on the cover page there was a foreword from *SS-Gruppenführer* Walter Kruger, where he approved of this award recommendation and draws attention to Schreiber's special courage. The remaining pages of the document read:

'On the 8.7.43, the *III./SS-Pz.Gren.Rgt. "Deutschland"* had the order to secure the main road on both sides of Teterewino. The enemy were holding this area with strong tank support and attacking into the positions of the *Battalion*. (In the positions of the *Regiment* they destroyed 83 enemy tanks.) At 16:00 hours the enemy succeeded in breaking into the exposed flank on the left of the *III./SS-Pz.Gren.Rgt "D"*. The enemy began to dig in.

SS-Hauptsturmführer Schreiber recognized immediately this threat to the *Battalion*. He collected a *Zug* from the *Kompanie* and took the decision to attack. After a hard and difficult fight, he was able to throw the opponent out of their

A formal, autographed photograph of Helmut Schreiber showing his many awards for bravery, which include the Knight's Cross.

positions. *SS-Hauptsturmführer* Schreiber then exploited this situation and decided to attack the enemy further. He advanced out of his own positions on the higher ground and moved into the enemy positions, taking these in a spirited attack. Through this improvement of their own lines, they had the better positions to deal with the enemy attacks coming in against the *SS-Pz.Gren.Rgt. "Deutschland"*.

Against these positions the enemy met with heavy losses. This is to be attributed to the determination and bravery of *SS-Hauptsturmführer* Schreiber. On the 9.7.1943 the *2. Regiment* of the *SS-Pz.Gren.Div. "Leibstandarte Adolf Hitler"* attacked the main Bjelgorod – Kursk railway line out of these recently won positions.

SS-Hauptsturmführer Schreiber, was awarded the German Cross in Gold on the 28.3.1943 for repeated courage. He is typical of the *Kompanie-Chiefs,* mastering each situation through exceptional leadership qualities. Schreiber is a passionate soldier.'

This recommendation was approved on the 30th of July, giving *Das Reich* their 11th Knight's Cross holder in 1943 alone.

In late 1943 he assumed command of the *III Battalion* within *Deutschland* and had been wounded a further time. On the 5th of November he was awarded the Close Combat Clasp in Silver. He was promoted to *SS-Sturmbannführer* on the 20th of April 1944 and one week later received the Close Combat Clasp in Gold. He fought in the west during 1944 with *Das Reich* and received a heavy wound near Mortain. In January 1945 he was commanding the *Replacement Battalion* of *Das Reich,* positioned on the Westwall line. He also took part in the defense of the Remagen Bridge over the Rhine in early March. He was awarded the Gold Wound Badge on the 20th of April and ended the war in Austria with his old *Regiment Deutschland.*

It is known that he survived the war, but the author was unable to confirm the date of his death.

Alois Weber

Date of birth: 30.11.1915

SS Number: 156 963

Born in Blumenried, in the Allgau region, he entered the *Allgemeine-SS* at the start of May 1933. In October that year he volunteered for the *R.A.D.* and stayed with them until the start of June 1934. On the 1st of October 1936 he joined the *SS-VT* and was placed with *Deutschland.*

He fought in Poland, serving as a *Pioneer* by this stage. He followed this by fighting in the west during 1940, where he earned the Second Class Iron Cross on the 11th of June. In 1941 he took part in the Balkans campaign, then moved into Russia. He earned the First Class Iron Cross on the 25th of July, now holding *NCO* rank. His next award was the Infantry Assault Badge, which came on the 20th of July 1942. This was followed by the Russian Front Medal at the start of August.

He was back in Russia during February and March 1943 and earned further recognition for his abilities. He received the Black Wound Badge on the 15th of March, the German Cross in Gold on the 28th of March, the Tank Destruction Badge at the start of April and the Close Combat Clasp in Bronze ten days later.

Staying in Russia he took part in the Kursk offensive, holding the rank of *SS-Hauptscharführer* and serving with the *16. (Pioneer) Kompanie*. On the first day of this new push he conducted actions that were felt worthy of a Knight's Cross recommendation. He was recommended by Heinz Harmel and this was counter-approved by both Walter Kruger and Paul Hausser. The document was written on the 10th of July and covered the following:

'During the attack on the 5.7.1943 the *II./SS-Pz.Gren.Rgt. "Deutschland*" had the order to break open the deep fortified enemy lines near Beresoff. After they had annihilated the enemy combat outposts, they were to take the village itself, then storm the heavily secured high ground northeastwards behind Beresoff and take possession of it.

To support this attack of the *Battalion* a Tiger-*Kompanie* was attached, as well as the a *Pioneer-Zug* of the 16./*SS-Pz.Gren.Rgt. "Deutschland"* under the leadership of *SS-Hauptscharführer* Weber. After elimination of the combat outpost, the *Pioneerstosstrupp* got the order to penetrate the tank-ditch, together with the *6./SS-Pz.Gren.Rgt. "D"* before Beresoff and to knock-out the bunkers lying behind, which where in controlling positions.

After they penetrated into the tank-ditch they lay under enemy fire. Out of camouflaged positions came the *II./SS-Pz.Gren.Rgt. "D"*, who then gained a foothold in this tank-ditch. Further movement was prevented through well-aimed and non-stop enemy artillery, mortar and sniper fire. A further attack appeared impossible and high bloody losses began to mount; mine damage was also caused to the supporting Tiger-*K*, who as a result could not give further support.

Within this *Battalion*, through which the enemy artillery fire was causing higher losses hour after hour, shown through our dead and wounded, the leader of the *Pioneerstosstrupp, SS-Hauptscharführer* Weber took the bold decisions to take control of this tank-ditch. Without Tiger support he alone took his *Zug* and

Alois Weber seen in a formal setting, wearing his Knight's Cross.

stormed towards the bunker line in order to get relief for the *II./SS-Pz.Gren.Rgt. "D"*. In the strongest enemy fire, he explored any attack possibility. He took his *Zug* through the running trenches and moved through the violent enemy barrage. Moving through this tank-ditch his men threw the enemy out of one position after another and reached the Soviet bunker system that controlled it.

They exploited this success further and Weber stormed on with his Pioneers and avoiding the enemy in Beresoff, he quickly took the calm decision to move through the village and onto the controlling high ground. In bitter close combat with his group, they attacked the bunkerfield there (around 15 bunkers) and forced the Soviets out of each position. This also forced the enemy to abandon the north and southern parts of Beresoff, who retreated in a wild flight over the high ground and moved northwards. Through this, it was possible for the *II./SS-Pz.Gren.Rgt. "D"* to begin their advance out of the tank-ditch and push the enemy northwards, also gaining access to the main road to Kursk.

The go-getting advance, the outstanding courage and the superior leadership of *SS-Hauptscharführer* Weber (his attack group had only six casualties), as well his bold decision done on his own initiative, his *Pioneerstosstrupp* made the attack possible. They had a decisive share of the 20km breakthrough by the *SS-Pz.Gren. Div "Das Reich"*of the fortified Soviet field positions on both sides of Beresoff.'

This recommendation was also approved on the same day as Helmut Schrieber's, the 30th of July 1943. He was recovering from wounds at this stage and there is a photograph of him receiving his award whilst still in his hospital bed. It would appear that Alois Weber also received a field-commission as a result of his actions, as he is listed as holding *SS-Untersturmführer* rank from July 1943.

He was with the *SS-Pioneer Replacement Battalion 1,* stationed in Dresden, from the start of September. This could be at a time when he was getting ready to return to active duty? His next listing shows him as the *Commandant* of the *Pioneer School* in Gradischka from late August to early October 1944. He is listed as being promoted to *SS-Obersturmführer* on the 9th of November, although his unit is not listed along with this. He next appears back with the *2. Kompanie, SS-Pioneer Training and Replacement Battalion 1* in March 1945. He did survive the war and died on the 19th of January 2003.

Gunther-Eberhard Wisliceny
Date of birth: 05.09.1912
SS Number: 41 043
Born in Regulowken, East Prussia, he was a member of the *Hitler Youth* from October 1930 until mid-July 1932. It would appear that he then joined the *Allgemeine-SS* immediately after this. He next made a move to the newly created *SS-Stabswache Berlin (LAH)* in mid-March 1933 with the rank of *SS-Mann,* therefore he was one of the first 117 men who were hand-picked to form this unit. He gained quick promotion and in October the same year he was holding the rank of *SS-Truppführer (SS-Oberscharführer).* Two months later he had moved to *SS-Obertruppführer (SS-Hauptscharführer).* In the autumn of 1934 he attended training courses, then on the 10th of March 1935 he was commissioned an *SS-Untersturmführer,* although it does not list which officer school he attended. He is also listed as being the *Adjutant* for the *LAH's, II Battalion* then. Promotion to *SS-Obersturmführer* came just over one year later, on the 9th of November 1936. At the start of June 1937 he was a *Zugführer* in the *8. Kompanie,* staying there until the start of May 1938. At this stage he moved to the newly created *SS-Regiment "Der Führer",* remaining as a *Zugführer* in their *8. Kompanie.*

On the first of September 1939 he was back in the role of *Adjutant* for *Der Führer's II Battalion.* However, two months later he had moved to the *4. SS-Totenkopf Standarte 'Ostmark'* and was commanding their *12. Kompanie.* This unit had been part of *Heimwehr Danzig,* but by this stage they were in Prague. He made another quick move to the *8. Kompanie,* within the *SS-Totenkopf Infantry Regiment 11* in early December. On the 2nd of April 1940 he was promoted to *SS-Hauptsturmführer.* His file lists him as being in Holland during 1940 as part of the coastal defense. At least part of 1941 was spent in France.

He did go east with his unit in mid-1941 and suffered his first wound on the 24th of July, earning the Black Wound Badge for this. Three days later he was awarded the Second Class Iron Cross. This was followed on the 7th of November by the award of the First Class Iron Cross. By this stage *SS-Totenkopf Infantry Regiment 11* had been disbanded due to heavy casualties and the surviving men were sent to the two remaining regiments of *Division Reich.* It does not state which of these Wisliceny was moved to, but it can be presumed that it was *Der Führer,* as by February 1942 he was with their *Replacement Battalion.* This was followed six-weeks later by a move back to the *II Battalion, Der Führer.* Back at the start of December 1941 he had been awarded the Infantry Assault Badge. Whilst in France in the second half of 1942, he received the further award of the Russian Front Medal at the start of August.

An autographed photograph of SS-Obersturmbannführer Gunther Wiscileny, pictured after his award of the Knight's Cross, added to his many existing awards, clearly visible.

He fought in the Kharkov battles in early 1943, and for his display of bravery and achievements in that area he received the German Cross in Gold on the 25th of April 1943. Five days earlier he had been promoted to *SS-Sturmbannführer.* In between then and the start of Kursk, he had made a move to take command of *Deutschland's III Battalion.* He had received his second wound by then, although the date of this is not listed.

He, like Weber, conducted actions on the first day of the Kursk operation that resulted in him being recommended for the Knight's Cross. It was also written by Harmel and was counter-approved by Kruger and Hausser. It was written on the 11th of July and contained the following:

'In the attack on the 5.7.1943, the *III. /SS-Pz.Gren.Rgt. "Deutschland"* under the leadership of *SS-Sturmbannführer* Wisliceny, were ordered to take the combat outposts around the village of Jachontoff and to position themselves there for the further attack.

In a resolute storming attack, *SS-Sturmbannführer* Wisliceny, with his Grenadiers, destroyed the combat outposts, took possession of them and stood ready for their next attack. After this the Sturmgeschutze advanced together with the *III. /SS-Pz.Gren.Rgt. "Deutschland"*, under the cover of a Stuka attack and their own artillery fire. They achieved a deep penetration into the fortified tank-ditch and snatched these strong positions from the enemy.

During the night, heavy rain descended on them and delayed the attack with the Sturmgeschutze by 2-hours. The Stuka attack and artillery fire were not able to exploit this situation, therefore they needed an immediate attack by the Sturmgeschutze, which should start after the last shell had been fired. Upon their own positions lay strong enemy artillery fire. Recognizing this danger, that threatened the entire undertaking, Wisliceny took the bold decision, in spite of the enemy artillery and infantry fire, to attack into the enemy positions and break them.

Nevertheless he himself was severly hindered by a knee injury, but he was at the lead of his Grenadier and fought through with strong momentum, into position after position within the tank-ditch. With the occupation of the tank ditch, *SS-Sturmbannführer* Wisliceny created, with his advance and through his good decision, the largest portion of the break-in, which was the prerequisite for the further advance of the *SS-Pz.Gren.Div. "Das Reich"*. He himself stormed from there in the afternoon and reached the next objective, despite the unfavourably wet conditions and against the hardest enemy resistance.

The meaning of the attack undertaken by *SS-Sturmbannführer* Wisliceny is to be recognised, as through this, the further attack by the mass of the *II. SS-Panzer*

Korps was started. These advances in this sector made possible the division of the strong enemy resistance.

SS-Sturmbannführer Wisliceny has typical courage and go-getting, through his heroic manerisms in all pushes forwards and through his inflexible defiance. This is typical for Wisliceny that his go-getting attitude also brought with it only slight losses.'

This recommendation was approved on the 30th of July 1943 and gave *Das Reich* their third new Knight's Cross holder on this day. This award would not finish Wisliceny's association with this award or its' higher grades, but we will cover that in future volumes.

Kurt Sametreiter
Date of birth: 09.04.1922
SS Number: 319 530
Born in Bockstein, Austria, he joined the *SS* on the 1st of April 1938. His choice to volunteer for the *Waffen-SS* was an antidote to the high unemployment in Austria at that time. His acceptance nearly did not happen though, with Sametreiter deciding to leave the long recruiting queue before his turn. This was due to seeing so many fit looking men being rejected. Luck played a part and he was stopped by an officer, who talked to him and asked him some questions, then brought him in front of the doctors, who in turn passed him fit for service.

He was initially placed with one of the pre-war *Totenkopf Standarte,* then moved to the *Heimwehr Danzig* in early 1939. He fought with this unit during the opening battles of the war in Poland. Like many of his *Heimwehr Danzig Kameraden,* he moved to the newly formed *SS-Totenkopf Division* in October 1939. It was also in this post-Poland period that he was promoted to *SS-Sturmmann.* He advanced through France with this unit during May and June 1940 and was there in all of the critical engagements, including the British tank attack near Arras. With the successful conclusion of that campaign, he went to the southern French coast, near Spain, before then moving to Metz in the closing phase of 1940. He was holding the rank of *SS-Rottenführer* then.

His next move came at that time in Metz, when he was ordered to move to the *LAH.* He spent a spell with the *3. Kompanie, V (Wach) Battalion, LAH* in January 1941, but was back with the frontline unit in time for the Balkan Campaign. After fighting in Greece, he went into Russia in mid-1941. He was awarded the Second Class Iron Cross on the 13th of July. This was followed in December the same year with the award of the Tank Assault Badge. He had also been promoted to *SS-Unterscharführer* in 1941.

Kurt Sametreiter seen in a formal pose to show his award of the Knight's Cross, one of many armour related Knight's Crosses awarded in the early part of 1943.

Another (previously unseen) photograph of Kurt Sametreiter (right), standing next to Werner Sternebeck who was one the LAH's Panzer Abteilung's Kompanie Commanders

At the start of September 1942 he was then awarded the First Class Iron Cross. He was back in Russia in early 1943 and took part in the battles around Kharkov, receiving the Black Wound Badge in mid-April 1943 for wounds suffered during those actions. This was followed on the 20th of April 1943 with a promotion to *SS-Oberscharführer,* thereby skipping the rank of *SS-Scharführer.* His actions in this region continued with the Kursk Offensive in July. He was serving with the *3. (Heavy) Kompanie, Panzerjäger Abteilung 1, LAH* as a *Platoon Leader.* During the difficult fighting within the Kursk salient in July, he conducted actions that his *Abteilung Commander, SS-Sturmbannführer* Hanreich, felt worthy of the Knight's Cross. He penned the following document on the 13th of July 1943:

'On the 11.7.1943, *SS-Oberscharführer* Sametreiter was with his *Zug* and the *II. /1. Pz.Gren.Rgt. LSSAH* in the attack on Swch. Stalinks and forest located south of there. During a night battle they threw the enemy out of Sowchose.

On the 12.7.1943 at 06:30 hours, the enemy advanced out of Jamki and Storostrowoje with around 40 tanks carrying infantry and also supporting infantry, and counter attacked Sowchose Stalinks and Hill 245.9. Under the determined leadership of *SS-Oberscharführer* and *Platoon Leader* Sametreiter, he succeeded with 4 of his 7.5cm guns to prevent an enemy breakthrough. Making his own decision, Sametreiter went with his *Platoon* over the foremost infantry line and out towards the enemy tanks and continuously shot up these tanks, which counted 24 tanks of different types, for over an hour. Out of his leadership of his *Platoon,* they shot up 24 enemy tanks. All of his *Platoon* shot at the enemy with their tank rounds and this explosive attack caused the enemy to retreat.

After they had shot all of their shells, he gave the order for his vehicles to drive against the enemy infantry and give further cover to the men. It is due to his determined leadership that the tank attack was defeated. The *Platoon* of Sametreiter gave combat covering fire to the men.'

This was signed by his *Abteilung's Commander,* but there was also an additional few words from *SS-Obersturmbannführer* Albert Frey, *Commander* of the *1. Panzergrenadier Regiment LSSAH.* These read as follows:

'The *SS-Oberscharführer* Sametreiter prevented the break-in of the enemy tanks with his *Platoon* and removed a heavy threat for the *Regiment.* I hold that Sametreiter is worthy of the honour of the Knight's Cross to the Iron Cross.'

Kurt Sametreiter was approved for this award on the 31st of July 1943, the last such award for an *SS* soldier in this month, but not the last that would be given for actions during the Kursk offensive.

His notification of this award came on the 8th of August as the *LAH* were speeding towards Italy. There was a brief stop at Innsbruck, where the actual award ceremony took place. This had been preceded by everyone on the train celebrating this news with brandy.

After their stint in Italy, they returned to Russia once more.

He moved to the *LAH's, 7. Kompanie,* within their *Panzer Regiment.* This was in the latter stages of 1943 and was followed by a promotion to *SS-Untersturmführer* on the 9th of November. He remained with this unit throughout 1944 as the *LAH* fought their difficult battles in Normany, France. He was in a Panzer IV during this time and he was one of the soldiers who managed to make it out of the Falaise Gap in August.

One source lists him as serving in the *8. Kompanie,* but one soldier who served alongside him at that time was *SS-Unterscharführer* Manfred Thorn. They both fought throughout the summer of 1944 with the *7. Kompanie,* especially during the intense battle for Tilly.

Following these intense and costly battles, the remnants of the *LAH* moved towards the Westwall defences. The *7. Kompanie* had only one useable tank left at that time – driven back to Germany by Manfred Thorn. They were moved to the Luneberg Heath area for a rest and re-fit with men and machines. Sametreiter himself underwent an operation at that time. When he recovered, he was posted to the *Nederland Division* and was given command of one of their Stug *Kompanies* on the orders of *Divisional Commander,* Jurgen Wagner; due to the previous *Commander* being killed the day before Sametreiter arriving. He fought with them in Poland, Danzig, Stettin, Frankfurt am Oder and finally near Berlin, where the remnants surrendered. The date of their surrender was in June 1945, four weeks after the official surrender! Kurt Sametreiter had incredible luck at the end of the war and avoided becoming a prisoner of war. The details of this are something that the author found very interesting and possibly unique? We will save the details until the final volume of this project, as the relevance and full interest of what took place for this soldier will be more in context in that volume. At the end of the war he held the rank of *SS-Obersturmführer,* being promoted on the 20th of April 1945.

Kurt Sametreiter survived the war and was living in his home town at the time of writing this volume.

•••

Volume 2 Summary

This brings to an end this second volume of this overall project. The original intention was to cover the whole of 1943 in a single volume, but as this volume has unfolded, it has become clear that the intense activity in the first half of 1943 and resulting awards gave enough material for a single volume. To cover everything that took place in 1943 for the *Waffen-SS* would have resulted in a very thick volume indeed!

This volume started with the crisis in southern Russia in the wake of the German Stalingrad defeat. The loss of the whole southern sector was looming, so the placement of the *SS-Panzer Korps* into this region was intended to help prevent that. You have read how they did indeed put a stop to the seemingly unstoppable Russian advances. They had therefore wrestled the initiative from the enemy and got ready to advance further.

They were ready for their further advances within a short space of time, but the personal involvement of Adolf Hitler put paid to this and added delays that lasted over two months. This intervening two months only allowed the Russians to further extend and strengthen their extensive fortifications, defensive belts and camouflaged positions. The enemy sat and waited on the advance of the Germans, whilst receiving up to date information on the German intentions from their friends in England.

Adolf Hitler's direct involvement decided the eventual outcome, when he extracted the *II. SS-Panzer Korps,* at the point when they were making their most notable gains! That decision removed one of the strongest barriers that stood in the way of Russian advances, something that was noted by the senior *Commanders* responsible for this region, at that time.

Cast your mind back to mid-February 1943 during the height of the crisis unfolding in Kharkov. It took a soldier of the *Waffen-SS* to directly disobey an order from Hitler to deliver the eventual successful outcome, rather than lose his entire *Korps*. What would have happened if *Totenkopf* had been allowed to continue their push forwards, possibly assisted by *Wiking,* whilst the *LAH* and *Das Reich Divisions* held strong enemy forces in their fighting west of Prochorowka? Here we are with speculation once again!

Back to facts. It is this author's opinion that Adolf Hitler's direct involvement and decisions during 1943 are what started the unstoppable road to the German's eventual complete defeat just under two years later. His decision to hold firm in the winter of 1941 had been the correct thing to do, but his decision to do the same in February 1943 was incorrect, as has been proved. So too, was his decision to smash into a strongly fortified enemy defensive line, instead of pulling back to a better line and rendering these strong enemy defensive positions useless!

The initiative had been re-taken by the Germans in mid-March 1943, only to be thrown away again four months later, all down to one man's decisions.

What lay ahead was two more painful years of losses and intense fighting, all the way back to the doors of the Reichs Chancellery. In those two years, the men of the *Waffen-SS* would find themselves fighting on all fronts, against an increasing number of enemy forces. This fighting would allow them to further demonstrate their bravery and fighting abilities. Their numerous battles to come will be detailed in the future volumes of this project.

For now however, let us finish by recapping on the successes and recognition to date. In the period from the start of January to the end of July 1943, saw the award of 46 Knight's Crosses, 7 Oakleaves to existing Knight's Crosses and 1 set of Swords to an existing Knight's Cross with Oakleaves. Therefore, 54 separate awards connected to the Knight's Cross for the soldiers of the *Waffen-SS*. This amounts to 85% of the awards made to *Waffen-SS* soldiers in the period from 1940 to 1942, a very busy seven months indeed!

With this volume now complete, I hope you, the reader, feels that another 'chunk' of the overall jigsaw is now completed. This overall project has now detailed 116 separate awards connected to the Knight's Cross or its' higher grades. I also hope that you have found these opening months of 1943 of interest to you. My quest is continuing on into the remaining months of 1943.

APPENDICES

Appendix 1
List of *Waffen-SS* units raised in 1943 (to end of July)

SS-Hohenstaufen-Division
SS-Frundsberg-Division
Sturmbrigade Reichsführer-SS
Lettisches-SS-Freiwilligen-Brigade
SS-Lettisches-Division
Croat SS-Freiwilligen Division
SS-Sturmbrigade Langemarck
SS-Sturmbrigade Wallonie
SS-Nordland Division
SS-Hitler Youth Division
SS-Freiwilligen-Division Galizien
Estonian SS-Freiwilligen Brigade (1942)
SS-Karstwehr Kompanie/Battalion (1942)
SS-Freiwilligen-Brigade Nederland
SS-Sonderkommando z.b.v. Friedenthal
I. SS-Panzer Korps
II. SS-Panzer Korps
III. (Germanisches) SS-Panzer Korps
IV. SS-Panzer Korps
V. SS-Freiwilligen Gebirgs Korps

Appendix 2
Overview of awards of the *Waffen-SS* Knight's Crosses, Oakleaves, plus Oakleaves and Swords

1943 (to end of July)
The total (54) breakdown of all awards made between January and July 1943 as follows:

Leibstandarte Adolf Hitler	16 Knight's Crosses, 2 sets of Oakleaves & 1 set of Swords
Das Reich	13 Knight's Crosses, 1 set of Oakleaves
Totenkopf	6 Knight's Crosses, 1 set of Oakleaves
Polizei	1 Knight's Cross
Wiking	5 Knight's Crosses, 1 set of Oakleaves
Prinz Eugen	2 Knight's Crosses
SS-Legion Niederlande	1 Knight's Cross
SS-Kavallerie Division	2 Knight's Crosses
SS-Kampfgruppe Schuldt	1 set of Oakleaves
II SS-Panzer Korps	1 set of Oakleaves

1940 – 1943 (to end of July)
The total (116) breakdown of all awards given from the start of the war is as follows:

Leibstandarte Adolf Hitler	22 Knight's Crosses, 3 sets of Oakleaves & 1 set of Swords
Das Reich	26 Knight's Crosses, 1 set of Oakleaves
Totenkopf	23 Knight's Crosses, 2 sets of Oakleaves
Polizei	10 Knight's Crosses, 1 set of Oakleaves
Wiking	14 Knight's Crosses, 2 sets of Oakleaves
Prinz Eugen	2 Knight's Crosses
4. SS-Totenkopf Standarte	1 Knight's Cross
SS-Legion Niederlande	1 Knight's Cross
SS-Kavallerie Division	4 Knight's Crosses
SS-Kampfgruppe Fegelein	1 Knight's Cross
SS-Kampfgruppe Schuldt	1 set of Oakleaves
II SS-Panzer Korps	1 set of Oakleaves

The rest of the *Waffen-SS* units in existence up to the end of July 1943 did not have any Knight's Cross recipients.

Appendix 3
Ranks of *Waffen-SS* Knight's Cross Holders (plus Oakleaves, Oakleaves and Swords)

1943 (to end of July)

Knight's Cross:

SS-Obergruppenführer	1
SS-Oberführer	3
SS-Obersturmbannführer	4
SS-Sturmbannführer	16
SS-Hauptsturmführer	6
SS-Obersturmführer	5
SS-Untersturmführer	2
SS-Hauptscharführer	3
SS-Oberscharführer	4
SS-Unterscharführer	1
SS-Sturmmann	1

Knight's Cross with Oakleaves:

SS-Obergruppenführer	1
SS-Standartenführer	2
SS-Obersturmbannführer	2
SS-Sturmbannführer	2

Knight's Cross with Oakleaves and Swords

SS-Obergruppenführer	1

1940 - 1943 (to end of July)

Knight's Cross:

SS-Obergruppenführer	2
SS-Gruppenführer	2
SS-Brigadeführer	2
SS-Oberführer	8
SS-Standartenführer	6
SS-Obersturmbannführer	7
SS-Sturmbannführer	32
SS-Hauptsturmführer	14
SS-Obersturmführer	9
SS-Untersturmführer	4
SS-Hauptscharführer	4
SS-Oberscharführer	6
SS-Unterscharführer	4
SS-Rottenführer	1
SS-Sturmmann	2

Knight's Cross with Oakleaves:

SS-Obergruppenführer	2
SS-Gruppenführer	1
SS-Brigadeführer	2
SS-Oberführer	1

SS-Standartenführer	2
SS-Obersturmbannführer	2
SS-Sturmbannführer	2

Knight's Cross with Oakleaves and Swords

SS-Obergruppenführer	1

Appendix 4
Skills of *Waffen-SS* Knight's Cross Holders (plus Oakleaves, Oakleaves and Swords)

1943 (to end of July)

Knight's Crosses:

Infantry	17
Aufklarungs	2
Motorcycle Battalion	2
Panzerjaeger	2
Pioneer	4
Artillery	3
Cavalry	2
Sturmgeschutze	1
Panzer	11
Mountain	2

Of note in the above list, is the number of Panzer related Knight's Crosses, bearing in mind that the *Waffen-SS* only received its' first Panzer unit in the second half of 1942, with the majority of the 4 separate Panzer units only seeing their first action in 1943!

Knight's Cross with Oakleaves:

Infantry	4
Aufklarungs	1
Motorcycle Battalion	1
Panzer	1

Knight's Cross with Oakleaves and Swords

Infantry	1

1940 - 1943 (to end of July)

Knight's Crosses:

Infantry	54
Aufklarungs	6
Motorcycle Battalion	4
Panzerjaeger	5
Flak	2
Pioneer	6
Artillery	6
Cavalry	4
Sturmgeschutze	2
Panzer	12
Mountain	2

Knights Cross with Oakleaves:

Infantry	8
Cavalry	1
Aufklarungs	1
Motorcycle Battalion	1
Panzer	1

Knight's Cross with Oakleaves and Swords

Infantry	1

Appendix 5
List of deceased *Waffen-SS* Knight's Cross holders during 1943 (to end of July)

Harry Polewacz	12th January 1943
Theodore Eicke	26th February 1943
Helmut Pfortner	28th February 1943
Erwin Reichel	28th February 1943
Hans Reimling	7th March 1943
Hermann Dahlke	5th July 1943
Karl-Heinz Worthmann	6-7th July 1943

List of deceased *Waffen-SS* Knight's Cross holders during 1941-1943 (to end of July)

Erich Rossner	30th July 1941
Hans-Christian Schulze	13th September 1941
Gert Pleiss	17th November 1941
Ludwig Kochle	9th June 1942
Harry Polewacz	12th January 1943
Theodore Eicke	26th February 1943
Helmut Pfortner	28th February 1943
Erwin Reichel	28th February 1943
Hans Reimling	7th March 1943
Hermann Dahlke	5th July 1943
Karl-Heinz Worthmann	6-7th July 1943

BIBLIOGRAPHY

Buss, Philip. H. & Mollo, Andrew. *Hitler's Germanic Legions, An illustrated history of the Western European Legions with the SS, 1941-1943*. Macdonald and Jane's Publishers Limited, 1978.

Haupt, Werner. *Army Group North, The Wehrmacht in Russia 1941-1945*. Schiffer Publishing Ltd., 1997.

Haupt, Werner. *Army Group Centre, The Wehrmacht in Russia 1941-1945*. Schiffer Publishing Ltd., 1997.

Haupt, Werner. *Army Group South, The Wehrmacht in Russia 1941-1945*. Schiffer Publishing Ltd., 1998.

Kratschmer, E.G. *Die Ritterkreuztrager der Waffen-SS*. Verlag K.W. Schutz KG, Preussisch Oldendorf, 1982

Kumm, Otto. *Prinz Eugen, The History of the 7 SS Mountain Division "Prinz Eugen"*. J.J.Fedorowicz Publishing Ltd., 1995.

Lehmann, Rudolf. *Die Leibstandarte III*. J.J.Fedorowicz Publishing Ltd., 1990.

Moore, J.P. *Führerliste Der Waffen-SS, Parts 1 to 4*. J.P.Moore Publishing, 2003.

Scheider, Jost. W. *Their Honor was Loyalty (2nd Edition)*. R. James Bender Publishing, 1993.

Strassner, Peter. *European Volunteers, 5 SS Panzer Division Wiking*. J.J.Fedorowicz Publishing Ltd., 1998.

Trang, Charles. *The 'Florian Geyer' Division*. Heimdal Publishing, 2000.

Ullrich, Karl. *Like a Cliff in the Ocean, The History of the 3. SS-Panzer-Division "Totenkopf"*. J.J. Fedorowicz Publishing Ltd., 2002.

Weidinger, Otto. *Das Reich IV, 2 SS Panzer Division Das Reich*. J.J.Fedorowicz Publishing Ltd., 2008.

Yerger, Mark. C. *Waffen-SS Commanders, Volume 1, Augsberger to Kreutz*. Schiffer Publishing Ltd., 1997.

Yerger, Mark. C. *Waffen-SS Commanders, Volume 2, Kruger to Zimmermann*. Schiffer Publishing Ltd., 1999.

Tieke, Wilhelm. *In the Firestorm of the Last Years of the War, II. SS-Panzerkorps with the 9. And 10. SS-Divisions "Hohenstaufen" and "Frundsberg"*. J.J.Fedorowicz Ltd., 1999.

Tieke, Wilhelm. *Tragedy of the Faithful, A History of the III. (Germanisches) SS-Panzer-Korps*. J.J.Fedorowicz Ltd., 2001.

Lepre, George. *Himmler's Bosnian Division. The Waffen-SS Handschar Division 1943-1945*. Schiffer Publishing Ltd., 1997.

Brandt, Allen. *The Last Knight of Flanders. Remy Schrijnen and his SS-Legion "Flandern"/Sturmbrigade "Langemarck" Comrades on the Eastern Front 1941-1945*. Schiffer Publishing Ltd., 1998.

Silgailis, Arthur. *Latvian Legion*. R. James Bender Publishing, 1986.

David Westwood. *The Waffen-SS. An Organisational and Operational History 1933-1945*. MLRS Books Ltd., 2004.

Nipe, George M., Jr. *Last Victory in Russia. The SS-Panzerkorps and Manstein's Kharkov Counteroffensive, February-March 1943*. Schiffer Publishing Ltd., 2000.

Laar, Mart & Suurmaa, Lauri. *The Estonian Legion in Words and Pictures*. Grenader Publishing Ltd., 2008.

Skorzeny, Otto. *Skorzeny's Special Missions. The Memoirs of 'The Most Dangerous Man In Europe'*. Greenhill Books, 1997.

Meyer, Hubert. *The History of the 12. SS-Panzerdivision Hitlerjugend*. J.J.Fedorowicz Ltd., 1994.

De Bruyne, Eddy and Rikmenspoel, Marc. *For Rex and for Belgium. Leon Degrelle and Walloon Political & Military Collaboration 1940-45*. Helion & Company, 2004.

Agte, Patrick. *Jochen Peiper. Commander Panzerregiment Leibstandarte*. J.J.Fedorowicz Ltd., 1999.

Schneider, Wolfgang. *Das Reich Tigers. The Tigers of the 8./SS-Panzer-Regiment 2 "Das Reich", schwere SS-Panzer-Abteilung 102 and schwere SS-Panzer-Abteilung 502*. J.J.Fedorowicz Ltd., 2006.

Agte, Patrick. *Michael Wittmann and the Tiger Commanders of the Leibstandarte*. J.J.Fedorowicz Ltd., 1996.

Logusz, Michael. O. *Galicia Division. The Waffen-SS 14th Grenadier Division 1943-1945*. Schiffer Publishing Ltd., 2000.

Munoz, Antonio. J. *Forgotten Legions. Obscure Combat Formations of the Waffen-SS*. Paladin Press, 1991.

Also: Various letters and face-to-face interviews with surviving Kameraden of the various *Divisions* and other units of the *Waffen-SS* from 1998 to 2009.